A Nightmare in Jamaica

Tommy Kennedy IV

NEW HAVEN PUBLISHING LTD

Published 2021
NEW HAVEN PUBLISHING LTD
www.newhavenpublishingltd.com
newhavenpublishing@gmail.com

All Rights Reserved
The rights of Tommy Kennedy IV, as the author of this work, have been asserted in accordance with the Copyrights, Designs and Patents Act 1988.
No part of this book may be re-printed or reproduced or utilized in any form or by any electronic, mechanical or other means, now unknown or hereafter invented, including photocopying, and recording, or in any information storage or retrieval system, without the written permission of the Author and Publisher.

Some names and identifying details have been changed to protect the privacy of individuals.

Cover design ©Pete Cunliffe

Copyright © 2021 Tommy Kennedy IV All rights reserved
ISBN: 978-1-912587-64-3

A Gripping journey into a nether world of
Violence and mayhem
Shaun Attwood

Tommy Kennedy lives on the dub side of life. Which sounds romantic until you find you are sentenced to three years in the General Pententiary in Kingston, Jamaica, one of the most terrifying jails in the wortd. Which gives Tommy time enough to think about how he got there. An extraordinary story.
Chris Salewicz

Acknowledgements

Firstly, I would like to thank Thomas Rees and Anna Carrington, for their vision for this book, and Jay Hirano, for the inspiration he gave me to actually write anything at all. I am also grateful to Janice Stretton for typing this (creating sense from my ramblings) along with Emilie Harper in the early stages.

I would also like to say a huge thank you to my family all over the UK and beyond, especially my elder sister Lynn and younger brother Anthony who shared my formative years.

My autobiography would have remained a pipe dream if I had not had the firm support from my friends in the Notting Hill community, around the UK, and the world, who encouraged and helped finance this book to come to fruition.

To my mother and father, who have both passed away, all I can say is 'Let he who has not sinned cast the first stone.'"Rike deserves a special mention for igniting in me a spiritual awareness which set me on this new long and winding road back in Thailand 1999. 'Little did you know that the words you uttered to me on that fateful day were going to be taken literally when I set out on this journey leaving the Island of Koh-Samui.'

My childhood friends Robert Albert Taylor, AKA The Rat, and Malcolm Lawless, AKA Tank, both now deceased: 'see you on the other side muckers.'

I would like to thank all the bands I have been involved with over the years, especially around the Notting Hill area, some I managed, and some I promoted. All of them taught me something, in one way or the other. Over a twenty year period here are just a few - there were way too many to mention them all - NRG-FLY, Steve Dior Band, Pink Cigar, The Electrics, Kult 45s, Dirty Strangers, Stolen Colours, Carnival of Souls, Angie Brown, Killing Joe Band,Freak Elite, Smiley and the Underclass, Slydigs Warrington, Mentona K, from Liberia, Rotten Hill Gang, Whalls, Etchoo Band, Serratone Warrington, Taurus Trakker, London Ghost, Alabama3, Alan Wass R.I.P, Ted Key and the Kingstons, Black Swan Event, Midnight Poem, Healthy Junkies, The SD5, Brady Bunch, Garage Flowers, Santa Semeli and the Monks, Guinea Pigs of Meta Data, Stanlees, The Stage Invaders, My Drug Hell, Anarchist Wood, Slow Faction, Relaxin Doves, The Loves, David Sinclair Four, Prisoners of Mother England, Albie Deluca, Sugar Lady from Holland,

Big Mackoofy, Anna Pigalle and Nick Farr, Aunty Puss, Raindogs, Paper Rock, Ray Hanson, The Vulz, Dave Renegade, Pistol Head, Chubby Letouche and his Band of Whores, Natural Mystery Museum, Jem and Helenna, Dave and Paolo, Key Mcloud, DJs, Alex Pink, Dr Philgood and Naughty Di, Steve Holloway, Rude Boy Ray Gange.

And I'd like to thank all the staff at the Mau Mau Bar and the Legendary Bullit Hardway, who runs the Sunday Night Reggae there for over 10 years. Rudy and Dexter on the door and the owners, Jay and Frank. Acklam Village Market, on Portobello Road, owners Dermott and Caroline and all the staff there, Pavell, Gina, Music Promoter Chris Sullivan. Inn on the Green, Dave and Tina. Portobello Gold, Mike Bell.

And I'd like to thank Emma Rule from Musicians against Homelessness.

And especially the organisation Prisoners Abroad, who did so much for me.

Finally, and most importantly, this book is dedicated to the lights of my life -my daughter Sophie and her three beautiful children, Barclay, Theodore, and Penelope, and my 11-year-old son Tommy Junior V, who has provided me with an opportunity to relive my own childhood in a much more satisfactory way.

This is not a pretty story, but I am a survivor and what I lacked in my early years has been repaid tenfold in later life.

I have retained my sense of humour and optimism, which to some may seem incomprehensible given my experiences in jail.

I love life and all the people I have come across in my lifetime have made me a much better person and given me a richness that money could never buy.

I salute you all, the good, the bad and the ugly - life is so short it 'will pass you by in the blink of an eye.'

My advice is always to savour every moment and really appreciate being alive.

'Get out there and live!'
Tommy Kennedy IV London June 2019

'The people you meet on this journey of life will make it wider - but the people who you part from will make it much deeper' Jay Hirano Japan

Content

Getting My Life Back	11
The Paedophile	15
Beamont Technical School 1971	21
More Trouble	25
The Summer of 1976	28
Everthorpe Borstal	31
Stoke Heath Borstal 1977	35
Factory Life	40
God Loves a Trier	43
Wymott	50
Chester	54
London	56
Horseferry Road Magistrates	62
Leaving the UK	65
Australia 87-88	68
Sydney to Mexico	70
Back to Asia	72
Jersey, Channel Islands	76
Australia 1991	81
1992: Ringing the Changes with Supreme Confidence	83

Monkey House	91
Manchester	101
Back to Thailand	104
Dunstable	109
Rasta Man	111
Kingston	115
Back to Jamaica	118
Trenchtown - Rema Remand Centre 2001	123
General Penitentiary	125
Dynamite	127
An Uneasy Feeling, Jamaica	131
One Love Football Game	155
Skin of my Teeth	157
Howard Marks	164
A Stroke of Luck	170
A Surprise Visit	174
Christmas	176
Red Yardie	187
Time Waits For No Man	197
A Glimmer of Hope	204
Hell, on Earth	207

Introduction

This is the first volume of my autobiography and it is a brutally honest account of the trials and tribulations of my life until the age of forty-three.

I have hidden these secrets for many years, and I believe now is the appropriate time to reveal them. I began writing in January 2018 and, as the words tumbled onto the pages, I came to the realisation that I was not to blame for many events in my life. However, today, with wisdom fashioned from years of introspection and spiritual enlightenment, I take responsibility for the decisions I have made. This is also accompanied by a profound sense of sadness and regret regarding how my negative behaviour has affected those around me.

Living a lawless life enabled me to love and fight in equal measure but I also experienced and observed intense suffering which continues to haunt me to this day. Somehow, I stumbled through and gradually I began to learn from the mistakes I was making. I survived! Many of my friends and family were extinguished before their time. I appreciate my life and if my story can help in some small way to steer even one life in the right direction then my experiences would not be in vain.

I now understand that a dysfunctional childhood in and out of institutions led me to search for adventure, which took me to many countries around the world. I desired to escape from the mind-numbing repetition of the daily grind of life and work forced upon me by my own lack of imagination. Deciding to rebel, I hit the road. Predictably, there was a rapid descent into alcoholism and drug abuse combined with a spirit of adventure which would not be quelled.

Inevitably karma descended upon me in the harsh realities of prison sentences in Thailand and Jamaica. The latter was my 'hell on earth' and where on reflection I began to truly understand myself and my self-destructive behaviours. Although I had previously consorted with prostitutes and drug dealers around the globe, I began to crave a different kind of life.

On my release from the General Penitentiary in Jamaica, I headed for the streets of London's Notting Hill and immersed myself fully into the music scene. I was experiencing the familiar feelings of passion and excitement, but it was punctuated with a focused and creative aspect. Did I continue to live a lawless life? Yes. Did I continue to make many unwise decisions? Yes. But I was also aware of an internal shift happening in my mind.

I had changed the direction of my life and my transformation had begun.

'With age comes wisdom, but sometimes age comes alone.' Oscar Wilde

Chapter 1
Getting My Life Back

It was a steaming hot day in July 2003, and I was standing near the gate inside the prison walls of the notorious maximum-security unit of the General Penitentiary in Jamaica, when I heard a voice that startled me: 'Don't forget, white man, when you get back to England, you tell everybody I'm an innocent man.' I realised it was Leppo, convicted of three murders in 1987, including that of reggae superstar Peter Tosh and his friends. All I could think was, *Get me the fuck out of here!*

I had just completed my sentence, over 700 nights, during which I had witnessed many murders, a vast amount of beatings and stabbings, and met some heavy duty Yardies who would, and have, cut people's throats in the blink of an eye. Members of the Shower Posse, who used Uzi submachine guns, so named for the way they would rain a shower of bullets down on their victims. Their leader Christopher Coke had ruthlessly used a chainsaw to dismember one of a gang who had stolen drugs from him.... while he was still alive, the rest of the Shower Posse looking on laughing while the guy died screaming in agony. You did not fuck around with these guys if you valued your life.

Eventually, the police turned up to take me to the airport. Even then I was never sure if I was getting out. When the gates swung open and we drove through, I smiled to myself and gave a brief wave to Leppo as we left him standing, glaring at the departing police van. We arrived at the airport to find out my plane had been delayed.

Fuck, they stuck me in a holding cell at the airport in Kingston until I got on a plane! I wasn't really sure if this was going to happen; I started getting paranoid, maybe it was a wind-up. Eventually, my time came to board. They led me handcuffed until I was let onto the plane and the stewardess took over. As we took off, I thought of all the days when I used to see the British Airways flights leaving Kingston, heading from Jamaica to the UK, which I used to watch from my prison cell regularly (mental torture). And now, finally, at last, I was on the plane, leaving. The stewardess greeted me with 'Welcome aboard' and gave me a wink; she could see how happy I was to be leaving police custody. I winked back and said 'Nice one.'

I breathed a huge sigh of relief whilst ordering a beer off the good-looking stewardess and thinking, *Yes! Got my life back, on to further adventures and god knows what else.* But I also remember pondering: *Whatever happens from here on it can only be up after this.* Little did I know what lay ahead. All I knew was I had to get back to London to resume my passion for music. This had become all-consuming and gave me a purpose, something that had been lacking for so many years in my life. By the time we landed at Manchester airport and I cleared customs after a two-hour grilling by immigration officers, I was buzzing. I stepped out into the English summer and the first person I saw was my younger brother Anthony, who stuck a camera in my face and took a photo. I looked a right twat, none of my clothes fit, my hair was down my back, but I didn't give a toss, I was out, I was free! We hugged, and our Anthony said, 'Long time no see.' I got down on my knees and kissed the ground, and we both laughed. Man, was I happy to be on home turf.

The only good thing about prison is the day they let you out. It beats all the birthdays and Christmases, nothing better than getting your freedom back. It's almost worth the experience just to have that feeling when they set you free. Anyway, we jumped into our kid's car and headed back to my hometown of Warrington, where he still lived at the time with his wife Paula and their kids, Alfie and Mia. This was Anthony's second marriage and they seemed really happy together.

I hadn't sat on a toilet or had a bath in over two years. It was heaven soaking in the bath and using a proper toilet. Our kid gave me some money and some new clothes to wear. He really is a star and I love him dearly, even though he can drive me crazy at times; we are brothers and I love him unconditionally. We had food and Paula made me feel welcome; it had not been easy for the family with the situation I had landed myself in, they had been worried about my safety.

Later that night my cousin Jack turned up and we had a few beers and a laugh about the predicament I had just been through. I didn't want to dwell on it just yet and caught up on all the news. It turned out Jack had been hanging around with Noel Gallagher from Oasis for a few years before he became famous. They had met from the rave days many years before at the Hacienda. Our Jack was like a brother to me. His mum and my mum were sisters, and both loved each other's company, so as kids we were always together. Noel always puts him on the guest list of various gigs, and they are still in contact over 25 years later. Jack and Noel still text each other, although he is quite shy and not one for bothering people, including me. Jack is five years my junior and very respected in Warrington. He gave me some cash and said, 'Spend it wisely' when he departed later that night.

The next day I went and saw my dad, who has been a constant throughout my life. He always did his best by me, along with my sister Lynn, and our Anthony. My dad had joined the Merchant Navy when he was 16 and spent 12 years sailing around the world in the 50s and 60s, later regaling us with stories of exotic places. It was through my father that my love of travel came. All through my school days, the only thing I wanted to do was join the Navy and see the world, but sadly it was not meant to be. From 13 to 21 I hit a rebellious streak and spent most of it in detention centres, Borstal and prisons around the country. I applied for the Merchant Navy and the Royal Navy numerous times, but with my criminal record, it was a no-go!

It was great to see my dad. He had given up the booze at the age of 52 after a lifetime of boozing, which I was thankful for, or else he would have died. We hugged, and he gave me some money. I was totally broke when they let me out and was really thankful. One of my good friends, Liz, came over and also gave me some money. Liz was a great girl and a good friend; she is now living in Australia, and I wish her all the best. I had met her when she was on the front desk of Legends night club in Warrington, taking the door money. I think she liked my cheek, and I amused her. Her brother Sean started Legends in the early 90s! Legends was at the forefront of house music in Warrington, and people flocked there from all over the UK.

Liz was a nurse and had a caring nature at the best of times, but she did a great job dealing with people, and Legends was making so much money it was packed every weekend. Gangsters started coming from Manchester issuing death threats to her brother Sean, threatening to blow his car up if they couldn't get in on the action, but fair play to Sean, he took it all in his stride and went on to put Legends on the map, big time. Scousers and Mancs were always coming to Warrington for the nightlife; some carried guns and knives, but the Warrington crew were just as bad and never backed down from them. After a few days I realised I had to get back to London: I was missing the buzz of city life and I knew Warrington only spelled trouble for me. So, after a few goodbyes and laughs with family, I hitched a ride with Eny, an old school friend who lived in Canary Wharf and was quite successful. I'd always admired him: he took the straight road and studied hard, and now he lives in Qatar and has done really well for himself. We are like chalk and cheese, but we are mates and always have a laugh when we meet up.

I had nowhere to live when I arrived in London. One of the Jamaicans who I met in the General Penitentiary, Carrot, had a flat in Brixton and told me to go there. Eny dropped me off and I knocked on the door. A woman came down and I explained who I was. Next thing I was upstairs with her and three Jamaican guys who took an instant dislike to me. I stayed there and nearly had a brief affair with the Jamaican woman, but I think the guys got wind of it and kicked me out after about a month.

Luckily my good mate from Warrington, Rob Taylor, rang me. He lived in Ladbroke Grove and told me his mate had a flat with a box-room on Westbourne Park Road, just off Portobello, £50 a week. Fuck, there is a god! I was no stranger to London. I had lived all over it since the early 80s and had been living around the Grove for a few years before I got nicked in Jamaica. Tony, who I moved into the flat with, was a man after my own heart, intelligent, a heart of gold, born and bred around the Grove, and better still, the local drug dealer. Fuck, we hit it off from the moment we met. Let's have a beer he said, and we hit The Castle on the corner of Portobello Road that used to be called The Warwick, Joe Strummer's boozer from the Clash back in the day.

I love London. Having lived all over the country and travelled all around the world, I've lived in many countries, but this is a special city: 300 languages are spoken, people are here from every corner of the globe and there's a buzz in the air. The summertimes are wicked in London. I'm learning to appreciate the winters too. I was born in wintertime, October 16th; wow, I'm still here when so many of my friends and family are dead and buried.

'I'm in love with cities I've never been to and people I have never met.' John Green

Chapter 2
The Paedophile

I entered the world on Friday 16th October 1959 in the working-class town of Warrington, famous for its factories and Warrington Rugby League. Warrington is situated right smack bang in the middle of two major cities, Liverpool and Manchester. Nicknamed The Wires, because of all the wire factories dotted around the town, it suited the Warrington fans: they were lairy and stood behind their team fanatically.

My mother said I had a full head of ginger hair and was a huge baby. She said the nurse had to smack me twice, to make sure I was alive, before I burst into tears! Ma was 22 when she gave birth to me, and I was the third child she had given birth to in less than three years. She had twins, my sisters Lynn and Donna, but sadly Donna passed away after only a couple of days leaving Lynn alone without her sister. She always felt she should have got twice as much love later in life, to make up for the loss of her sister. My father was in Japan the day I was born, and it would be another three months before he saw me when his ship docked back in January 1960. My aunty Rita had spoken to my dad by phone while he was in Japan and told him, 'You have a brown-eyed handsome son, Tom.'

Ma was born in Ireland, but by the time she was two years old her mother, Alice, had separated and left her first husband and moved to Glasgow, in 1938. So Ma had grown up in the tenement blocks in the roughest part of Glasgow, the Gorbals. In those days it was extremely run down, and poverty was rife. Along with the rest of her brothers and sisters, the kids grew up with that crazy Glaswegian attitude. Years later, when Ma was 11, she was placed in a convent, and I never found out why. When she was 16, she finally left the convent to rejoin the rest of her family in Warrington, where they had settled a few years previously, after leaving Glasgow to find work.

Uncle Benny, Ma's brother, had met my father when they were both serving in the Merchant Navy in the 1950s, becoming great friends, and in turn a few years later Benny had introduced my dad to my ma. Within a few months, Ma found she was pregnant, and they duly married; Ma was 19, my dad was 20. Dad's mother had told him, 'You made your bed son and now you lie in it.' Within a few months, Dad had to rejoin his ship in New York and flew out of Heathrow leaving my ma to cope by herself. Once again, he had been away when my sisters were born, and I think Ma found it very difficult by herself with no man at home, and she secretly started drinking, maybe to alleviate her loneliness. When I came along three years later, they were renting a house in Phillip Street, not far from the town centre.

My earliest memories of Ma were how much she used to drink, and that she was always playing music. She kept the house spotless though and was very house-proud, just like her own mother, Alice. My sister Lynn and I were always well dressed. Ma never bought us presents or anything like that at Christmas or birthdays, it was always a new set of clothes. Ma was a real character: she had been blessed with good looks, but she could scare you to death when she was in a rage, shouting at you in her Glaswegian accent. She really was not a lovey-dovey kind of mother, which all my friends' mothers seemed to be. She never thought twice about using a belt on you, especially if you upset her in any way. I would have constant red welts on my legs from the strap.

If she wanted a bottle of sherry, she would send me across the brickfield outside our house to the off-licence when I was about five. You would never get away with it these days, but back then they would just take your money and smile and say, 'Is this for your mum?' and wrap it up in brown paper. We had an outside toilet with no lights, and the tin bath hanging on the wall for our weekly bath, and the coalman would deliver the coal and the milkman delivered the milk. It would always be a struggle getting money out of Ma, and many a time we would all hide behind the couch when the rent man came to collect the weekly rent! The rent collector would be peeping through the letterbox, and finally when he gave up Ma would laugh and sing 'The rent, the rent, the rent is spent'; she really did have a wicked sense of humour, Ma. She would think nothing of hiding a bar of chocolate in my pram when we were out shopping, or she would say, 'Stick this up your jumper.' I thought shoplifting was normal back then. She would let us run wild playing outside; half the time she would be half cut and not care.

My younger brother Anthony was born in that house on 12th of January 1966; now I had a little brother to love and care for. A few months after he was born, we were so far behind in the rent that the council decided to evict us all, and my ma had a nervous breakdown and was committed to Winick hospital. We were then placed in care. I was six years old, and my sister Lynn was nine; my younger brother

Anthony was fostered out, and Lynn and myself were taken by car to Liverpool and placed in a convent, or more likely dumped there, and left to be raised by nuns for the next 12 months. It was a massive shock. I really had no idea what was going on in the 1960s, it felt like I was in hell. The nuns were a strange bunch; I really thought they were evil witches at the time. Dad was still at sea and had no idea what was going on at home. I remember I was very scared of the nuns; they were not very kind: they were very strict and would punish you for the slightest infringement of the rules. I was placed in a new school in Liverpool. By the time I was six years old I had seen things no child should have seen at that age; my dad was never around to see my ma's antics because he was always away with the Navy. When I started the new school, I was constantly in fights and got involved in shoplifting, and the nuns would punish me brutally. It was a real shit time in my life and it took me months to settle into the convent.

Dad was born in 1935, on 13th of March; he always said he was born unlucky, but he grew up in a loving family, along with his brother Roy and his sister Val. My grandfather was also named Tommy, and he had been a master bricklayer and could build anything with his hands. They were one of the first families in their street to own a television. The Kennedys had left Ireland in 1874 on my dad's side and settled in Warrington. Grandad Tom had died before I was born, in 1955; he died in agony with lung cancer at only 42. Grandmother Lily was left alone with three children, but she did a wonderful job, and she loved her family with all her heart. We loved to go and visit her, and she always made us welcome and made a fuss about giving us sweets and money. There were businesspeople on the Kennedy side of the family who owned shops and building companies across Warrington. Dad had huge respect for both his parents.

I never met my grandfather on my ma's side either, as sadly he had passed away before I was born. Nana, on my ma's side, was a warm loving person and I never could understand why Ma was not. Nana would tell us all the stories of growing up in Ireland and we would love to hear them, sitting by the fire in her front room. She was an excellent cook, unlike my mother who couldn't boil an egg, even when she tried. All the family loved music, and the record player would be blasting out loud continually. The Irish loved to sing and dance, and our family was no exception.

It took a year for Dad to leave the Navy and he found work on a power station in a place called Fawley not far from Southampton, finally bringing all the family back together again. We were so happy to be leaving the convent behind, we spent all day in the convent awaiting the arrival of Ma and Dad. Lynn ran down to greet them, almost euphoric to see them. I can still see it in my mind's eye, something you never forget, and I have been blessed with an excellent memory, although sometimes I wish I hadn't. We were bundled into Dad's car and didn't really have a clue where we were going; we were just so happy to be escaping the clutches of the nuns and leaving the convent behind to start a new life.

We eventually arrived at a caravan site in a place called Calshot, by the Solent. On a good day you can see the Isle of Wight. This was to be our new home for the next four years. My father hadn't been much of a drinker but living with my mum he started to drink heavily as time went by. The combination of the two of them drinking turned into a nightmare for us kids growing up in that environment, and sometimes I just wanted to run away from it all. The real happy memories would be when the music was playing, and they were both happy together, but that was far and few between. Somehow you learn to cope when you are a child, but it never did us any real good.

I have memories of Winston Churchill passing away, the Kennedys being assassinated and man walking on the moon, but no real memories of my ma kissing or loving me. I have had a problem with jealousy in my life; I'm older now and over it, but when you feel unloved by your mother it makes you insecure: you've nobody to turn to with your problems. My mother was a drunk, good-looking and had loads of affairs when my father was at sea. Born in Ireland and raised in the Gorbals in Glasgow in the 30s, my mother's favourite saying to me was 'Ya wee bashtard, I should have phissed on ya and drowned you at birth' - said in Scottish accent - she would laugh and kick me up the arse or give me a slap. Thanks Ma.

On the campsite at Calshot, I went exploring. I was about seven years old and went swimming in the sea in winter. I went out to a reef and couldn't pull myself up: freezing, choking on the water, I was drowning. Some old man on a small boat spotted me, dragged me in and revived me. I never even bothered telling Ma or Dad. I keep things to myself; they say children of alcoholics do that. It makes you secretive, it makes you ashamed to tell your friends or anybody what's going on back at home. I didn't care that we lived in a caravan for years, but soon all the local kids at school would be taking the piss out of me: dirty, stinking gypsy bastard. I had endless troubles and fights, and I felt ashamed and embarrassed most of the time. I didn't know what we had done wrong to suffer such abuse, and I remember my mother lifting her skirt up at the caravan door to my friends and laughing at me - that sure didn't help things either. Probably Ma did it for a joke, but I was humiliated and the butt of endless pisstakes. I didn't have the coping skills to realise it was probably all just in jest; when you are seven or eight you are still learning about life.

When we moved down south, Mum was drinking all the time. She missed one of her lovers from Warrington probably. She was always taking it out on me, threatening me with knives, dragging me out of bed and beating me, taking fake overdoses. I look back now and realise she was young, and I was no angel at her age either. My dad was working on Fawley Power Station, having left the Merchant Navy to become a steel erector or rigger. They were so busy drinking and fighting they didn't realise the local paedo had befriended me. His name was Bill. He ran the local cinema and told me he had gone to school with the Scottish actor John Laurie from *Dad's Army*. He was about 60 then. He started buying me things, toys, taking me out, giving me money. I started staying overnight at his, and then he started touching me up, what a twat. I knew it was wrong, but he never went too far. Even at that age I knew something wasn't right but once again I told nobody. Who gave a fuck about me anyway? He took me on trips to Birmingham and Scotland, and he threatened to kill me if I told anybody about our little secret. I didn't know which way to turn so I kept quiet. I never really understood what he was doing really, I was far too young and gullible.

My ma would send me up to stay with the old nonce Bill during the school holidays the first year, till I told Ma I didn't want to go anymore and wanted to be with my friends. She should have known, but she acted like she was oblivious to it all, and that was her all along when it came to me. I have never been quite sure if she knew, or even condoned it one way or the other, and I am sure he gave her money. Ma had come from a hard background and really thought differently about things to other people. It is a hard thing to say about your own mother, but if she had any feelings for me, why did she let it happen? I think she just didn't give a fuck.

The old paedo tried to get me back many times when we eventually moved back to Warrington a few years later. I was determined I would never clap eyes on him ever again, and I never did. I've carried that shame with me for a lifetime, and now I'm letting it out. I did no wrong. If anyone did that to my children, I would kill them with my bare hands without a shadow of a doubt. If the truth is known I was glad to get away from that sick bastard in the end, but he made me feel I was special when I was at my most vulnerable, buying me presents, taking me on trips. I now know he was grooming me, but he was also threatening me, as if I didn't have enough shit going on in my life at home.

Is it any wonder things turned out the way they did for me? It's not something I think of constantly - I buried it deep in my mind - but it is there, and something I will take to my grave. It's not something you lightly drop into a conversation, is it? People really don't want to hear this kind of stuff, do they? But I am old enough now not to care what people think: you like me, or you don't, it's that simple.

It's not easy to write this in print for people to judge me, or even think how this will affect my children or family. Do I want to make a good story? Do I really have to reveal this? I have learned that there are a lot of people out there who look to gratify themselves by grooming children, usually a friend of the family. You really should be ultra-careful with your children and fully make them understand under no circumstances should they allow any adult to abuse them or their trust. It is not something that should be taboo either: in any household where children are, they must totally know about paedophiles and the way they operate. Any sign of it, and they immediately must run and tell an adult. If I had known or understood in those days this would never have happened under any circumstances. It's not ruined me, but it should never have happened, full stop.

He will be long dead now, and good riddance!

'Childhood: One of the worst things that can happen to them is to have their childhood stolen from them'

Chapter 3
Beamont Technical School 1971

Back in Warrington things never really changed, although I did pass my 11 plus exams, god knows how; and Mum and Dad's drinking started getting more out of control as I was getting older. I was becoming more feral, unable to concentrate at school and always getting into trouble. Trying to do homework was nigh on impossible under those circumstances, and I ran away many times, sleeping in derelict houses and stealing from shops, anything to stay away from home and the constant arguments between my mum and dad. As I grew older, I would be getting into more mischief, not differentiating right from wrong, constantly playing truant and misbehaving. I got a paper round; I had a bike and I was also a grafter. I had been good at sports, rugby, football, and running; nobody praised me though, nobody seemed to care, so I rebelled.

Around this time, I started to take notice of girls, and going to the local youth clubs and dances where I met the local legendary DJ Peter Rigby. He was about 27 when I was 11 or 12. Pete was famous in Warrington for bringing the mop-tops to town, The Beatles, long before they became household names. The Bell Hall and the Co-op dances would bring all the kids together and I learned to love music, it was escapism from the shit going on back at home. We used to go back to Pete's house and listen to music - Pink Floyd, The Rolling Stones, Elvis - he introduced me to lots of music, and eventually I would start to roadie for him, carrying his records from gig to gig all over the North West of England. He became like a father figure to me. It opened my eyes up to a whole new world: I loved going out and seeing all the grown-ups in various nightclubs dancing and interacting with each other, having a good time.

I started to meet all the scallywags in the town. I became great friends with Terry and Johnny; we clicked, and we became a team. They were always looking for adventure and led me on some serious crime sprees. I went along wholeheartedly; I wanted to be like them. I was just doing it for the buzz, and I wanted to be accepted. Terry and I burgled houses, taking anything of value and squandering the money in local arcades. One day Johnny suggested we burgle his dad's house while he was at work. He wasn't getting along with his dad and thought it would be a good idea to piss him off and teach him a lesson.

So sure enough we did: we took everything of value and all the cash lying around the house, convinced we would never get caught. It was the summer of 1974. Shortly afterwards we took the train to Rhyl in North Wales and lived in a tent on a campsite; I think it was called The Robin Hood Camp, aptly named. I had already done a few tattoos on my arm. A.C.A.B - All Coppers Are Bastards, or, as I used to tell the police, Always Carry A Bible. Stupid really, but how did I know; or more to the point I didn't care anyway.

After a few weeks in Rhyl, we were running out of cash and decided to head to the bright lights of Blackpool. We hitchhiked, and when we arrived in Blackpool it was pissing down with rain. We were broke and went looking to rob somewhere, but it wasn't long before a sharp-eyed policeman spotted us loitering, and proceeded to stop and question us both, asking what were we up to, and where we were from. He quickly realised we were both underage and radioed back to the police station; we were both placed under arrest and taken back to the police station for further questioning. After a few initial enquiries, it turned out we were wanted by the police back in our hometown of Warrington for the burglary of our friend's house. The game was up, and I think we were both relieved to be heading back home, as we were cold, hungry and completely demoralised by this time, and in the morning we were taken out of our cells and transferred back to Warrington to face the music. We still had items from the burglary on us - a camera and a watch - so it was pointless denying it and we were both charged, and bailed to go home to await our fates, after being collected by our parents. My dad went mad, but I just laughed, and within a few days I was out stealing again. I never bothered going back to school after that. Terry and I just kept meeting up and carried on with our crime spree while we were both out on bail.

I was appointed a probation officer, Ian Chalmers, who was to write a report on me. My attitude did me no favours: I was a surly teenager who thought he knew it all. A few months later we appeared in the dock at Newton-Le-Willows Magistrates Court and the charges were read out. The lawyer then said his piece on our behalf, and then my probation report was read by the magistrates. They then went back to consider our sentences in the back room.

I had plans to go out that evening, but I was due for a big shock when the magistrates returned. My probation officer had recommended a custodial sentence, and the magistrates had agreed. We were both sentenced to a short sharp shock of three months each in a detention centre. We were parted and sent to different intuitions. I was taken down to the cells below, had my property taken from me and was placed in a cell to await the arrival of the van to take me to god knows where. I had started smoking when I was 11, stealing fags from my ma and buying them in ones from the local shop, and the policeman said, 'Where you are going, there will be no smoking son.' Later that day I was placed in handcuffs and taken to a police car and driven to a detention centre called Whatton, near Grantham, a huge place surrounded by a chain-link fence, holding hundreds of boys from around the country aged between 14 and 21. Here I was to meet my peers, who loved fighting; most of them came from dysfunctional families and violence was rife.

The emphasis was on punishment. You had to march everywhere, scrub floors, and you were constantly on the go from morning till night. I was processed on arrival, had my shoulder-length hair shorn off, given my prison number, placed in one of the dormitories and left to await my fate. I was 14 years old and instinctively knew I had to hold my own with the other boys, or they would have bullied me relentlessly. I was dying for a smoke but there was no chance. Smoking wasn't allowed anywhere in the detention centre.

Four or five of the boys in the dormitory set about me, for no other reason than that I was the new boy on the scene. They gave me a good kicking in a whirl of fists and feet; I tried to fight back, but in the end, I just curled up in a ball until they left me alone. I kept my trap shut and never mentioned it to the screws: a grass was the lowest of the low, and I would really have been in trouble then. After about a week I started to understand the rules of the dorm. I became familiar with who was who, and nobody bothered with me after the last kicking I got. One on one, I would have had a go, and I think the boys knew that. I became friends with some of them and at the end of the day, we all just wanted to get our sentence over with and go home. I came in in early October, and was due out the first week of December with good behaviour.

It was a pain in the arse no smoking, but I could see the light at the end of the tunnel and made the most of it. Some of the screws had homosexual tendencies, you could feel them watching you in the showers and the gym. One of the screws said I should have been a woman with legs like mine, and while he looked at me he had his hands in his pockets rubbing his groin, the dirty bastard. Who would want a job locking young boys up in the first place? They were perverts, ogling the young boys.

I met other kids from around the North West, Bri, Chris, people I knew from home starting out on their criminal careers. We all used to eat in a big dining room together. You could always see the new boys when they arrived; some were scared and crying for days, others were fearless and didn't give a toss. I wasn't really interested in being rehabilitated, but I played the game with the system and awaited my time to come before they would release me, which they did in early December of 1974. Released and dropped at the nearest train station, I bought my cigarettes and boarded the train back to Warrington. When I arrived home, I was in for a massive shock. My mother had left my dad for another man. I was secretly glad it was over: it was for the best, they weren't good for each other, they had tried for 18 years.

'The world is a tragedy to those who feel, but a comedy to those who think.'   Horace Walpole

Chapter 4
More Trouble

Dad was drinking heavily and becoming more bitter since Ma had left. I was out all the time, taking drugs, smoking hash, taking speed, going to Wigan Casino. There was no parental guidance whatsoever and that suited me. I loved Wigan Casino: the atmosphere was electric, dancing all night and just losing myself in the music. It was a special time, and a special place in my life, which really taught me the power of music. I started burgling chemists for the DDA boxes, ripping them open and selling the drugs at Wigan Casino to the dancers who wanted to stay up all night and be young, free and crazy. I was burgling houses constantly to fund my lifestyle of debauchery.

I hadn't long been out from my last spell behind bars when with a friend I broke into a house in broad daylight. He shit in the kitchen and pissed all over the furniture just for kicks, then we heard a door open and a woman shout, 'Who is that?' We were upstairs and had no way out; my mate had a screwdriver and said, 'Rush downstairs and push past her,' but I said, 'No, let's jump out of the bedroom window.' He went first, crashing in the garden below, and I quickly did the same just as the woman realised and came out of the front door; luckily, I just missed landing on her, but sprained my ankle. I tried to run, but she started screaming, 'Stop that thief!' I got a few hundred yards away before a passer-by grabbed me and the woman called the police. I had jewellery and cash from her house on me when the police arrived.

I was caught red-handed. My mate got away and I kept his name out of it. The police suspected me of dozens of burglaries, and when after a night in the cells I appeared in front of the local magistrates, the police asked for me to be remanded in custody until further inquiries were made. I was then taken to Risley Remand Centre. The locals nicknamed it Grisly Risley. It held a large amount of Scousers and Mancs. I was still only 15 and placed on the Under 21 Wing. It was three to a cell and you would be guaranteed fights and arguments; you grew up quick and had to be on your toes at all times.

I was held for a week and returned to court to face my charge of housebreaking. I admitted to that one charge and was sent back weekly until finally I was sent to Chester Crown Court with a recommendation of Borstal training in the month ahead. I was getting visits from friends, and in those days, it was behind a glass screen, so you couldn't pass anything over. I was young and cocky and really had no idea what I was doing with my life. The time came for me to be sentenced at Chester Crown Court, where a decade earlier the Moors Murderers had been sentenced to life, Myra Hindley and Ian Brady, the infamous child killers. My crime was read out in the open court facing the judge in his red gown and wig. After hearing my defence, they decided to give me a further chance, so instead of Borstal training the judge gave me a further three months in the detention centre. I couldn't believe my luck: I would be back on the streets in two months.

I was once again taken to Whatton detention centre for another sharp shock, only this time I knew the ropes and all the dodges. The screws knew me, and I knew them; you didn't call them paedos in them days, nonces they were, but many of the screws were too.

A short sharp shock it had been the first time, now it was just a pain in the arse to get it over and done with. I started using the gym and playing football, basketball, volleyball, doing classes and keeping my nose clean. They had a game called murderball where anything went; basically, it was a chance for all the boys to knock the fuck out of each other and get rid of their aggression in the gym chasing a ball around. My time passed quickly and in June 1975 I was back on the streets once more. I had the world at my feet, or so I should have thought.

Girls I was shy around. With my ginger hair and teenage spots, I was no Brad Pitt, but I had started to make a name for myself, albeit for the wrong reasons, with the girls in Warrington, but I learned quite quickly that some of the girls liked my bad boy reputation, even if it was just for the night. I lost my virginity with a girl called Debbie, who was a sweet girl whom I had fancied for ages. I thought, *At last, I am a man*! Laughable really. Back in Warrington I never went back to school; I had been due to leave in 1976 but technically had left in 1974. I was always playing truant; this went on for two years. My plan was to follow in my father's footsteps, to join the Merchant Navy and see the world, so I could see no reason to go back to school. I didn't have to sit any qualifications, and indeed I left school with nothing. You cannot put an old head on young shoulders; what a waste of a good education.

I started to notice a young girl called Wendy. She had grown up in Canada and her family had recently moved back to Warrington; her mum and dad, and her sister Carole, were living close by to me. I'd had a brief fling with another girl, Ange, who went to my school, but it never went further than kissing. I was no Don Juan; but Wendy was different, a year older than me, a bit more worldly-wise, and I fancied her like fuck. She hung out with all the boys, and we all loved her Canadian accent; it was sexy. I thought so anyway. I would see her at the local clubs and discos when I was with the DJ Pete Rigby, and plucked up the courage to ask her out.

I was still getting in trouble for petty offences. I went joyriding and causing breaches of the peace but somehow I was getting off with small fines. A couple of times they placed me in care homes, but I would run away to see Wendy. I had a probation officer for over seven years; he would shake his head at my antics and really did his best to keep me on the straight and narrow, but I was far too young and angry to take any notice. Things were progressing well between me and Wendy, and she introduced me to her parents. Her dad worked for the council, and her mum ran the local corner shop; they were great people and made me very welcome. I stayed nearly every night at their house, and they treated me like a son, fed me, gave me money and looked after me. My younger brother Anthony never saw me, it took him years before he knew who I really was, or that he had a brother.

I was also staying in old houses that were derelict. I had a mattress in there, where I and Wendy would go to satisfy our teenage passions. But I was still hanging around with my mates and being a nuisance all the time. I did odd jobs and worked on the fairground when it came to town; I was still stealing to survive and have fun.

'You can be childlike without being childish. A child wants to have fun. Ask yourself, am I having fun?' Christopher Meloni

Chapter 5
The Summer of 1976

I went away camping with Wendy, my Uncle Dave and Aunty Val, to Newquay, in Cornwall, along with my cousin Darren. We had great fun. Cornwall is beautiful in the summertime: you could well be in Australia, with its white sandy beaches and stunning coastlines. I was now 16 and thought I knew it all.

We got back from Cornwall, glowing with happiness, but my problem was I loved my mates and going out with them all the time. Somehow Wendy persuaded me to go to Belgium with her by coach. We passed through London and onto Dover for the ferry across, but I missed my mates and couldn't wait to get back.

I was still seeing and working with the local DJ Pete Rigby, and a character called the Longford Lover, who had brought the Rolling Stones to Warrington. Warringtonians love music: there were always parties and fights, Warrington was renowned for them. I was always giving Wendy excuses and slipping out to meet my mates around the town. I would meet up with all my friends and just go on the rampage, getting pissed, and being boisterous, and after the pubs closed would head to the hotdog stand called the Hogie Wagon, run by Ken, which was near the River Mersey which meanders its way through the town at Bridgefoot. Everyone came there after the boozers closed, either for a burger or a fight.

One particular night we all met up at the Hogie Wagon at gone midnight, Terry, Johnny, Alan and a load of others, all in very high spirits, drunk and being abusive to the local coppers. One of the policemen told us to shut it. We all laughed and started singing! 'Who's that twat in the big black hat. Doo dah... doo dah... dah day.' A group of the lads were dropping their pants and we were all laughing. The policeman was getting angrier and called for backup, and my mate Johnny rammed a burger in the copper's face. Tomato ketchup was running down the copper's face, I was so pissed I didn't know what had happened, but a car full of police jumped out with their batons drawn, and it kicked off big time. I really couldn't remember much after that.

I awoke the next day in the police cells in Arpley Street in Warrington, with a banging head and a dry mouth wondering what the fuck had happened. Nothing like waking up in the cold light of day and thinking, *This is not looking good.* I was hoping we would be charged with drunk and disorderly, but when we appeared in the dock after being brought up from the cells, they read the charges out: police assault, breach of the peace, and the serious charge of an affray which carries 14 years. It was really not looking good. It was that scorching summer of 1976, and I really was not looking forward to being caged up for one stupid night of high jinks either.

The prosecution said the boys were running around with their pants down, to the chants of 'Get them off, get them off.' We all just burst out laughing, probably through nerves. The magistrate told us to be quiet and then remanded us into custody for a week. Alan and I were 16, Terry and John were 17, and Johnny had a lot of previous for violence. We were all taken back down to the cells to be transferred to Risley.

Anybody who was alive in 1976 will remember how hot that summer really was - it never rained for three months - and we were now facing the prospect of lengthy sentences behind bars, for fuck knows how long, all for stupidity.

When you arrive at Risley as an unconvicted prisoner you are allowed visits and food to be brought in. Wendy and my dad came to see me, and the local lawyer Peter McKenna; he was almost like a mate he represented me so much over those years. Pete probably made quite a lot of money over the years defending the scallywags of the town, and good luck to him, he was a decent fella. But we all knew we were not getting out on these charges and would definitely get a jail sentence.

We kept going back to court week after week getting the case adjourned; in that summer heat, it was stifling. Luckily the affray charges were dropped and finally our cases were sent on to Chester Crown to be sentenced in October 1976. Johnny and Terry were sentenced a week before me and Alan, as they were slightly older. Johnny got three years and Terry got eighteen months and they were sent off to Walton prison in Liverpool to serve out their sentences. A week later Alan and I were up before the judge ready to take our punishment. He gave us a dressing down and then sentenced us both to Borstal training, and we went down to the cells below to await our transfer to Strangeways prison, Manchester. Strangeways was where you got sent to before they allocated you to Borstal. We spent six weeks there, then were sent on to Low Newton in Durham, before finally being sent to Everthorpe Borstal in Humberside.

Alan was a game little fucker who loved Northern Soul and fighting at the Warrington rugby games. He was small and wiry but had bollocks, and he had a girlfriend, Lynn, who had been with him for a couple of years, a really nice girl.

I remember Elton John and Kiki Dee were at number one that year with 'Don't Go Breaking My Heart.' We both had baggy trousers and spoon-shoes; we were in for a shock the following year.

'Things are so hard to figure out when you live from day to day in this feverish and silly world' Jack Kerouac

Chapter 6
Everthorpe Borstal

If you stayed out of trouble in Borstal you could be out within six months, or two years; they called it 6 to 2.

When we arrived, they split us up and we went on different wings. For the first six weeks, it was circuit training, marching around being shouted at constantly, and scrubbing floors. You had to keep your cells spotless, they would always be blowing whistles and you ran everywhere. When you finished the induction period things became easier. Alan worked in the kitchens and I did a building course, and we tried to make the most of a bad situation.

I was getting weekly letters from Wendy. I don't know how she stuck by me, but she did, and kept me connected to the outside world. I was doing night classes, reading and using my brain. I made a good friend called Tiger from Sheffield; he was a lunatic, but not a bully, he would assault screws and had been moved around from Borstal to Borstal, but we became good friends. I often wonder how he is now, and if he's still alive. He used to get hash smuggled in and we would get stoned and listen to music, when the screws weren't around that is. He served the full two years of his sentence.

By this time, I was getting postcards from friends who had joined the Navy, from places like Hong Kong, Japan and South America. What the fuck was I doing with my life? I was raging through my rebellious teenage years. Quietly in my mind I knew I was on the wrong path, but I stayed on this path for many years to come. I loved reading and writing letters, and short stories, and I wish I'd had some encouragement back then, but better late than never.

What was I now? In my 17th year, a Borstal boy with no qualifications, a string of convictions and a further nine months to serve ahead of me.

Christmas 1976 came and went, and into the New Year of 1977, Dad came to see me; he was now living alone, raising my younger brother Anthony, who was now 10 years old. My family lived all over the UK, and they all moved around. On both sides of my family we have Irish and Scottish connections: Celtic blood ran through the family. Dad seemed to be coping, and things were getting easier for him and my brother Anthony, and I was glad for them both.

I get along quite easily with people: I do like people, and growing up around music and parties. I can have the gift of the gab, and other times I can be very quiet; maybe I have a split personality. I am sure some people who know me would agree. Children of alcoholics do suffer, especially in their formative years, but on the whole, I think I'm a good person. I do like helping people, but when you are young, and your life gets screwed up in some way, life can turn out to be quite different from what is expected.

Alan was doing fine in the Borstal by now; he had a good job and was just getting on with his sentence, obviously looking forward to his release date, as we all were. I was attending classes and courses keeping myself busy. I had a few minor fights with boys on the wing but nothing too heavy. When you're that age teenage boys like to assert their prowess by acting the tough guy.

Time was passing by, and I started to hear new music on the radio; there was to be a major shift in youth culture. This was the time of power cuts and the miners' strike; the youth was getting angrier and more unsatisfied. The working class were doomed to be cannon fodder for the local factories or mines in their area, scattered all over the North of England. They wanted more, I wanted more. Football hooliganism was a direct result: they wanted excitement and they got it on the terraces of football grounds across the UK. I met loads of them in jail, young, cocky and extremely violent. They thrived on the buzz of violence; they had the mob mentality. Luckily, I was never drawn into it. Although I loved playing the sport, I was never really into watching football, although I occasionally watched an England game, or went to the Warrington rugby games for a laugh more than anything. I loved watching boxing, in the days of Ali, Roberto Duran, Marvin Haggler, Tommy the Hitman Hearns; it was exciting for me, but watching football was a bit like watching paint dry, but there you go, different strokes for different folks.

In Borstal, guys made up poems about their times inside. Kids had a spot tattooed on their faces, a mark on the cheek, a badge of honour to prove they had been to Borstal. Luckily, I never bothered: when you are young and angry you will do the most outrageous things.

In wartimes the working class were the backbone of this country, led into battle by the politicians and the rich to do their bidding; the politicians would have been fucked without the working classes fighting their battles. You rarely see a rich kid take up boxing seriously, step into a boxing ring and make something of themselves. They are not hungry enough; they don't have to fight their way out of poverty. Working class kids see a way out through boxing, football - they see a chance to shine and lift their families out of poverty. Some working class kids get lucky and break through into the sports arenas across the globe, but for most, they are left having to work for a pittance to sustain their families. Others turn to crime, drug dealing, theft, murder: the working class have the hunger and are great in dangerous situations, but have been exploited for centuries, which is why they are called the salt of the earth, they really are. Then you have the underclass; they don't even merit a look on the street by passers-by, but they are there, living under the margins, breathing the same air as you and I.

In jail time drags by slowly. I kept imagining myself to be outside. I had family in London we used to visit in the 60s, my uncle Barney who was a friend of the actor Arthur Mullard. Through my family, I knew there was a big wide world out there to be explored. I didn't know how, and I didn't know when, but I knew one day I was going to see it. When you're alone in your cell you have plenty of time on your hands, and I turned to books. I read everything I could get my hands on: I loved reading. I read *War and Peace* by Tolstoy twice; it can take a week to read such a magnificent book. I read *Papillon*, and *Banco*, and they gave me a sense of adventure and a love of reading that I carry to this day in my life. My love of reading really came from those days of being locked up as a child. I have met people who have never read a book in their lives; they cannot concentrate on the books, but reading and the classics especially can enrich and expand your mind so much. History I find fascinating; I may not be a scholar, but I do love to learn, and I do like to learn about life and its experiences.

After about six months in Borstal, you have been carefully monitored and watched closely, and reports are made on you. I was classed to be a daydreamer, perhaps I am, always lost in my own thoughts, away from reality, it suited me. I remember near the end of my sentence they offered me a 5-day home leave, where they let you go home and you have to come back and finish the rest of your sentence, of perhaps another three or four weeks. I decided to take it sometime in June of 1977. I stepped into my own clothes, baggy pants and spoon shoes once again, and left Borstal behind me, headed to the nearest train station and boarded the train back home.

I felt like I had landed on the moon in that summer of 77: all the kids were in drainpipes and jumping around to the punk rock that had suddenly broken through that year via four guys from London, The Sex Pistols. What a contrast - here was I in my baggy pants. That weekend I still went to Wigan Casino, and I stayed up for days speeding and having a whale of a time. Within five days I was back in my cell in Borstal. I was absolutely exhausted, closed my cell door and slept like a baby until the following morning. I still had weeks to go. My mate Alan had left Borstal by now, as he had been recommended to go home earlier than me, and good luck to him.

Finally, I served out the rest of my sentence, and three weeks later I was back on the street. It had been a rough 12 months for some poxy stupid offence, but I did learn my lesson, and I have never hit a policeman again; it's all 'Yes sir, no sir, three bags full sir.' I realised they are only doing a job. I really did fight the law, and the law definitely won. Violence and getting locked up for it was really a mug's game, you make no money and you lose your liberty - what a moron I had been. Football hooligans didn't give a toss; I did though, no more of that for me I thought. I was 17 years old and thought I was wising up to myself. Little did I know, as I left Everthorpe Borstal, that day back in 1977.

'The road to hell is paved with good intentions.'

Chapter 7
Stoke Heath Borstal 1977

Fuck me dead! That didn't last long: had I really been out, was it all a dream? After another spell, I was yet again being shipped out from Strangeways to another Borstal in Shropshire called Stoke Heath, not far from Crewe. How could I have been so stupid? How had this happened yet again? The words of the judge were ringing in my ears: Thomas James Kennedy, we have decided to recall you to Borstal. In the cells below Warrington Crown Court, I saw scrawled on the wall: No ale, no bail, no tail, all jail.

Was this to be my life? Rotting away in institutions? I punched the fuck out of my cell door, I was so frustrated, my knuckles were bleeding and red raw, another Christmas and New Year on the horizon, and all I had to look forward to was a fucking cell again. I couldn't believe it: honestly, I had not expected this, the Warrington police must have been pissing themselves, laughing at me. I had no choice; I was so pissed off at myself. The only good thing about this whole scenario was the judge had recalled me to Borstal rather than given me a further sentence of 6 to 2. I was to serve an extra four months and I would be released on Valentine's Day, February 14th, 1978. But it was a fucking ball ache; *Thanks for nothing your Honour*, I muttered under my breath as they led me down below to serve my sentence.

A new Borstal, same old routine. Bumping into faces I knew from previous spells inside. I was becoming a face in the penal system; not something I wanted, but I had to deal with it in the best way I could. They gave me some shitty job in the laundry where I learned how to fold and press shirts, and it was mind-numbing. I had just turned 18 the day before, and I was on the road to nowhere, for sure. I really had no time for knob heads, nor indeed was I in the mood for bullies trying it on: I was becoming an old hand at dealing with them. I was more than ready for a punch up and they left me alone. There were some really violent kids in there: a lot of them went on to serve life sentences years later.

Wendy still stuck by me. Since we had lost our child in 1975 when she miscarried, she had been loyal and loving, but I must have tried her patience at times. She had a heart of gold that girl. She passed her driving test while I was on that sentence, and I was made up for her.

I was meeting creative people in there, kids who really could paint and draw, and I bought many things from them to decorate my cell and make it homelier. But I was just another prison number, marking my time until they set me free. More reading was essential to improve my mind, help me to forget my surroundings and go on adventures around the world, in my mind at least. My gipsy soul was yet again being constrained and confined to a cell. I really had plans to live an adventurous life: no settling down with a mortgage and 2.2 kids for me, no sir. A house and a mortgage were the last things on my mind. My dad used to say, 'Don't think about marriage until you are 40, and forget about it when you are 50.' I have to agree: some of us are not cut out for that life, although I was a long way from being 40, and I was hardly Warrington's most eligible bachelor with my ginger hair and spotty face, but somehow Wendy loved me.

My friends and family wanted to visit me, but I decided it made things worse as after a visit, it would put you on a downer, so I would sit out the rest of my sentence and see them on my release. My brother Anthony was 11 now and barely knew me, and my sister Lynn had left Warrington many years before and was now married, and the main reason I was now locked up.

After my short release from Everthorpe Borstal, my sister had decided to get married in the July of 77. I had no money and was invited to her wedding in Fareham just outside Portsmouth. Wendy's mum gave me twenty quid to buy a wedding present, and I went around the town with my mate Chris, who took me into Timothy Whites in town. I explained to the shop assistant I was going to my sister's wedding and needed a good present. She was showing me around, and unbeknown to me my mate had stolen an expensive canteen of cutlery out of the display in the window. He beckoned me by waving, so I followed him outside and he pulled out of his jumper this rather fine and exquisite silver canteen of cutlery, which was worth two hundred quid, and said he would sell it to me for a score. I stupidly agreed, and thought nothing about it.

The following week I went to the wedding. Lynn was made up with the present and so were her new in-laws, who were quite middle class, compared to the Kennedys at least. We had a great time, and I thought nothing of it. A few days later, having come back from Fareham, I was in the town centre in Warrington when the police arrested me and brought me into the police station. I had no idea why they asked where

I'd been the last few days. They had been looking for me. I said I was at my sister's wedding, not having a clue why I was pulled in for questioning. The CID officer then said, 'What did you get her for a present?' and then the penny dropped. I said, 'I got her nothing,' and he said, 'We will have the police go to her house, and we will have her arrested for receiving stolen property if you do not admit to the charge.'

I was fucked, I had to admit it; even though I never stole it, I couldn't involve my mate as I would have been classed as a grass, so I had to swallow it. The police went to my sister's house and took the canteen of cutlery away from them; my sister was mortified and so was I. I was charged and released on bail, with restrictions and a curfew to stay home at night.

Wendy had previously booked three weeks in Canada, for a holiday for me as a surprise before I was arrested. It meant I couldn't go along with her, so I was fuming. But then I decided to take the risk and just go, even though I was on bail and not even supposed to go out at night. We flew to Canada a few days later for the three-week holiday, and we stayed in Edmonton with her family. We went by car to the Rocky Mountains, and I learnt to water-ski on the lakes out there; I even had the Canadian flag tattooed on my wrist. I came back to England at the end of the holiday, and the police had been none the wiser, luckily for me.

The whole episode had cost me dearly though. I had to buy another canteen of cutlery for my sister, costing me more money, I had embarrassed my family, and to top it all off I was in the local newspaper under the headline 'MAN STEALS WEDDING PRESENT FOR HIS SISTER'S WEDDING', naming and shaming the family. My dad went mad, and I went back to Borstal. Unbelievably, even the other kids in the Borstal were taking the piss when they heard what I was in for.

Dad was still working, and he had bought a house on Liverpool Road in the town; he was still boozing heavily though, he was unhappy, I knew that, and I just hoped things would get better for him, especially as he was looking after our kid.

We were now in January 1978, and I just had to keep my nose clean and I would be out in six weeks. I was always smoking hash through and had to be careful not to get caught by the screws, but it made life more bearable in Borstal with its petty rules and the monotony of it all. Luckily, I didn't get caught, and it always put a smile on my face. I had learnt to drive cars by joyriding and borrowing my dad's car at nights when he was asleep, and I was determined to pass my test on my release, but never seemed to be out long enough. But the way my drinking was, when I was out, I probably would have killed myself or others in the process.

I was meeting a lot of Londoners who had been caught committing offences around Birmingham, usually burgling manor houses for paintings and jewellery, and large amounts of cash sometimes, if they were lucky. I was loving the London attitude: they didn't have that small-town mentality, and they would regale me with stories of the East End, and the tourist area of the West End and Piccadilly. In jail, you meet a lot of bullshitters, but if the stories were good, I didn't mind. They had great stories of the Kings Road and the punk scene where the phenomenon had taken place, and how the punks and Jamaicans would throw parties and mix freely together. I was still into Northern Soul but my musical horizons were being broadened, even though still locked up. I have a way of connecting with people who want to be friends, which has stood me in good stead over the years.

Wendy wrote to me and told me her dad had found me a job in a local factory called Lockers in Warrington, wire weaving; it was not what I'd had in mind, but for now it would do, and at least I would be earning the readies legally and hopefully keeping out of the penal system. I was getting down to the last few weeks of this sentence and getting gate fever, just wanting to be back on the road, although wanting to read and learn, never having had the best education in the world, but at least I did try to improve my mind, and the books taught me about the world.

Most of my friends at that time were in and out of jail, not all of them but most of them. I didn't really hang around with the law-abiding ones, I thought they were too straight-laced; once again how stupid was my thinking in those times. It was inevitable with my background that I was heading for trouble. Crime never paid for me at that time, but it did give me a fix, something I unconsciously sought, and it made me the centre of attention for all the wrong reasons.

Ma had left my dad for an Irishman called Mike. I never really took to him, although he did get Ma to stop drinking. I blamed Ma for destroying my childhood, with her drinking and wild ways, but at the end of the day, she was still my mother.

There were plenty of kids who came through the penal system from broken homes with far worse stories than me; still it broke my heart, you should love your kids and be kind with them. There were plenty of nonces in the penal system who had abused kids and they would be targeted by the other cons: hot water would be thrown over them, they would get razored. Most of them were on the protection wing under rule 43, but even the screws would turn a blind eye if you caught up with one of the nonces and gave them a good hiding. It was a sport and a great way of getting rid of your aggression on them. I dished it out to a few of them on occasion.

I was now 18, coming to the end of my sentence and ready to go home to try and sort my life out. Or was I? With my track record, I couldn't be sure. Well, my time was up on the 14th of February, Valentine's Day, when lovers spend the night together. They gave me a giro, 14 quid, dropped me off at the train station in Crewe and left me to my own devices: nobody telling me what to do, able to eat whatever I wanted, and finally able to get laid, and at that age I was dying for it. The train pulled into Bank Quay station in Warrington, and I started to make my way back to Wendy's house when I bumped into some mates who persuaded me to go on the lash. I was supposed to be going straight, and I did - straight to the pub. I arrived at Wendy's house late that night, smashed out of my nut, and her mum went mad.

I fell asleep on their couch in the front room. What a thoughtless bastard I was. Happy Valentine's Day, it was not, but as usual the next day Wendy forgave me: she truly did love me, only the way youngsters do with their first love.

'Love makes you stronger.'

Chapter 8
Factory Life

Wendy's dad had sorted me with a job, so on a Monday morning, I reported for work at the local factory. The noise was deafening: the wire looms were going all day long, about a hundred of them in unison, making chain-link fences and weaving wire mesh. I decided to give it my best shot for the sake of Wendy, and the family. Some of the guys had been there 30 or 40 years, and there were plenty of women working there also. I soon got the hang of it after about a month, but my soul was dying; the money came in handy though, and I had to stick it out at least for a while. It wasn't long before I reverted back to old habits, going to Wigan Casino, taking drugs and getting into all kinds of skulduggery.

I was late for work dozens of times, and they started to warn me if I was late or took any more days off, I would be fired. I took no notice as usual and after a couple of months the foreman came along and told me my services were no longer required, or more to the point I was sacked on the spot. It had been so boring, but I did miss the money. I told Wendy I was sorry, and I was going to look for work down south the following week. I hitchhiked to Newquay, Cornwall, looking for work, as I had friends there. I couldn't find anything. I had another mate in Torquay, Devon, Scouse Ray, and decided to chance my luck down there, so once again I stuck my thumb out and headed back towards Devon.

Ray was a big lad and he worked the doors; he was happy to see me and offered me a job on the door. It wasn't what I had in mind, but he found me work on the doors in a pub called The Yacht, near the Marina. The money was good, but I soon realised it wasn't for me, chucking people out: I was usually the one getting chucked out, and hated telling people 'You can't come in.' After about a month I quit and went back home to see Wendy. I stayed at Wendy's house, and once again her dad got me a job at another factory, the Longford wireworks. Jeez, was I doomed to purgatory working in these factories for the rest of my life? It felt like being in jail, clocking in and out, doing shift work, 6am till 2pm and 10pm till 6am, this was even worse, but I made some good friends, Dave and Frank, who were young and up for a laugh, which made it more bearable and the days flew by.

One time I had been driving a brand-new forklift truck and crashed it outside the factory, and the next day when we came back it had been set fire to and was a complete write-off; how they never sacked me I will never know. When I wasn't at work - and why, I don't know - I was out stealing cars, going on joyrides, until I got caught. They gave me bail, and eventually I ended up back in court, but for some reason they gave me a three-month suspended sentence. Probably having a job helped. I was so lucky this time.

So back to work it was. I was spending my wages on clothes, music, drugs, blowing it like there was no tomorrow. Still, Wendy and her family stuck by me. Her mum and dad must have been pulling their hair out with my carrying on. I did feel bad, but I just couldn't seem to help myself, I seemed to thrive on drama and mayhem.

Within a few months, I was back in court, this time for shouting my gob off at a Warrington rugby game. I was pissed and acting like a twat again, arrested once again, and brought before the magistrates. On a suspended jail sentence, I was guaranteed time in the slammer. Unbelievably, the judge in his wisdom let me off again because I was working, and gave me a fine of 125 quid; wow, I was really pushing my luck and I was still only 19.

Having a job didn't keep me straight, but it did the next best thing: it kept me out of jail, for a while at least. I had been with Wendy four years now, but I was really trying her patience, big time. I was a walking one-man disaster. Fighting around the town became a sport, especially when I was pissed; fights were going on just simply because of drink and drugs. Finally, in August 1979 I was sacked after getting caught again, joyriding in stolen cars. I appeared at Warrington Crown Court, and the judge shook his head, banned me from driving for three years and gave me community service, changing shitty sheets in the local doss houses.

When I lost my job, I went on a small crime spree, burgling pubs and clubs, ripping open gaming machines, anything that wasn't nailed down, to get cash. I went on thieving trips across Europe, always on the rob, always on the mooch; I was so reckless, I was a dysfunctional kid who seemed to be destined for a life sentence at some point in the not too distant future. I had tried working but couldn't hack it, I could only live in the moment, and the moment was all I had. Robbing cars, driving to London, Manchester, Liverpool, anywhere, looking for excitement.

I was caught burgling yet again in the summer of 1980, but

surprisingly the judge set me free with probation. My probation officer advised me to see a shrink. I refused. I just carried on. I was now 20 years old, taking huge amounts of drugs: acid, speed, smoking hash - I was out of it most of the time and was driving my family nuts. I had hardly seen my dad or brother: I was like a ghost to them, they saw me fleetingly. I spent a few weeks here and a few weeks there.

'An ounce of blood is worth more than a pound of friendship.'
Spanish Proverb

Chapter 9
God Loves a Trier

Finally, Wendy and I split: she couldn't take it. I had always been loyal to Wendy, but who could blame her?

I met a new girl, Caroline, through a friend of mine called Tony. She was his sister. I was so crazy, I was out burgling all the time, and finally my luck ran out and I got caught.

Up in front of the judge on 12th of January 1980, my brother's 14th birthday, I got six months, and a further six months for breaking my community service order. I was back where I belonged, behind bars. I was a habitual criminal and my life was a mess, why oh why? What was wrong with me? I met old friends from previous spells, Dave, Bri, Ray, Craig, Charlie, George, the list went on. I was literally throwing my life away for what? Cheap thrills and a few quid. The screws in Liverpool were like the screws in Manchester, racist cunts, but I had only myself to blame. There were always fights on the landings, and you were locked down 23 hours a day; an hour out for exercise, and that was it.

They put me in a cell with an ex-boxer, a fucking tosser and brain dead; I could barely stand the sight of him and his bullshit stories that I was forced to listen to nightly. He drove me mad, he was such a liar. I had to grin and bear it though; I was stuck with the cunt for the next six months. I soon found out he wasn't really a boxer when he offered me out in the cell about three weeks later. I couldn't take any more, and I belted him a few times and he soon shut up after that. Just like most bullies, he was all mouth. I got him moved out of the cell, and one of my mates moved in, happy days. My love of books kept me sane in those days. I was always on the hustle for baccy, soap and shampoo. I went to the gym at any opportunity to get out of the cell and unleash the energy coursing through my body. You had to keep yourself busy somehow. The cells were filthy, so we kept them clean, you had to. My Borstal training came in handy: I was good at keeping myself and my cell in tip-top condition.

The more time you spend in prisons the more you learn. Armed robbery was on the rise in the 70s and 80s. I wasn't interested in violent crime, but I was interested in other scams and soaked them up like a sponge. It almost becomes a way of life, crime, like an addiction, and very hard to break away from. It has you moving up the ranks. I wasn't a hard man, but I held my own when it was really needed. The best way to find out about a man is to put him in a corner with no escape route, and then you will know if he's got bollocks after all.

Caroline kept in touch, but she was young and met somebody else; good luck to her, I respected her for trying. Life is a gamble, and I was flipping the coin continually in the wrong direction, but I still saw it all as an adventure, and you have to take whatever comes your way and deal with it like a man.

I stayed in Walton jail for all of that sentence, made a few good friends and a few enemies, just like life in general. Again, my time was up, and I walked out of the gates of 68 Hornby Road, Liverpool, with two empty pockets and a sense of humour about it all, if nothing else.

After a week back in Warrington I decided to try and go straight again and try my luck on the building sites of Germany and Holland. With a few friends, Bri, Chris and Ray, I boarded the ferry in Hull, to head over to Germany.

There was shed loads of graft in Germany around 1980. Agents and scam artists were thriving, hiring British workers, sending them all over Germany and Holland. I had building experience from Borstal and was ready to blag my way into anything. We met an agent in Holland, and he offered me work as a painter, in a place called Bremen, Germany. I had no experience painting, but if you can piss you can paint, right? We all went our separate ways to various parts of Germany.

I loved Germany, the beer, the women, the way of life; it was fun. Bremen, the home of Becks beer, in the north west of Germany, some 40 miles south of the River Weser on the North Sea, was a stunning place to be. I started work in a school, painting the classrooms, rough but easy work, nothing too complicated. In the mornings the Germans would have their 10am break, and out would come the Becks beer in huge bottles. I wasn't used to it, but still got stuck in. I kept getting smashed and blundered my way through the work, for a few weeks anyway. I was staying with a young lady and her boyfriend; they rented a room to me in the town centre. I was getting so pissed on the job the foreman caught me, and yet again I was sacked. I had to wait to get my wages a few days later. I was fuming: they paid me a pittance, so I painted 'We won the War', and a swastika, on the wall. Childish I know, but it made me smirk. I was truly a walking disaster. That night I stayed with the young couple, and in the morning bade them my farewells and boarded the train for the six-hour journey to Amsterdam. I stayed the night in Holland getting stoned and wasted, and the next day I was in Rotterdam to catch the ferry back to Hull.

I arrived back in Warrington less than three weeks later, with nothing, but I had had an adventure, and if nothing else I survived. I was sleeping at mates' places once again; the cycle started all over, getting pissed, out on the rob, to fund my erratic lifestyle - what a winner I was.

I just couldn't seem to stay out of trouble - talk about the Nowhere man - was I descending into madness? I was my own worst enemy. Time after time I was getting so drunk, to blot out the memories of an unhappy childhood more than likely. Did anyone notice I was on a one-way ticket to madness, sinking to the depths of insanity with my behaviour? I was getting in trouble constantly, crying out for some kind of guidance; I just couldn't verbalise how I was feeling. I always kept things inside my head: outwardly I was Jack the Lad, but deep down this was not the life I wanted or indeed deserved.

It seemed I couldn't stay out of trouble in Warrington. I had to leave, but I kept coming back. Why? It was madness, I was reckless to the extreme and I was fucked. I had my demons, and I really think they came from Ma; something terrible must have happened to her but I never found out what. The thing is, I never spoke to anybody about this, school, probation; my mates would have laughed and taken the piss, so I just carried on as if everything was fine.

I have always been drawn to the bright lights of any town or city; in fact, I just couldn't stay in, I had to be out every night, and if something was going on, I had to be part of it. Warrington was full of pubs and clubs in the 70s and early 80s while I was there. It was a crazy time in my life; everybody loved a good piss up or punch up. We used to go to The Lion, run by Scouser Bill Medland. Bill had put David Bowie on there. The Lion had great bands playing every night, and The Carlton, run by Manchester Dereck, was for dancing. Warrington had some posh areas - Lymm, Daresbury, Grappenhall, Stockton Heath, although I never went there unless it was on the mooch. I always went to the town centre, looking for fun as usual.

I had friends who played for Warrington: Alan Rathbone, AKA Action; he had been a good amateur boxer too, a good all-round sportsman. My mate Carl Webb, from Penketh, played for the Wires. Warrington games were always played on a Sunday, and the pubs and clubs would be heaving. I never paid to get into the rugby games, ever;

always jumping over the walls. I remember one time I jumped over a copper's head while he was taking a piss - he could hardly chase me with his cock in his hand, could he? I was laughing my bollocks off as I quickly disappeared into the crowd. By this time, I was well known to the police in the town, and with my ginger hair, I always stood out in a crowd. The kids used to take the piss at school calling me Gingernut; it drove me mad and usually ended in a brawl.

If my younger brother Anthony got into trouble or a fight, I would take care of him. I was also a bit harsh with him myself looking back, but I didn't want him to be a weakling, which he wasn't anyway. He was a good-hearted kid and he should have been looked after much better by his mother, but she only seemed to bother when it suited her purpose. Anthony loved our dad; it was our dad who raised him when she split with her new fella. No wonder Anthony can be a handful at times after being raised mainly by Dad. Our Anthony had lots of mates with names like Cheedy, Browny, The Ruane brothers, the O'Malleys - their uncle had been Mr Universe - the town was awash with Characters.

Trouble was never far away for me though. Most of my friends were involved in scams of all kinds, in one form or another, from credit cards to Post Office books, the bookies, and even gaming machines in pubs were making money for them. I had some good friends from school, and one of our most famous pupils was Ossie Clark, the fashion designer who had dressed the Rolling Stones. He came back to revisit our old school Beamont Technical in the 70s. He was being filmed by *Granada Reports*. He came on stage to give a speech in a white suit and a huge green dickie bow with white polka dots on it. When he opened his mouth, he sounded so obviously gay, all the kids laughed at him, and he ran off the stage crying. I felt sorry for him though; he was one of the people who had inspired me, showing me there was more to life outside of this town. Ossie lived in Holland Park, West London, close to where I live now. He was later murdered by his gay Italian lover. What a tragic waste of a great talent.

Warrington has had its fair share of famous people: Lewis Carroll, the author of *Alice in Wonderland,* was born there, Ian Brown from the Stone Roses lived there until he was six before moving to Manchester, the actor Peter Postlethwaite, the radio DJ Chris Evans, Pete Waterman has a house there, Roger Moore had a house there, so there must be some attraction to the town. It was close to the major cities of Manchester and Liverpool, and people moved to Warrington from both cities. Oliver Cromwell fought battles there. Warringtonians are a proud and feisty bunch who love the crack and follow the Wires. I carried on drinking and drifting through life pretty aimlessly, in and out of petty crime. It was inevitable I would get nicked again, either through sheer boredom, or that rebellious streak that ran right through me.

Sure enough, I and another lad called Tommy got nicked burgling a workingmen's club in Stockton Heath. It sounded like a good idea at the time. We broke in through the roof and ripped open all the gaming machines whilst the alarm was going off, but the police arrived in droves and caught us on the job, and we were arrested on the scene. Yet again we appeared in the dock. My brief got up, said his piece in our defence, and the magistrate told him to sit down, and five minutes later sentenced us both to six months. In the van on the way to Strangeways I thought, *Here we go again*. This was getting out of hand; half the time it was just drunken escapades, spur of the moment stupidity that kept leading to my downfall, and although not a long sentence, it was still enough to make me wonder what the fuck I was still doing in this town.

My reputation was logged in the police notebooks, and if anything went wrong and red hair got mentioned they would soon come looking for me. It wasn't good: my life was panning out like a car crash. People were giving up on me, although my dad always stuck by me, god knows why. I was back in Strangeways, where I remained for the next four months, walking around the exercise yard again, where fights often kicked off to relieve the boredom. I was kicking myself yet again.

The town drunk, Henry Marshall, was in there too. I'd never seen him sober on the outside. He had won medals in World War Two; his ship had got blown up somewhere in the Atlantic, and Henry suffered shellshock for the rest of his life. He became a full-blown alcoholic, drinking methylated spirits daily around Warrington town centre. He was a figure of fun to a lot of people, but I liked him. He had a childlike quality about him, and who was I to look down on anybody? I heard his wife suffered living with him, and I can only imagine the headaches he gave her.

I heard around this time that our kid, 14 by now, had just got three months in a Detention Centre. What kind of role model was I? It really gutted me when I heard the news.

I was doing more and more reading in Strangeways, trying to educate myself, and listening to Piccadilly Radio. I was constantly thinking: why am I doing this bullshit way of living, I have got to give my life of crime up. I knew it wouldn't be easy, but then nothing in my life had been easy up to now. My spirit was always strong, and I had so much energy sitting in a cell all day long. It really made me feel like a caged animal, which in a way I was.

I was now 21, and on the men's wing of the prison with all the adults. I preferred it. It was better than being on the under 21s where fights were more common, and kids would want to fight you over some trivial nonsense at the drop of a hat. Strangeways and Walton were becoming like my second homes - how freaking stupid was that? Life was just passing me by, and what had I achieved in my life so far? I wouldn't wish this life on a dog, and most of the other cons were probably thinking the same.

I shunned all visits. What could I say to anybody? I was becoming a hopeless case; would I ever get my head together?

I had friends from all over the North West of England, but they were mainly people I would meet in prison, blaggers, drug dealers and the like; we all mixed freely together on the exercise yards courtesy of HMP. Occasionally the prison would show films in the cinema and I remember watching the life story of the singer Buddy Holly, who tragically lost his life in a plane crash at just 22 years of age, and here was I just throwing my life away, for what? Cheap thrills and a few quid. The Probation Service was beginning to think I was a lost cause, and really, I was.

I started to think I wanted a place to call my own on my release, so I set about writing to various people to see if somebody could find me a place to live. I wasn't sure if anybody wanted to house an ex-con, but it was worth a go. My sister Lynn had left Warrington years before, when she was 16, and now had her own family. We were like strangers, but she wrote to me and we kept in touch; she had her life going on and she seemed happy.

My old man was still working, and he was still very bitter about the way my mum left him. He had loved her with all her faults - he had been happy - and it hurt him deeply. Life moves on, and you have to get over things, and never get bitter about it: that's just a real waste of energy, and I saw what it did to my dad. He was a good man and he always tried his best with all three of us; he had no favourite, but I think as Anthony is the youngest of the family, he kept more of an eye on him. I think out of all of us Anthony knew my dad the most. If my dad said he would do something, he did it, while Ma would promise the earth, and forget about it the next day.

I was now a grown man and able to make my own choices in life. I had somehow slipped into this life of criminality, and the old saying was *If you can't do the time, don't do the crime*; well, you somehow had to deal with it the best you could, and my deep love of books helped me through all the sentences. I do have a vivid imagination, and I needed constant change, new places, new faces, but mine were all coming through the prisons I was frequenting, it was almost laughable if it hadn't been so true. I was the architect of my own downfall.

Some friends had moved to London and I always envisaged I would be living there one day; if I ever got my act together that was. The energy of big cities would suit me, I hoped. There is only so much you can do in a small town, and I was too well-known in my hometown: I couldn't do anything without being noticed. Time passed by slowly but pass by it did, and some time in the summer of 1981, I was set free, leaving behind Strangeways, with another shot at freedom and with the greatest intentions of leaving this life behind.

'The definition of insanity is doing the same thing over and over and expecting different results.' Albert Einstein

Chapter 10
Wymott

I quickly found a one bedroom flat in Orford, Warrington, and set out to find some kind of work. I just couldn't get that motivated, and it wasn't long before I was slipping back into old ways, buying and selling hash, dealing from my new flat. I was surviving but my life of crime was still going on all around me. The flat gave me a base, and I always had people coming and going after the pubs closed. I would buy a few ounces of Lebanese Hash, or Gold Seal, sometimes speed or acid, whatever my punters wanted. At least I was not burgling any more, I thought to myself.

I was going out every night, getting bladdered, getting high, meeting girls, generally having a good time and thinking I was making up for lost time. Some friends were getting married, settling down and raising families, but not me, that wasn't in my mindset one bit.

I would sometimes go to Holland and bring back hash, not large amounts but I enjoyed the buzz of coming back through customs and not getting caught. I would go with friends who drove there on shoplifting expeditions. I would join in. I was like a kleptomaniac; my mum had taught me well. I really was crazy. I was also buying and selling off the shoplifters and there were loads of them; anything to make money, and keep the party rolling. I would sporadically do a bit of work on local building sites, which never lasted long, a few days here and there. Warrington was like a playground for me. I was in all the pubs and clubs around the town and you made your connections there; I nicknamed it 'Party Town.' I was meeting all the local girls, or getting pissed predominately. With no real trade to my name, I could only do factory work, and I knew this was not for me. I wanted to be a bricklayer, but I wasn't skilled enough. Getting out of bed was hard work when you have been up all night.

I was seeing a few women, but nothing serious: I was enjoying being single and having nobody to answer to. Blackpool is about an hour away, and I would frequently go there to have a break from the town. When you are dealing you are always risking being caught with it, and in the days before mobile phones you would be carrying it around constantly, risking being stopped and searched. I never had a driving licence, but I still drove; you could get away with it in them days. I was borrowing cars from friends and sometimes my dad. I used to go to Manchester and Liverpool; I knew loads of people from jail, the drugs were cheap, and I loved the buzz of both cities, and going to the pubs and clubs of both of them. My accent was a combination of both of them; some people thought I was either a Manc or a Scouser, but I never put it on. I was proud to be from Warrington; it was the place I was born and spent my early years. So, life went on, in a foggy haze, either drunk or stoned, on a permanent rollercoaster of debauchery.

And so it was, one night drinking in the Carlton Club, that I ran into my old mate Terry, fresh out of jail a few weeks before. He told me about a pub that had a lot of money, and the warning light in my head went off. What was I thinking? He was telling me one of the windows was left open; it would be easy money. We had a few more beers and it started to sound like a good idea, so we agreed to meet the following night after the pub closed, and I would be his lookout.

When I woke up the next day, I started to think this wasn't such a great idea, but for some reason I didn't want to let him down and back out. That night, we met up and waited for the pub to close, and a couple of hours later when the pub was in darkness he pulled out his gloves and screwdrivers to open the gaming machines. My job was just to keep watch. Sure enough, the window was open on the side of the pub in a quiet street, and it was very dark outside.

He climbed up to get in the window. I give him his due, he was fearless and game for anything. My heart was pounding, and I was sure I saw some people in a car further up the road, so I shouted to him to come down. He was well pissed off with me and thought I was losing my bottle - perhaps I was - but we both approached the car to check it out. Fuck me, it was an unmarked police car, and two CID jumped out and told us we were both under arrest. It transpired that the pub was under surveillance as the police had been informed it was going to be targeted; some low life grass had set us up, and we had walked right into their trap. I couldn't believe our luck. We were bundled into the police car, and I just remember thinking, *Aw fuck, not again.* I had only stood in the street keeping watch, but they charged us both with attempted burglary and going equipped to steal. The next morning in court I pleaded not guilty, but we had no chance of bail and were both sent to Risley Remand Centre yet again. I was so pissed off with myself. I should have gone with my instincts in the first place, but no.

I was sure my friends and family thought I had a screw loose, and indeed I was beginning to think it myself. What was I achieving? Sweet fuck all, and once again I was looking at jail time.

We spent a couple of months in Risley, back and forth to court, until we finally appeared in the dock of Warrington Crown Court just before Christmas 1981, in the final sessions of the court before they closed for the Christmas holidays. I had changed my plea to guilty hoping to get a lighter sentence, and sure enough, I got the Christmas present I really never wanted: the judge handed me a nine-month prison sentence, and Terry got fifteen months. I muttered to the judge under my breath 'You cunt' as we were led down to the cells below. We were both dispatched to Walton prison in Liverpool where we spent another month before they sent us on to Wymott, a new prison in Leyland, just outside Preston. I said to Terry that night, 'I am finished with jail, and I will never be back.' He laughed and slapped me around the back of the head, and said, 'Shut up you soft twat, you'll be back.' He was almost right, but it would be many years later and in different countries. I never went back to Strangeways, or Walton, and nor do I wish to, I might add. I was determined to give up this wayward life, but first I had many months ahead of me to serve.

I hated Wymott: it was full of dickheads, and I just wanted to get it over and done with. I had said many times it was over, going to jail, and this time, I really had to prove to myself that I really could do it. I was assigned a job to work in the kitchens cleaning the steel trays that the men had their food on. It was hard work, three times a day cleaning up thousands of steel trays after each meal the prisoners had finished. I spent months doing that job. It really drove me nuts constantly collecting the trays and washing them; it was a hard job with no perks whatsoever. The time was passing by and I was like a greyhound chomping at the bit to finally get back onto the streets and put my plans into action.

On the final night, I wrote 'Fuck jail' on my cell wall before they released me in the morning.

Leaving Wymott behind me, I was confident I was going to make it and stay out of jail forever. I was now 22 years old, and I had fuck-all money behind me, but I had a burning desire to get out of Warrington and make some kind of life for myself that had nothing to do with crime and being locked up behind bars. Within a few weeks of my release I met a girl called Karen. She was gorgeous and had a twin sister Jackie; they were both from Chester. I fell in love with Karen, and she really helped me to calm down. The Council had set me up with a flat, but I wanted out of Warrington; but first I had to work out how I was going to do it.

'Whether you think you can, or you think you can't - you're right'
Henry Ford

Chapter 11
Chester

A few months on, Karen had been helping me out with money and I had been doing odd jobs. When I applied to do a bricklaying course in Runcorn I was accepted. Karen and I decided to move to her hometown of Chester and leave Warrington behind.

Life was good with Karen. She had a great sense of humour and really had a calming effect on me, for a while anyway. Her family accepted me, and I really did think the world of her; she was a good girl, but I still had that wild streak in me. I came to realise that my life of crime was really just a rebellious period in my life, when I did things out of anger and frustration, and wanting to be accepted by my peers, who were the rebels of the town. We both settled down to living in Chester, which is a wonderful old Roman town on the banks of the River Dee.

Karen found a job and we rented a room in the city centre; we were happy and settled there for six months whilst I attended the Skill Centre at Runcorn every day. I just had to stay away from Warrington, and it did me the world of good going to work every day learning a trade, and I started to enjoy mixing with the other trainees. I never took a day off; it was a new way of living, being with people who had no criminal links, and who just wanted to better their lives.

In the back of my mind, I had my heart set on moving to London. After the course was over, I knew London had plenty of work on the building sites, and I concentrated on learning as much as I could. I gave up drinking, as I had to be up early each morning and I wanted a clear head. I had given up my life of crime, and at long last, I was beginning to see some kind of hope for myself, and more importantly some kind of future. I enjoyed living in Chester, but after a few months there I was tempted to go back to Warrington, for the weekend. I fell off the wagon and got hammered, but luckily some mates who were time-served bricklayers convinced me to go back the next day. They said, 'When you finish the course, come back and we will all move to London, and help you on the trowel, to get better.'

I love women, but I never played around if I was in a relationship. Call me old-fashioned but I'm a one-woman man; but living with me is not an easy task, especially with my foibles, and I did have a one-night stand one time, and I felt really guilty about it. But Karen and I got on well at that time, and her family made me see a different side of life, and I look back on those days with fond memories. It was a turning point and I had the best of intentions of turning my life around, which I did for many years, and meeting Karen helped me to do that, and I know I owe her big time. I was fully intending to leave the north and head south when the course was over. Karen knew I was getting itchy feet and it would only be a matter of time.

The money I earned from the course was a pittance, but Karen was working, and we paid our rent; we managed to have the odd weekend out, but for the most part, I was living a quiet life. I never really got to know people in Chester, but that suited me. I know how easily led I can be. I found the course interesting, and I had to learn a lot in that condensed six months. My grandfather had been a master bricklayer and had served an apprenticeship of seven years back in the 40s. Six months wasn't enough, but I learnt the basics, and I would be going to London with friends who were great brickies.

Kenny and Ste were so different from each other but both great brickies. Kenny was a massive rock fan and would shag anything that came his way, and he made me laugh. Ste was quieter; he loved Northern Soul and speeding his tits off. My best mate was Rob Taylor. Rob had worked in Spain and Cornwall; he loved Man City and was well handy in a punch-up, and he was also a massive Northern Soul fan who was funny as fuck. These were the friends who were going to come to London to chance our luck when I finished the course. So, I had a plan of action, and something to look forward to when the course was finally over. I realise now I have a very obsessive nature: when I go for something, I give it my all, sometimes for the good, and sometimes for the bad. I stuck the course out and passed with flying colours.

I told Karen my plans and decided within a few weeks of finishing the course I would be heading to London.

'Know thyself' Socrates

Chapter 12
London

I found myself at Bank Quay train station, on a one-way ticket to Euston, London, to start a new life. There were about ten of us, as the ranks had swelled and loads more wanted to come. Karen stayed behind. She knew she couldn't stop me, and we promised to carry on seeing each other. She came to London a few times, but as time passed, we both knew it was over between us.

There was so much work in the 80s right across London, you could pick and choose. We lived in a hotel in Victoria for a few weeks before finding rooms in Chelsea, off the Kings Road. I had a bedsit on Oakley Street, opposite the fire station. I fell in love with this great capital of ours and worked all over London, having a great time watching bands and going to clubs, and the first couple of years just sped by. We were young and feisty some of us had come out of the punk scene and some from the Northern Soul scene and we knew how to party. We were out every night chasing women, doing drugs, getting into punch-ups, going to the 100 Club and the Mud Club. I was making good money, going on holidays to Spain and Greece; earning money, we had it to burn. I was getting forty quid a day in the hand, whereas back in Warrington you were lucky to get a tenner a day. I opened a bank account and for the first time in my life was saving money.

Every few months we would go back to Warrington for the weekend in the early days, and I went looking for an old friend called Gill, who was a mate I had known for five years. Gill was a good mate and we had never been out together, but somehow, we spent the night together, and in the morning, I headed back to London. I saw Gill seven months later on a visit back and she was seven months pregnant. I was completely shocked. Gill smiled and said, 'Tommy, it's your child, but I want nothing from you.' She was a strong girl; we were friends and she sure never wanted a relationship with me, she knew me too well.

I went back to London, confused. On April 22nd, 1985, she gave birth to our daughter Sophie. I wasn't there as I thought it best not to interfere in her life and make things awkward for her and our daughter. I stayed out of her life for 13 years. I regret it now. I love my daughter, but I must have hurt her badly. Many years later I heard that my daughter Sophie had spoken to my ex, Wendy, and said, 'You know my dad, I don't like him because he doesn't like me.' When I heard this, it made me feel so bad, and I started to try and repair the damage I had done, but Sophie was 13 by then and going through adolescence and really never wanted to speak with me at that time, and who could blame her? It took years for her to want to speak with me. We talk on the phone now; she is a very strong girl with a mind of her own and doesn't suffer fools gladly. Life is never so black and white, and I realise I fucked up big time.

In my own defence, what can I say? Gill and I were friends and Gill was very happy for me not to be around; it was not the best solution but if I kept popping up it would really confuse things. Gill had another daughter, Gemma, and rightly or wrongly I stayed out of the picture and Gill carried on with her life and eventually met a decent guy and they were both happy. Gill was a friend and in all those years she really was a lady about the whole thing and never made me feel bad about it all. But in reality, I was the one who missed out on my daughter growing up, and I have to live with that till I go to my grave.

More people were coming to London from Warrington - Alan Moye, the McPake brothers Bobby and Pete, Bobby Houghton, Tommy Connor, Stewart Maloney, Dave Sleigh - we had a small army that first couple of years. We moved around a lot, living in South Kensington, Maida Vale, a spell in Streatham, South London which I hated. Earls Court, which was full of Aussies and gays in those days, was more fun and vibrant. Kenny went back to Warrington because he missed his family; Rob met a girl called Theresa from Ladbroke Grove, and I started to see her sister Veronica who worked in a bank.

West London is great. I was going to work daily, and I started buying hash again and selling it to guys on the building sites. I never looked on selling hash as a criminal way of living; I was doing friends a favour. I was living a normal life. My cousin Darren came to live with me when he was 17. I was living above a dry cleaners on the Earls Court Road, which was run by a German guy who was constantly telling me to buy a flat. He had a string of properties and offered to help me buy one near Gloucester Road tube station. This was around 84/85, and flats were only £60,000, but I wasn't interested - stupid I know, as they go for over a million pounds these days!

Earls Court had so many Aussie backpackers in the days before they gentrified it, coming from their travels across Asia and South America or some other route, and loads of them had hash from Nepal to sell on to fund further travels across Europe. Wheeling and dealing was second nature and always going on.

Darren became my hod carrier, and we travelled all over London working together, exploring the city and having a crack. I reckon you can live in London for 100 years and still not know it, every nook and cranny. People from all over the planet and all walks of life come here to seek their fortune or escape from whence they came. I really started to think this was the life for me. I was getting used to getting up in the mornings, going to work and collecting my wages on a Friday, and staying out of jail. I was really appreciating my freedom without looking over my shoulder. I was just another face in the sea of faces in this city, and nobody bothered me. I felt like I was growing up, and by now aged 25, I was meeting interesting people who had no idea about my past and took me on face value. It's not easy surviving in London, but if you persist things can really start to come together.

Earls Court is a very transient place, people are always coming and going, but that suited me: I love people and I enjoy the tales they have. London was vibrant, and it gave me great energy to go on and do many things, and it really opened my eyes to the world and beyond.

Our Darren was a real live wire, with boundless energy and a lust for life, and that was contagious: he made me howl with laughter at times. Friends can come and go, but family was always there for me, and it felt good having him by my side.

I'd been making a few mistakes in the early years of bricklaying and got sacked a few times, but there was never a problem as there was so much work about, you could virtually start again the next day, somewhere else across London; the construction industry was booming. I was learning the trade, and after two or three years I became good at it. I made a great friend from those days, Martin, an Irish bricklayer from Cork, Ireland, with a personality to match. He could drink like a fish and had the blarney by the bucket load. He taught me well and we spent a couple of years working on various jobs. We had so much in common. I went on to see him in random places and would just bump into him over the years in such places as Australia, Jersey and America. It was quite strange how we would meet, but it is true that the interesting people who come into your life on this journey you will always remember; you never remember the boring ones, do you?

I've not seen Martin for nearly 30 years now, and I often wonder how he is and would love to meet him again one day. I believe he may still be in America. I've tried the Internet but no luck. His father owned a shoe shop in Cork city, which I believe was called O'Brien's.

There were plenty of hotels around Earls Court. There was also a large gay population living around the area, but they never bothered me: my motto is live and let live, we are all part of the tapestry of humanity that makes life so colourful and interesting. I observe people; life evolves by people exchanging ideas and communicating with each other, and I try to learn from people no matter who they are or where they are from.

In the days before computers they used to say television killed the art of conversation, but computers are doing it now; is it a blessing or a curse to be constantly on them, being checked and monitored by them? This generation are now born into them and have to be savvy in this age of tech, but at least make them play outside and engage them in real life conversation so they can develop their characters, their personalities, reach their true potential in life and not become quite soulless and withdrawn. I wonder what would happen if all the computers crashed around the world, would people be able to cope? I don't think so; it is quite scary when you think about it.

I was living and working around West London close to Ladbroke Grove, Notting Hill, Holland Park, Shepherds Bush and within walking distance of the West End, a very interesting place to explore, and I liken it to a playground. The Royal Borough of Kensington and Chelsea is rich in history, the heart of the British Empire, where the extremely wealthy live alongside people in council blocks. The history and the museums and art galleries all mesh to create the kaleidoscope of colour that interests me immensely. Venturing further afield, south of the river, Battersea, Balham, Stockwell, Brixton and beyond… East London, Shoreditch, Brick Lane with the best curry houses and bagel shops in the UK, Columbia Road, Petticoat Lane, Billingsgate Fish Market, and a whole host of things to satisfy your curiosity.

North London, Hampstead, Camden, Highgate Archway, Finsbury Park, all connected by tube and bus, 33 Boroughs, with over 8 million people going about their lives; I was a very small piece of it all, and even if you have never travelled the world you feel you have when living in London; I embraced it all with a passion, almost like a lover. I had some crazy encounters with all kinds of people. I thrive and survive off people; I really do enjoy the company of strangers, rich and poor, from the Sloane Rangers of Chelsea, privately educated, living in huge houses in the Borough, to the hordes of beggars. I would talk to them all and felt my life was enriched by doing so.

I can and do enjoy my own company, and appreciate the simple things in life; riding along the Thames, the streets and alleyways fascinated me no end. I went back to Warrington randomly, but I was always glad to get back to the city, and my dad was glad to see me go back. He really urged me to stay away, as he knew how much trouble I could get myself into around the town.

My brother Anthony was now married and had his first child Jamie with a different woman, and four months later his first son Anthony Junior was born with his future wife Cath when he was 18, and his daughter Sarah came along 18 months later. He was still a child himself in my eyes, but he seemed happy; he was his own man, coping with life as best he could. He probably has his own demons to cope with. Life had not been a bed of roses for him either growing up in the Kennedy household. I always thought our kid missed his forte: he should have been a comedian, he is a naturally funny guy who can chat with anybody.

Working on the building sites in wintertime is not much fun, and living in Earls Court meeting Antipodeans from Australia and New Zealand, who were bricklayers travelling, living and working their way around the world, got me thinking, *If they can do it, why not me?* But I felt my criminal record was holding me back from many countries including Australia, America and Japan. I had constantly been checking out airfares in shop windows, and I started questioning people about how to get around my criminal record and get a visa. I was always daydreaming of escaping these UK winters which were bleak and miserable, in my eyes at least.

Veronica wanted to travel, and she persuaded me to have a go at the Aussie Embassy, never believing they would let me in, but thinking I must try. *God loves a trier* was going around my mind. So off I went a few days later to find out one way or the other. Luckily for me there were no computer checks in them days. I filled out all the forms to apply for a visa, and when it came to the question, *Have you ever been convicted of any crimes?* I wanted to say, *I didn't think you needed them anymore to enter Australia!* Obviously, I didn't. I just lied through my teeth and told them, *No, I had never been convicted of anything whatsoever.* After a few hours, they granted me a visa to enter Australia anytime in the next twelve months. To say I was ecstatic was an understatement. I was over the moon with joy: at long last I could put my plan together to travel the world!

I loved London, but I was looking forward to seeing more of the world. London would still be there. I had a great feeling my luck was changing for the better, and indeed it was.

'When a man is tired of London, he is tired of life.' Samuel Johnson

Chapter 12
Horseferry Road Magistrates

I had just started saving money but over the next few months I went on a massive budget and saved as much money as I could. I started reading everything on Australia and the tourist trails of Asia and the States, learning as much as I could, as I was determined to make this a reality. I cut down on my boozing and Veronica and I were both saving like mad, and finally in 1987 we went to the travel agents and booked the round-the-world ticket that I had been dreaming of since I was a kid, growing up listening to the tales of my dad from when he had travelled the world as a teenager. The Navy had refused me, but now I was going under my own steam. It may not sound such a big deal these days, as you can view every country on the planet via the Internet, but in those days, I was so excited I couldn't wait to set off.

I really didn't give a toss about leaving Earls Court and my room, having nothing on my return and having to start all over again; none of that concerned me, I was ready and willing just to go and see how it all panned out. You also have to remember I had a record as long as my arm and should never have been going to Australia or America at all, so it really was a big deal in my eyes. I had been working in Sloane Square with a right bunch of characters, and then the unbelievable happened: I was arrested.

I had been working on one of the big houses in Sloane Square in Chelsea for a couple of months; the money was great, building a huge extension. There were a lot of other trades there working on the job. I seem to remember the *Sun* columnist Gary Bushell's brother-in-law, a plasterer, was working on the job also. I was working with a huge bricklayer called Graham who seemed to be a bit of an oddball. I couldn't put my finger on why; but I didn't give it much thought, he was only a workmate.

The job was coming along nicely and one day Graham said, 'Why don't we have a drink after work next Saturday, have a few beers around your manor, Tommy?' I thought about it and said, 'Yes, why not?' I had been saving hard and could do with a bit of a blowout. So the following week at work Graham was excited about going out after work on Saturday; I don't think he had many friends and probably wanted a bit of a blowout himself. On Saturday we worked until dinnertime, then we knocked off and changed out of our work clothes and into our good clobber, and we set off down the Kings Road, Chelsea. We had a few beers in the Chelsea Potter, and a few further up the road in J Henry Beans, and Graham was having a laugh and started to open up a bit.

From there we jumped in a cab and carried on to my manor, Earls Court. I used to drink in Cromwell's on the Earls Court Road in those days and knew the landlord who ran it, a little fat guy from Manchester; it was just near my flat above the dry cleaners. After a while and a few more beers we headed off to the Courtfield opposite Earls Court tube station. This was in the days of the pubs closing at 3pm to reopen at 6. We must have drunk six or seven pints that day and I was bursting for a piss. Not having eaten anything, I was feeling quite pissed; last orders had been called but I told Graham to get the ale in while I headed to the toilets. On my return five minutes later, I asked Graham where my pint was and he said we had missed last orders. I thought nothing of it until a few minutes later when three coppers came over and said we were under arrest for impersonating police officers.

I thought they were joking and told them to piss off, which led them to start grabbing hold of us both and trying to escort us out of the door and on to the street. I was so pissed I started shouting at the coppers and Graham started to threaten them; he really was a big guy, so the policemen pulled out the handcuffs and shackled us both, got us out of the door and into a waiting Black Maria. We were driven to the police station near Kensington High Street. I started to sober up quite quickly and realised my world trip was now in jeopardy, and the last thing I wanted was for that to be fucked up. I had already booked the ticket, but I could go to jail and the whole trip would be ruined. The police had us both in different cells and I found out the whole story later that evening...

While I had gone to the toilet in the Courtfield pub that afternoon, Graham had tried to get served, but the barmaid had refused him, saying last orders had been called. Instead of leaving it at that, he told her we were off-duty policemen and it would be ok to serve us. It sounds unbelievable; the landlady rang up the coppers, and they turned up to investigate. In the morning I was charged with threatening abusive behaviour to cause fear or provocation of violence. They charged Graham with the same, plus impersonating a police officer, but to give him his due he told them it was nothing to do with me. We were then both bailed to appear at Horseferry Road Magistrates in three weeks' time. I couldn't wait to get out of that police station.

Back at work on the Monday, after finding out what had happened the lads at work started taking the piss big time. Graham was really nervous, and I was fuming: how the fuck had this happened? I never told my family or Veronica; I had been out of trouble for a few years now. The next three weeks dragged by. Graham had quit the job a few days later, and the next time I saw him was in the Magistrates Court standing in the dock looking shady as fuck. I had made my mind up I was going to plead guilty and hope for the best.

I found out why Graham was so nervous after my charge was read out. It turned out he was on licence from Broadmoor. He had a solicitor and it turned out he'd done 14 years for rape and attempted murder 10 years previously. The magistrate sentenced me first, and I had my fingers crossed thinking, *Please don't jail me*, but this wasn't Warrington, and in London, it was a minor offence; they fined me 30 quid. I was so relieved. Graham got a 200 quid fine and was also let off. I couldn't look him in the eye; I left the court in a hurry and never saw him again. It just goes to show, you never know who you are talking to in this life, do you?

'False friends are like autumn leaves found everywhere, true friends are like diamonds, precious and rare.' Author unknown

Chapter 13
Leaving the UK

Veronica was born in Ladbroke Grove, along with her two sisters Catherine and Theresa from Irish parents. Portobello Road was a great place to be in the 80s. I fell in love with the Grove, and we used to drink a lot in The Elgin, a few doors down from her family home. It was more real and less transient than Earls Court, and it was a big step for Veronica, leaving home and her family to go travelling for a year. Her younger sister was still going out with my mate Rob, and it was through Theresa and her sister Veronica that we discovered the buzz of the Grove. Veronica had a best mate, Mandy, and it was a big wrench for Veronica leaving it all behind. We had planned to go for a year, but in my mind, I had other plans. A couple of more mates turned up from Warrington, steel fixers Alfie and Bri, both good lads, and we all hung around together before Veronica and I set off travelling. After my brush with the law that could have ended in disaster, I had a feeling my luck was changing for the better, and it sure was.

On the final night before we set off on our travels, we had a leaving party. Friends came from all over, including an old friend called Bagga, aka Gary Jones, from back in Warrington. He was 5ft 6ins, with a mouth that could make grown men cry; he was the ultimate piss taker, but I loved his character. I woke in the morning and he had covered me in margarine and was laughing his head off; they had done it for the crack, and it was highly amusing to him. I was fuming, as it took me ages to get cleaned up.

I met Veronica at the tube station a few hours later that morning and we boarded the tube to Heathrow airport to catch our flight to Bangkok for the first leg of the journey, a place I have since gone back to time and time again. Thailand was promoting Visit Thailand in 1987. When we arrived at Don Muang Airport, we had no real idea what to expect, and this really was part of the appeal to me in the first place, exploring the unknown.

We quickly found a cab, sped over to central Bangkok and found a hotel close to the infamous Soi Cowboy, a red-light district full of lady bars. It was so named after an American black guy had decided to stay in Asia after being in Vietnam during the American-Vietnam conflict; he always wore a cowboy hat, and after opening the first bar there in

1970 the name stuck. We had a great time exploring the city and all it had to offer, from the Buddhist temples to the markets. The heat was incredible, mixed in with the hawkers and the tuk-tuk drivers whizzing by every few seconds looking for farangs to pick up; the city was alive and teeming with people and energy.

One day we took the bar girls out to the Crocodile Park, where men would put their heads inside the crocodiles' jaws. I took them all for dinner, about 10 of them, and paid for it all; it was so cheap I didn't mind, and my idea of travel is meeting the people who live there and sharing the experience.

We got ripped off, of course; we were naive this first time, but I never got offended, it was all a learning curve. I loved the Thais, and they were always up for a laugh. There were all kinds of scams going on involving cards, gemstones, anything to part the farangs from their cash. I nicknamed it the White Leg Sting: they saw you coming a mile away and you were fair game in their eyes, as this was a third-world country and people were desperate for money. Many unsuspecting tourists fell for their many scams and cons. From Brighton to Brazil, the world over, if you are a tourist the local businesses want your money at the end of the day, and let's not forget that. We weren't staying in expensive hotels or driving around in expensive cabs, we were doing it all on a budget, but nevertheless we loved it.

The Chao Phraya river runs through the city, and then onto the Gulf of Thailand. You could spend months trying to take it all in. There were lots of Westerners teaching English, and many seedy-looking types who smuggled drugs, gold and whatever else they could make money on; they had made Thailand their home, all living together in this huge metropolis, like Sin City with its neon lights and millions of people going about their daily grinds.

I was now on the straight and narrow and would have to find work when we finally hit Australia. So, after a few days, we took the train down to Singapore passing through the South of Thailand, crossing the Malaysian Border with its ominous signs of a hangman's rope, with death for drug trafficking; it was all a bit much to take in on that first trip. We winded on down to Singapore and further adventures in Jakarta, the capital of Indonesia, and onto the drug haven, the island of Bali, and all it had to offer. We spent a few weeks just chilling by the beach before finally boarding the Qantas flight to Perth, Western Australia, leaving the island of Bali behind us.

'Traveling - it leaves you speechless then turns you into a storyteller' Ibn Battuta

Chapter 14
Australia 87-88

I was still a bit apprehensive about whether I would be allowed in by customs officials at the immigration desk because of my criminal history, and I wouldn't be sure until we collected our bags after the five-hour journey and went to the queue to face the customs officials to hopefully be allowed into the country. I passed through customs after a few questions being put to me by the immigration officer; he stamped my passport and let me through. I was well happy. We stood outside in the Australian sunshine, and hailed a cab into downtown Perth. Looking out of the windows of the cab I was slightly disappointed by Perth; it felt more like a sleepy little town than what I had expected.

    I knew in a few months' time we would be off to Sydney, so I decided to make the most of it in Perth for the time we would be there. We were both pretty tired that evening and soon fell asleep in the room above a pub which we had rented that day. The next morning, we both woke up early and decided to go job hunting separately. I went scouring for building sites, not really having a clue where to look, but as luck had it within half a mile of where we were staying, I spotted a lean Australian guy laying bricks on what looked like a big garage. He had just started coming out of the foundations and was on the first course of bricks; this looked promising, so I walked confidently over and told him I had just arrived in Perth and was looking for a start. It turned out his parents were Scottish and had emigrated in the 50s. He seemed to like the look of me and offered me a start first thing in the morning.

    His name was Jono, and he told me to be there at 5am, start early and finish early, because the sun was scorching after 11 and we would finish at 2pm. I was quite taken aback - I had not really thought I would get a job that quickly - but I thanked him and said I would see him in the morning. I had one problem though: I had no tools. I quickly found a hardware shop and purchased the tools I would need: spirit level, line and pins, hammer and bolster, line blocks, a tape measure and two trowels, one for laying bricks and the other for pointing. I got a new bag to hump them all around in, and then went back to the room. A few hours later Veronica came back and told me she had got a job in a local restaurant. Our luck was in; we had a few beers to celebrate and then we had an early night. I had to be up at 4.30am - what a change had come over me, for the better.

In the morning I went straight to the job; it was only a few blocks away. The first few hours were fine, and I thought it was a doddle until it started to get hot and the sand flies were all over me. I was sweating my bollocks off and covered in flies. I could barely see what I was doing. I looked over at Jono and he seemed fine; we were out in the open with no shade, and I was feeling like I was going to collapse and couldn't carry on. Around midday when we stopped for a break, I said to Jono, 'How come the flies are not bothering you?' He looked at me and started laughing, and pulled out a big can of mosquito repellent. 'You cover yourself with this mate,' he said, 'from head to toe before you start in the morning.' He chucked the can over to me and I drowned myself all over in it. The flies really got to me that morning and I was so relieved when they left me alone.

That night I slept like a baby, and in the morning, I turned up with my own can of repellent, and after a week I'd started to get the hang of working outside in the blazing heat. I really had been a greenhorn. Jono and I got on really well; he got me a lot of work, building barbecues on large houses, and the money was flying in. He told me about places to go at the weekends, the white sandy beaches of Cottesloe; my favourite place was Freemantle with the boats and the pubs which were really lively. Veronica was doing fine, and after a few months, I was getting itchy feet and ready for the bright lights of Sydney. I told Jono I would be leaving the next week, and the following week I shook his hand, he wished me luck, and Veronica and I packed our things. Once again, we set off on our travels, flew out of Perth slightly relieved, and a touch excited at what lay ahead.

'Adventure may hurt you but monotony will kill you.'

Chapter 15
Sydney to Mexico

Landing in Sydney, it was just as I imagined it: a bustling city surrounded by gorgeous beaches. We found a place to stay in the red-light area of Kings Cross; this suited us, as we were central to everything around the city.

There were thousands of expats on the building sites from all over the UK, and they were crying out for bricklayers. I secured a job building a hotel in Sydney Harbour right opposite the Sydney Opera house. Walking into work in the mornings, I had to pinch myself to know it wasn't a dream. The guy I was working for, Tony, from Queensland, made me a foreman after a few weeks, and I was getting a hundred dollars a week more for training apprentices, on the job. Wow, my life really had been changing since I had left jail five years before. I was seeing parts of the world which I could only dream about years before. I had got myself a trade and money in the bank. Why hadn't I done this when I left school? *Better late than never,* I told myself.

Veronica and I were poles apart really: she was ambitious to acquire a property in London and be a homeowner. I knew I wasn't ready for settling down; we were living in the moment, but I knew she was far more sensible than me. After six months in Sydney we were ready to head up the coast of Queensland and explore some more, which we did, finally arriving in Cairns, where we both took a scuba diving course, which we both passed. I enjoyed the experience but have never done it since. We travelled back down the coast to Sydney and took our onward flights to Hawaii, America.

We stayed in Hawaii for three weeks. I got bored of watching the surfers and we decided to fly out to San Francisco, on to Los Angeles, and carry on down towards San Diego, entering the Mexican border at Tijuana. We carried on to Acapulco to meet Veronica's friend Mandy, who was there with her boyfriend on holiday. We travelled by train arriving in Acapulco a couple of days later, which was full of American tourists. My plan was to carry on through Central America and on to South America when our time was up in Mexico.

We spent a few days on the beach, and then we hired a boat to go deep sea fishing, something I had never done before. I got drunk and very burnt after a few hours out in the open sea, and all of a sudden felt a massive pull on my rod; it was a huge marlin, and somehow with the help of the Mexican fisherman we reeled it in. I was fucked and sweating profusely when we finally pulled the fish on board. It was the one and only fish I ever caught, and it was a whopper. I had my photo taken with it, and thought, *I'm sending this photo to my dad;* he had it on his wall for many years.

Afterwards, we went on to watch the famous divers dive hundreds of feet below into the Gulf of Mexico, while we were watching from a restaurant high above. It looked very dangerous, but they made money collecting tips from the tourists. Later that same evening we went to a Mexican night club where we drank tequilas all night. I staggered home with Veronica. We were accosted by two young men who pulled knives and robbed us both at knifepoint. Veronica was screaming, I tried to chase them, but I was in such a drunken state they quickly lost me. We went back to our shack and just collapsed on the bed.

In the morning, the sudden realisation dawned on us: we had no money, no passports, and we were a long way from home - this wasn't looking good. We went to the police, and they filed a report and sent us to the local consulate, a fat guy smoking a cigar; he was useless, but he told us we would have to go to Mexico City to get our passports reissued to sort this frigging mess out. Mandy helped by giving some money to us to cross Mexico by bus, to get to Mexico City, the world's most polluted city, where we spent ten days virtually penniless until we got our passports and Australian travellers' cheques reimbursed. After that fiasco, Veronica said she would go no further and we had to curtail our journey through Central and South America to go back to Los Angeles and get a flight back to London, which really was the last thing I wanted to do. We arrived back in London in the middle of a freezing winter. It almost made me want to cry.

'Change your thoughts and you change your world.' Norman Vincent Peale

Chapter 16
Back to Asia

I had quite a lot of money still saved up and made up my mind I wasn't hanging around in this English winter. Veronica had sourced a job; she was happy to be back with friends and family in Ladbroke Grove. Within a couple of weeks of arriving back in London I had booked a one-way ticket back to Bangkok. I told Veronica my plans, and I think she was secretly happy; the writing was on the wall for our relationship.

I arrived back in Thailand, and immersed myself into the Thai culture, going to the North of Thailand, Chiang Mai, trekking and trying the opium up there, then back down to Pattaya. After a few weeks, it was like Dodge City: every scam known to man was going on around me. I decided I'd had enough of Sodom and Gomorra and headed south to the island of Koh Samui, with its laid-back lifestyle and stunning beaches. It was a perfect blend and kept me entranced for months, smoking weed and meeting women from all over the world. I started hustling; when I befriended a Thai guy called Nang, he had the best Thai weed, and I would get it from him and sell on to fellow travellers to help to supplement my stay on the island.

Koh Samui was pretty quiet in those times. Lamai had the Flamingo Bar and a few smaller bars scattered around it. Koh Samui is a small island and it didn't take long to start to know people. I hired a Jeep and would go around the island; the beaches of Chaweng, Bo Phut, and Maenam were not yet fully developed, and it really was like being in paradise. I was hooked by it all. The little fishing village of Nathon, where the ferries would bring in the travellers from the mainland, was a good spot for meeting people. I would recommend my friends' beach huts to stay in: Sunrise and Whitesands were popular with the travellers, right on the beach and very basic, but more importantly very cheap, in the price range of 50p or a pound or two a night. That suited my travel philosophy for years to come: travel light and don't waste money on sleep. I got along with the Thais in general; one or two of them stabbed me in the back, but as I have found that can happen on your own doorstep. The favourite Thai saying, Mai Pen Rai, covered nearly everything.

After a few months, it was time to head on over to Australia and earn some more cash on the building sites in Sydney. I liked Australia but it was a first world country, and I knew I had to find work; I was always happy when the time came to leave and head back to Asia for more adventures. I travelled far and wide through Thailand, Malaysia, Singapore and Indonesia, with plans to go to India and Sri Lanka at some point, but for the moment I was content. I started meeting all kinds of people and made connections with them; there were many Vietnam veterans who had fallen in love with South East Asia in particular, and never returned to the States, much preferring Thai women. They used to call the western women silver bellies. I asked one of the guys the last time he had been with a western woman; 'Hell man, it was about 20 years ago, and I had to open my own beer, never again,' he laughed.

People could go mad in the tropical heat, and I saw many junkies who had stayed for years, lured by the cheap China white heroin that was plentiful in Asia. I travelled with all kinds of people, a few weeks here, a few weeks there; I was crisscrossing around the continent so much it began to feel like home. When I got tired of island life, I would always go back to Bangkok; it was like a magnet to me. Most people only stay a few days and then move on, but I was quite happy spending weeks there.

The sex industry in Bangkok was rife, although technically illegal; Patpong 1 and Patpong 2, along with Nana Plaza, and the infamous Soi Cowboy, would draw tourists in from all over the world. I quickly saw through it all: it was mainly young girls from villages across Thailand who were desperate to earn money to provide for their children back home. There is much more to Thailand than the sex industry: there are decent hard-working Thai women who worked in banks, offices, shops, very elegant, very ladylike and very polite.

The Thai men are very laid back unless you upset them, and if you make them lose face, they are a tough breed. Thailand has never been conquered in a war, and many farang men would disappear off the face of the earth, having their throats slit and buried in a shallow grave somewhere, never to be found.

If you were cool you usually had no problems, but you had to be careful not to upset people. I used to see stupid farangs getting in the ring with Thai kickboxers at local gyms, thinking they would easily win. I saw many of them hobbling around for days afterwards. Muang Thai is taught to all kids growing up in Thailand, much like football in England.

I was always fascinated by the sounds and stories of Asia. One of the popular books around these times was the story of Charles Sobhraj, half French and half Vietnamese, who had been a serial killer on the Asian hippy trail in the 1970s. He was highly intelligent. He would befriend people who were travelling and eventually rob and murder them, and he was caught and sentenced to life in prison. He was wanted for murders in Thailand, but after 20 years was up the extradition treaty was over, and he couldn't be extradited back to Thailand to face further murder charges. They released him from Tihar prison in Delhi when his sentence was over. He was deported back to France where he became a minor celebrity. Can you imagine letting a serial killer back on to the streets of London? The last I heard he had returned to Asia; he couldn't resist it. He was rearrested in Nepal in 2012, where he is now, serving a second life sentence, but I can fully relate to his love of Asia, it is a magical place.

Asia is also full of misfits from across Europe, Australia, Africa and South America, Nigerian conmen who had all kinds of scams to relieve you of your readies, Americans who were doing deals in the Golden Triangle areas of Burma, Laos, and Thailand for the best smack in the world. British football hooligans setting up bars used mules to bring high-quality cocaine to feed the ever-growing frenzy of tourists who arrived daily in Thailand. Japanese and Chinese gangsters were operating and living in Bangkok, bringing their brand of violence to the country. In those days you could quite easily buy yourself out of trouble, as corruption was rife, the police were paid such a pittance; if money changed hands you were swiftly released, but if you had no money you could be locked up for years with no chance of release in brutal and very harsh conditions, it was no joke.

I met travellers from Holland, Sweden, France, Germany and Spain who were hustlers, not hippies - they also preyed on their fellow tourists. It can be hard to distinguish who was who, and many, many tourists were robbed: their drinks would be spiked by these so-called farangs, it wasn't just the Thais who were committing crimes against the tourists, believe me. They would talk fellow travellers into smuggling drugs and gems across borders throughout Asia; they pretended to be your friend but in reality they were ruthless and calculating, using you for their own means.

False friends are like autumn leaves found everywhere, true friends are like diamonds, precious and very rare; this really rang true across Asia and beyond. Young travellers were very susceptible and easily conned and utilised by them.

I caught myself once or twice nearly being robbed or blagged. Pickpockets operated on the buses, slicing open backpacks with razors. I learnt to carry my valuables in a thin money belt tied across my waist just above my groin, and out of sight of prying eyes, especially after what had happened to me in Mexico, you can never be too careful. People jostled you on the streets, lifting your wallet, credit cards, money, leaving you with nothing. I saw Western women turn to prostitution, selling their bodies to get home or buy drugs; with their soulless pinned eyes, it was quite sad when you looked beneath the surface. There were brothels that catered solely for the Asian clientele, women sitting behind glass with numbers on them, being sold to the highest bidder for an hour of sex, or less.

There were also many paedophiles from across the world coming to Asia to gratify their lust with young children, quite sickening, and yet the police would turn a blind eye when money exchanged hands. I met many dangerous and devious individuals on my travels masquerading as friends or fellow travellers. If you were on holiday for a few weeks you would never really notice this, unless you were an unfortunate victim that is. I learnt to budget and survive on very little, five or ten pounds a day; you didn't need to spend thousands, although many tourists did. I enjoyed going off the beaten track - travelling is in my blood, the wanderlust runs through my veins, it still does to this day. I always wanted constant change, not mind-numbing repetition forced on me by my own lack of imagination.

One day I met the most stunning girl I have ever clapped eyes on whilst I was travelling on one of the local buses around the city. She was studying in Bangkok, half Filipino, half American, and she had green eyes and long dark hair; we hit it off and were chatting away during the course of the bus journey. When the time came for her to leave the bus and alight at her destination, I wanted to ask her out for dinner, but I was tongue-tied and didn't have the balls to ask her. I never saw her again and completely lost my chance. That taught me a valuable lesson though: if you see a chance you have to take it, even if you have to fight for it; anything in life worth having, give it your all.

'He who takes no chances wins nothing.' Danish proverb

Chapter 17
Jersey, Channel Islands

I had been offered a job on one of the fishing boats operating out of Indonesia by an American captain; he described the work as back-breaking with very long hours, but the money was good. We had been chatting in a bar, and I declined the offer, especially after he described the work as back-breaking. I decided to head back to the UK for summer.

Arriving back in London in the summer of 1990, I was now 30 years old and wasn't yet ready to settle back into the daily grind of London life. I had met people from the island of Jersey, Channel Islands, on my travels, and decided to chance my arm there. It was a duty-free island, and I had heard there was plenty of work. I took the ferry there and swiftly found a room in St Helier. I had my mind made up I would have to work, as funds were running low. I didn't mind working: it was a means to an end, to further my travels. Come that winter I would be leaving for sunnier climes. I had no intentions of staying for more than six months, and no girlfriend, and no plans to acquire one either. Jersey is a great place to be, for a while anyway. I found a job with a local building company and set about building my bank account back up to a reasonable amount.

Jersey is a small island, and you could go mad if you spent years there and never left, but I was living in the moment and enjoying it. It wasn't long before friends I had met on my travels were coming over, guys from Manchester, Warrington, Liverpool, who I knew or had befriended. Everybody wanted drugs, and I started obliging and set up my usual sideline of supplying, not large amounts but enough to make money without causing the local plod to notice me. I built up a small clientele, mainly people who I knew and trusted, and I enlisted the help of some English girls from Liverpool who grafted the pubs and clubs around St Helier. When supplies were running low, I made a few phone calls, and somebody would bring them over from the UK. I was still working, and no suspicion fell on me.

I was making money and life was sweet. I met a girl called Alice from Liverpool, who had been a policewoman until she got assaulted on the job. She gave the police force up and moved to Jersey. She intrigued me, and we started going out for a while, but after a few months I could tell it wasn't working out, we were both so different. She had never really been out of the UK and was talking about us both moving to Liverpool; that did it for me. That really was the last thing on my mind. It fizzled out and came to nothing - if she knew my mindset she would have understood.

My old sparring partner from Warrington turned up, Bagga. I got him a job hod carrying for me on the building sites. I liked Bagga, he was such a character and came from the nice part of Warrington, Penketh, but had split from his wife years before. He had turned to the beer and was drinking quite heavily; he'd heard I was in Jersey and decided to come over. We had known each other since we had been 11 or 12, so it was nice to see an old mucker. I was saving my money, as usual, ready for when the summer season ended, and I could follow the sun again.

With Jersey being tax-free, beer was cheap, so Bagga would be on the piss each night after work, and I must admit I wasn't far behind him on those stakes. It didn't take long before we knew loads of people around the town. Bagga was always taking the piss, he was famous for it in Warrington, and he'd had his nose broken a few times by various people for his insults, but it never slowed him down or shut him up. He just knew how to wind people up, he made it into an art form, it was always amusing if he wasn't directing it at me. Many a time I would have to step in and calm things down, as many people couldn't take his brand of humour. He suggested he wanted to come travelling with me when I set off again on my jaunt; I wasn't so sure but thought *Fuck it, I'll give him a chance.* We carried on working through that summer, and we both had a few flings with various women but nothing serious, just a bit of fun.

By the end of the summer, we both had a few shillings stashed away and it was time to leave Jersey. I had some great memories of that summer, but I had itchy feet once again and was ready to leave. We made our way to London and stayed with friends in Ladbroke Grove whilst we hunted for a cheap flight to Kuala Lumpur, Malaysia, which we found a few days later, and flew out to the capital. We spent a few days in Kuala Lumpur, jumped a bus to Penang, and from there to an island called Langkawi where the beaches were pristine, and the beers were dirt cheap. After a few weeks Bagga suggested going on to Thailand; we were having fun, but for me, Thailand was the fun centre of South East Asia, so I readily agreed.

When we arrived in Koh Samui, Bagga was drinking heavily and to tell the truth he was slightly getting on my nerves. I asked him if he could calm down a bit, but after a few more days it was obvious he wasn't taking any notice. Well, I am no angel, and he was a grown man, so I decided to leave him to it and go on alone. I said I would meet him in Australia in a few months' time, we shook hands and I left for Nathon, to get the ferry to Koh Samui. I intended to make my way on to Bangkok for a few weeks. To be honest, I was glad to be leaving him: nothing worse than when you are doing each other's head in, and to be fair I was probably getting on his nerves too.

The next few months were a blur. I went to Manilla, Philippines, onto the Islands. It was a wild time down there, and I took a plane to India for the parties in Goa. I came back to Thailand and made my way down south, only this time I went to Koh Pan Ghan for the full moon parties, smoking loads of weed, meeting lots of women, hustling where I could, travelling light and not wasting money on expensive hotels.

I was living on a shoestring, but I always had a good time. The old saying is 'Nothing good lasts forever'; well, the time had come, funds were low, and I had to accept it was time to go to Australia and look for work.

I was constantly thinking I was making up for the time I had spent in institutions; compared to anyone else my age, I felt I was seven or eight years behind them. I more than likely was with my mentality. Arriving in Australia was much like landing in London, I was getting blasé about it all. I found work, and soon enough friends were out there, Bri, Rob and Theresa from the Grove, our Darren; but after a while, you think you're back in the system. I felt constrained going to work daily in Australia. I saved more money quickly and went on to America, landing again in Hawaii, then on to New York. America is expensive in comparison to South East Asia so after about six weeks I found myself back in London for the start of the English summer. I only had one thing on my mind, and that was to earn cash, work over the summer and carry on with my travels.

In London it was easy to find work, and easy to find crack; it had exploded all over London, and New York, and there were crack houses all over the Grove. It seemed like everybody was on it. I have a very addictive personality and I sure didn't want to get sucked into that, no way. I had my travelling head on. I can be quite obsessive, so I tried my best to avoid it. House music was taking off in a big way, and everybody was a drug dealer, pulled in by the easy money that could be earned off thousands of punters in each of the 33 boroughs of London. Guns were carried, lives were lost.

Harlesden, North West London, had an epidemic of crack. The Yardies from Jamaica were behind it all. Harlesden is only a few miles from Ladbroke Grove, and people were taking crack in their droves, especially in the early 90s. London was at the forefront, closely followed by all the capital cities that had a Jamaican population; it spread like wildfire through the towns and villages of the UK. Illegal raves, house parties, E and coke were unlimited, and it was a sight to behold. I was up and down the country and watched it happen before my eyes. There was one good thing: the football hooligans calmed down on the Es; everybody was getting loved up and dancing to the music of deep soulful house from America, and it was a great time to be alive.

I still had my travelling head on, so after a few more months working in London I was ready to leave town and booked myself on a jet to Singapore, and onwards through Malaysia. I stopped over in Penang and started dabbling in smack with a good looking Indian bird who held up a few straws of cheap heroin in a squalid hotel in George Town. She fucked my brains out for hours before I realised you couldn't come on smack. We started scoring from Thai and Malaysian gangsters, sitting in the hotel room for days getting wasted. I was past caring, even though the death penalty was still in use. In the end, I had to leave before I fell apart at the seams. I headed back to my spiritual home of Thailand and the beaches of the south, hanging out in hammocks for months on end, smoking weed, drinking beer, reading books and meeting women left right and centre. Tourism was really picking up in South East Asia, tourists were flocking there, and I was having so much of a good time; I was addicted to the beach life, I couldn't and just didn't want to settle down. Mortgages were something I never even contemplated. I hung around a lot on Lamai Beach, and my friend Phum the owner thought I was mad, I am sure she still does. Phum is straight-laced but she has a sense of humour, and speaks Dutch after living in Holland for seven years. Her English is impeccable. I loved Koh Samui in those heady days, and I went back time and time again. The girly bars of central Lamai are fun, but I would spend months in my hammock, chatting to tourists drinking at the beach bar on Samui, and not even bothering to go to the other bars. I wasn't a sex tourist; I went there to recharge my batteries. I would swim in the South China Sea, read, relax by the beach;

I really did feel I was in heaven sometimes.

Travel is so good for everyone of any age, and I would urge people to explore and learn about different cultures if you get the opportunity, or make the time to do it, meet other people from across the globe before you are laid to rest six feet under and it's far too late.

I would help Phum by going to the markets bringing the vegetables back, showing the tourists around and amusing them with the northern sense of humour. My wanderlust was driving me on, and I couldn't seem to settle anywhere, but I could see myself settling in South East Asia one day for sure. I met so many different characters across South East Asia who were living in the moment, hardcore travellers who had escaped the mundaneness of life back home, kindred spirits. Travelling and reading were the only things on my agenda; money was a tool I used to buy me a plane ticket somewhere, anywhere to have fun. I had short-term goals, and that was me, travel light and don't waste money on sleep.

'Share your smile with the world - it's a symbol of friendship and peace' Christie Brinkley

Chapter 18
Australia 1991

I was like a boomerang, toing and froing, backwards and forwards to earn cash. Back in Sydney, staying with my cousin Darren and his woman Jill, they now had a baby girl Shelley, born in Australia. They were all living there illegally by this time, but they didn't seem to care; they loved the lifestyle and Darren was making good money working for a mouthy Jock around Manly. I could have scored umpteen jobs, but when I worked with them it really was just a means to an end, making money to set off on my travels again. I loved that freedom of movement; it was highly enticing, something we all can take for granted. After a few weeks of dossing at theirs, I found a place and moved out.

Once again, I had to get into work mode, and it was becoming difficult as my mind was always on the next trip, but at least I was working in the sun and not the bitter cold English winters, and I was truly grateful for that.

Manly, where we were living, is a great suburb of Sydney, on the northern beaches, with pubs and bars near the beach, and for sure there are worse places I have lived. There were so many backpackers I felt I was permanently on holiday, which in a way I was in those days. The live music scene was thriving, and you could see bands most nights; the Aussie Bush Weed was potent, so I started selling it on to friends and workmates to supplement my income. I had been out of jail for nine years now and was finally starting to feel my past was well and truly behind me. I would ring up my dad now and then, to check up on how he was doing. I didn't hear that much about either of my siblings, but they were both settled with spouses and kids; good luck to them, but it wasn't for me - rather them than me.

Time was flying by that Australian summer of 1991, and soon my mind was working out where to go next. I made up my mind to go to Darwin in the Northern Territories of Australia and visit Alice Springs on the way up there. When the time came to quit the job, I had about five thousand English pounds. I bid our Darren goodbye and left him with his family, and bought a one-way plane ticket to Melbourne. I spent a few days there and wanted to be free to hit the road, so I went hitchhiking. I always travel light: one pair of jeans, a few shirts and shorts, underwear, and that was me. I used to laugh when I saw people with huge backpacks, I just couldn't see the point. After reaching Alice Springs I went to visit Ayers Rock and then on to Darwin, where I booked a flight to Timor in Indonesia. I spent a few months island-hopping down the Indonesian Archipelago, finally making my way to the capital, Jakarta, and booking a one-way ticket to London.

Arriving back in London in the summertime once again, I wanted out of London, and found myself in Nottingham after hitching a ride. I went to see my old school friend Eny, who was living there. I spent about a month there before making my way back to London, catching up with Rob and Theresa, who were now back living in the Grove after their trip to Australia. My ex-girlfriend Veronica was now going out with my old friend Alfie, and they were very happy. Good luck to them: I don't hold grudges and life is far too short for all that nonsense. I had many friends who were now settled down, but no, not I.

'If you can't take care of yourself, you can't take care of somebody else.' Sahithi Setikam

Chapter 19
1992: Ringing the Changes with Supreme Confidence

Having just finished another trip to Asia, I had met an Australian girl in Malaysia called Simone. We decided to travel together. When we arrived back in the UK the rave scene had well and truly exploded. We went north, mainly for the parties, the drugs, and the cheap rents; also I knew people there.

My bricklaying days were over. I was living a purely hedonistic lifestyle: travelling, music and just having a good time were on my agenda, but where was the money going to come from?

'Ringing the changes' was a scam, and there were teams of them. It had been around since the wartime, involving £20 notes and blagging the shopkeepers, making an extra £10, £20, £30. It was unbelievably simple and some of the gangs in Warrington had made it into an art form. They were masters at it. They usually worked in pairs and drove all over the country and Europe, working the scam. You could make a good working-class wage, a grand a week, even two grand a week if you pushed yourself, tax-free. I fell into it because my brother Anthony and all his mates were heavily involved in those days. Once you were hooked into it there was no stopping you. We went all over the UK, everywhere, and we used to go to Ireland when the troubles were on. We were on the road continually clocking up thousands of miles. I mean, you couldn't stay in the same place, so it suited my sense of adventure, and boy, did we milk it. England, Scotland, Wales, Northern Ireland, southern Ireland - we had maps and would hunt out every little shop in even the remotest places. We took the piss and it was unbelievable how much money was being taken daily from thousands of shops all over the UK.

Summer times were the best, along the coastal roads. All the students working summertime jobs were easy pickings. In to one shop, and straight into the next shop - we would hit every shop, every till, and nobody was the wiser. People were making good money, buying houses, cars - living the life. We stayed in different towns and cities every night, literally living like rock stars, and at the weekends, man, we were taking so many drugs, crack, smack, Es, weed, just to clear your head of all the lying and bullshitting you were doing. Some of the lads developed severe drug problems and there were many casualties along the way, but we were having it large. I made 800 quid in one day; it's an unbelievably simple scam that people fell for continually, time after time. It was organised crime really, and everybody knew everybody who was in the game, and we tried not to cross paths on our travels, but occasionally we did, and the shopkeepers would be on high alert if we walked in their shop and they had just been done a couple of hours before we rocked up, and it usually meant we had to make a swift exit before they called the bizzies.

Venturing further out, guys were going to America, Canada, Australia, Sweden, Norway, Denmark, Holland, Germany, Switzerland - basically anywhere they could get away with it. I know people who have been doing it for 30 years. With all my travelling I started getting into Buddhism and believed in karma, and eventually gave it up. I could write a book on the adventures of ringing the changes, but in the end, it led to the downfall of many good people, including some very good friends who were killed in car crashes, or died of drug overdoses. It fucked them one way or another.

I was all over the UK on the rave scene. I was selling Es in Cornwall and had many friends in St Ives, whilst we were on the road ringing the change or tricking as we called it. In 1993 I went to Glastonbury with Simone, the Australian girl, who was gay, and a good friend. We were doing so many drugs, wires were getting crossed, lines were getting blurred. It really was a mad time in my life. At Glastonbury I bumped into Jo, the girl from Manchester, with Nick from St Ives, a very good friend of mine. Nick was born in Manchester and was raised in St Ives. Jo was a mad party-head in them days, but a great soul. We decided to move to St Ives, which we did, and I fell in love with Jo, and it wasn't long before we were living together. She was 21 and I was 33. She was a drug dealer, and she had three cars, moving kilos of speed and weed from Manchester to St Ives. She had a good head on her shoulders, and had guys grafting for her, but was probably doing far too many drugs, as was I; but we hit it off.

The Shire Horse in St Ives was fucking brilliant. I met the singer Angie Brown there. Parties were happening all over Cornwall; it truly was a magical place to be. I met up with Nicky, a young mate who was about 18 then, and my mate Sammy Baker from Warrington lived in St. Ives and knew everybody around the town. The house music scene was well and truly happening down in Cornwall, and I was more than happy to be there. This was the time of the White Doves Ecstasy and people were well and truly in party mode. I stayed up near Carbis Bay with Jo, and we partied around the town like there was no tomorrow. St Ives has some of the best beaches in England, a top surfing spot attracting people from all over the world. Loads of the surfers were into smuggling, and drugs were plentiful; they hid them in their surfboards. Lots of them were top grafters, which helped to explain how they surfed all through the summer months, before heading out to places like Hawaii, Mexico, Portugal, Australia, South Africa; they knew where the best surf was worldwide. There were a circuit of young drug smugglers from the skateboard community also, young and brash with a 'don't give a fuck' attitude, taking smack from Pakistan, moving coke and ecstasy to Japan, shifting kilos of hash and weed in and out of third world countries to the UK, Europe, the States; balls of steel, up for anything that involved making money, travelling and having fun.

St Ives is the closest you can get to paradise in England, more than anywhere I have seen on my travels around the UK, or in fact anywhere in the world. On a summer's day you could well feel you were in the south of France or Australia. The beaches and coastline are superb. It had been a fishing village for many years but now is predominately a seaside town for tourists. The small population of St Ives, around 13,000 people, kept the whole thing running in the summer months by working in the restaurants and bars that the tourists flocked to. If you have never been you are missing out big time.

We would drive along the back roads to avoid the police; we transported many drugs this way. It seemed like the whole town was on something or other. We used to go to Newquay about 15 miles up the road, but I was always glad to get back to St Ives. I thought Newquay was much trashier and never had the charm of St Ives; it was usually full of hen parties and stag dos, with loads of drunken people hanging about on the streets, fights and litter everywhere. I much preferred St Ives by a long chalk and was happy to call it my home for many months to come.

After a few months with Jo I realised we were getting on, and I started to take her on the road when we were 'ringing the change', but Jo wasn't content with sitting in the car, being a passenger, and so it wasn't long before she was coming into the shops checking for me, to make sure the shopkeepers were none the wiser that they had been conned, which was important: you needed to know if you had to skip town and get out of there. After watching how I did it many times Jo suggested she would have a go; she was tired of drug dealing and she knew if she was caught it would be a big jail sentence for the number of drugs she was dealing; whereas ringing the change was very, very difficult to prove. If they ever caught you, you would be brought before the courts, but it was such a silly scam, you would get just get a small fine. In all the years I had done it I had never been to court; it really was very hard to prove. The shopkeepers would be so confused, and I think the police couldn't be bothered with it either, it was such a petty crime in their eyes; which suited me, as we were making really good money.

So, I started checking for Jo, and would be behind her when she pulled a touch, and after a while she took to it like a duck to water. I reckon she was better at it than me, and once she was hooked into doing it there was no stopping her. It was good to work as a team, it made you more competitive, thus you started making more money. We took turns: she would watch my back, and then into the next shop I would watch her back. It was also good teaching somebody how to do it: it made you more confident and you wanted to prove how easy it was, and that any shop was fair game. We went all over the south west of England continually for months, along all the coastal roads, through the villages and towns during those summer months of 93, cleaning up and making a small fortune.

Simone, my Australian friend, went on the road with friends, and we were all bang at it and away for days at a time, returning back to St Ives with a shed load of money and ready to party. Jo started to veer away from selling drugs, which was a good thing, since the number of drugs she was dealing with had been tremendous and really would have got her in serious trouble.

My brother Anthony would come down from the north with one of his grafting partners occasionally and stay with us in St Ives. He was continually on the road right around the UK and Europe. He had three kids by now and wanted the money to support them. Anthony and Jo got on like a house on fire. Jo knew everyone in St Ives worth knowing, Neil the surfer from Nottingham, Jan and Ray, Alan the Scouser, Lisa and Sally the sisters; there were so many characters around it was just one big party and that summer was a belter, we had so much fun. I even contemplated living there for good at some point.

Sonia and Darryl were friends of my mate Nicky. Darryl had been in the army and was a great lover of house music, and we all went out and partied like it was 1999, even though it was 93! The Es were so good, they took you into another dimension, you were loved up and the world was a better place. I was addicted to them for many years and was spending loads of money on them, but it was worth it, we had a fucking ball. St Ives is such a small place though and the winters were long and cold. The police would know your every move after a while, so we contemplated going to India to do some serious travelling. Jo was well up for it; travel and having a good time was in her blood.

One night we were up at one of her friends' houses, and the party was banging. We ran out of booze, but we were high up in St Ives and had to go down about fifty steps to arrive at the shops below, and it was very late, in the early morning hours, and all the shops were closed. I said, 'Don't worry, I will get some more beer.' I was so wasted. I took a hammer with me and was going to do a smash and grab on the Costcutters in the centre of town. It was quiet: it was wintertime in early October. I came down the steps and approached the shop, and I could see where the booze was; I took a massive swing at the glass door, and gave it a mighty whack. Fuck me, the hammer bounced back onto my knee and it felt like my leg was on fire, and the alarm bells started going off; it was the dead of night and I had to leg it, or more to the point stagger away clutching my knee, get back up those fifty steps, and back into the house. Everybody pissed themselves laughing when I told them what had happened, and luckily for me nobody was the wiser... the things you do for a drink!

We started to save money for the forthcoming trip to India. I took Jo to Warrington to meet my dad, and she took me to Manchester to meet her family. Her mam and dad were sound. Jo also had a couple of brothers and a sister; she was the youngest in the family but had a good head on her shoulders. Manchester was full of gangsters and I thought Jo had made a wise move giving up the drug trade and moving away from there. She loved St Ives, but she also wanted to travel. We had met each other at the right time; we were both on a mission to see the world. We carried on grafting back to Cornwall, hitting all the shops on the way from Manchester. It became like a job really, a bit like being a travelling salesman. We were continually looking for shops to blag. We were spending so much time together, and when under stress we would fight and argue like two raving dogs. Jo had done a lot in her short life, and I really did respect her; my heavy drinking never really helped, but somehow, we did get along and had fun.

The Shire Horse in St Ives was something else, crammed with house music fans and was full of dealers. The place was jumping; we used to love going there and it became like our second home. Jo loved taking acid and mushrooms, along with sniff and Es, and she would smoke spliff continually, but I was doing the same and we were in love; it was a great time in our lives. We had only been together for three or four months, but we had clicked, and I felt I had known her for years, we were that comfortable in each other's company. Ringing the change can be stressful, and it took its toll mentally. When you are blagging and bullshitting continually every day, you really start to take more and more drugs to blot it out; we had the money and we didn't hold back one bit, even going out ringing the change when we were drugged out of our heads, sometimes way too much, so much so that we had to give up on that day, and try to get our heads together.

We would stay in good hotels; we had the money, and we would eat at great restaurants, but we were also saving money for travel in the near future. Jo was a good driver and we got to know each other very quickly on those trips ringing the change. Driving for long distances we had plenty of time for chatting.

We had access to the best drugs. We started to smoke a lot of crack cocaine and we were constantly high; it was mind-blowing how many drugs we were taking during the first few months we were together. We also started injecting cocaine; the rush would be unbelievable, but the comedowns were getting worse. We were drinking a lot in the Three Ferrets, St Ives, and I remember we had been up straight for three days with no sleep whatsoever, and I was ready to crash out when Jo popped a tab of acid in my mouth. I was so out of it, we drove to the Three Ferrets and I ended up rolling all over the floor of the pub on a Sunday afternoon. My mate Nick came in and took a photo of me on the floor, pissing himself laughing.

It was becoming too much and we had to get out of St Ives very soon, before we ended up losing it big time. Jo had sent off for a new passport, and as soon as it arrived, we went to London to get our visas for India. Simone, the Australian girl, had decided to return to Australia but was going to stop over in Goa on the way back, so we arranged to meet her down there about a month later. The one thing we didn't want was to be stuck in St Ives for that winter. We booked our tickets and were due to fly out from Heathrow in November 1993, three weeks from when we booked the tickets. We were both buzzing and itching to get on the road. We were due to fly into Delhi, India, and intended to travel overland from there down to Goa. Finally, the day arrived, and we left St Ives by train to make our way to Heathrow. We had a few thousand pounds each in travellers' cheques. When we arrived at Heathrow to the check-in desk, I realised I still had a couple of wraps of speed in my pocket, and for sure I didn't want this to fuck our trip up if we got caught with them, so we both swallowed them out of the wraps, and we were speeding our nuts off as the plane took off for India.

Landing in India we were totally knackered, as we had been up the whole of the ten hour flight. I was drinking beer, and Jo was on her favourite tipple, Jack Daniels and Coke. After we landed at Delhi and cleared customs, we jumped a cab and found a cheap place to doss where we both fell asleep instantly. Waking up the next day we set out to score some good drugs, and it wasn't long before we were approached by an Indian guy who had some great Manali hash. Jo quickly bartered with him and bought ten grams' worth for about two quid; wow, we were in heaven. After smoking a few spliffs back at our room, we went back out onto the streets of Delhi and just strolled around with smiles on our faces.

Jo could drink like a man and fight like a man, and she had a great sense of humour, but we fought like cat and dog at times on that trip. She put me on my arse a few times and I deserved it.

We split whilst we were in Australia; she went back to the UK and I was gutted. I flew back and persuaded her to come back with me. We set off travelling again, and this lasted three years; we went everywhere, Hong Kong, Singapore, South Africa. We went to South America and to Argentina on our way to Brazil. We spent so much money in the airport at Argentina that we decided it was too expensive and flew back to South Africa. We decided we loved Asia, so we flew to Kuala Lumpur and took the bus back down to Thailand. We arrived in Koh Samui where we had friends who lived on or around Lamai Beach and stayed at the Sunrise Bungalows. Previously we had paid for Robert, a Dutch guy from Amsterdam who was penniless and working at Sunrise, to fly back home; we had friends and we had money. After a few months of lazing about on the beach, Jo was working with the Thais in the kitchen, learning how to cook Thai. She really was a good cook.

Phum, the Thai owner of the bungalows and the restaurant, had a bar on the beach sitting empty, and she asked if we wanted to run it and split the profits. She knew I was good with people and so was Jo. Phum had known me for many years and trusted me, and I'd also spent a lot of money at her place over the years. Jo and I started to learn Thai and were quite good at the barroom talk. We set up a bar and called it Ten Million Dollar View, and it really was. The views were stunning. People from all over the island and the world came to the bar. We were having parties every night, and we started selling weed to the tourists. We were selling jewellery; we had the beach sellers selling hammocks for us. If there was money to be made, we were on it. It got really popular, we were working hard, and it was like a dream come true. We set up a sound system, music blaring, people were in party mode and so were we.

Every few months we would go on visa runs to Penang, Malaysia or Singapore just to have a break. We were doing some serious partying, and friends from London, St Ives, Australia and Warrington would come and visit. Happy days! We met a German lady called Rike, who described herself as a spiritual mover. Her husband Peter had just died. We became great friends and she helped to set me on this path, but more about that later. Life was good, Koh Samui was beautiful in those days, Lamai, Chaweng, great nightlife. We had friends all over the island, and I was teaching English to the bar girls, which was funny - me who had run away from school at 14 teaching English, with not one qualification to my name; I never took any.

My mother died in 1996. I hadn't spoken to her in over 12 years, but I came back for the funeral. She left £50,000 and her house to my brother Anthony, but our kid gave me £15,000. She had written me a letter a few years earlier and gave it to my brother, but I told him I didn't want to read it. At the funeral, I asked our kid for the letter, but he said he didn't have it anymore. I regret I never read the letter.

What an unhappy life my mother had as a child, left in a convent in Glasgow; in later life she had many breakdowns, for a time being sectioned at Winwick Hospital and receiving electric shock treatments in the 60s and 70s for mental health. I never knew what really happened but as I grow older, I have to think back to the times and realise how young she really was and how naive. She had been unable to read or write properly. She must have felt hurt when I refused to speak with her for over 12 years and we both never got to resolve our issues because death took her too soon, and now I am more mature I have to forgive her.

R.I.P Mum.

I went back to Thailand, but trouble was on the horizon.

'A fool and his money are easily parted.' Proverb

Chapter 21
Monkey House

One day whilst I was serving at the bar in Samui four Thai police turned up and said they wanted to speak with me. Fuck, this wasn't looking good. They took me back to my hut, where Jo and I lived, ripped the place to pieces and found our stash. We usually had it outside, but this was the rainy season, and they found it inside the ceiling. The policeman was laughing so much when he found it, but I certainly wasn't. They handcuffed us and next thing we were on the ferry to Nathon and taken to court. We had our passports taken off us and were given bail to come back a few weeks later. We returned to Lamai, dejected.

Phum wasn't happy we couldn't run the bar anymore. The party was over, and we were well pissed off. About a week later I met with the police and gave them a grand to get our passports back. We decided to jump bail, and moved onto Malaysia. We went on to Indonesia and India as we couldn't go back to Thailand, but after a year Jo had got herself a false passport and so we decided to go back there as we loved it so much. Big mistake.

Returning to Thailand was madness after jumping bail the year before, but I wouldn't be told. It had such a hold on me, it was like a magnetic force was pulling me back there to the rocks on Lamai beach, where sometimes I had sat for 18 hours a day just watching the comings and goings of people during the course of the day. The Elephant Rock at the southern end of Lamai Beach, behind the Grandfather/Grandmother Rock, gave you such a magnificent view right across Lamai, I was transfixed by it all. I knew it was a huge gamble to take the risk to return, but in my head, it was worth the risk, and one I was prepared to take a chance on. We had so many happy memories of Koh Samui and it truly felt like home; it didn't matter where we travelled, somehow, we always wanted to be back in South East Asia, and more to the point Koh Samui and Lamai beach in particular.

I really thought there would be no problem with Jo and her brand-new forged passport, but my heart was in my mouth when we finally landed in Don Muang Airport, finding out if we would be let through that day when we stepped on to the tarmac. We collected our things and proceeded to the immigration desk. I watched Jo sail through passport control without a hitch and silently gave a sigh of relief. It was now my turn to find out if they would let me into the country. I approached the desk and my arse was twitching slightly, praying there would be no problem. The Thai customs officer took my passport and looked at me quizzically, and then started to speak to one of the other officers at the desk. I knew something wasn't quite right when he stepped from behind the counter, and told me in broken English I was under arrest and would not be allowed into the country as a free man. They then realised I hadn't been travelling alone, and another officer went looking for Jo, and she too was arrested.

Shit, this really was not looking good. We were taken to a small room at the airport with no real clue what was to be our fate, but one thing was for sure: we wouldn't be savouring the delights of Bangkok for the foreseeable future. We were well and truly in the shit, and I couldn't believe how stupid I had been to return in the first place. Finally, after a couple of hours, we were placed in handcuffs, taken by two policemen and bundled into a police car. Not a lot of communication went on and we couldn't understand them at all really; where were they taking us? We hadn't a clue. As we left the airport in darkness, Jo and I both sat silently to await our fates.

The police car drove towards downtown Bangkok. We arrived at the gates of the Immigration Detention Centre, where we were taken out and handed over to the officials there. We were both tired, but the guards didn't give a toss, we were just a stupid couple of farangs who were to be processed and led to our cells. This was a whole new ball game to us both: it was one thing being a tourist and another being a prisoner in Thailand. They separated us and took Jo away; we were both in for a massive shock.

I was dragged towards a doorway, thinking this was my cell for the night. I was expecting a small room, but when the door opened it revealed a massive cell that resembled the size of a school assembly hall, with hundreds of bodies lying side by side and no room to move. We stepped over bodies until they found a place for me to lie down next to a huge Russian prisoner and a Vietnamese drug trafficker. The guards shouted for them to make room for me to lie down on the ground with them. Shit, our bodies were touching each other it was so cramped. I was in total fucking despair without a clue as to what was going to happen in the immediate future.

I was set about when the guards left: prisoners were looking for money, but luckily for me, I had none on my person and they gave up. The Russian guy said, 'Don't be scared.' That first night was torturous, and sleep was impossible; people who had slept all day were talking all night and vice versa, and the lights never went out, staying on continually. I was hemmed in between the Russian and Vietnamese guy and pretended to sleep, but the heat and the stench of the other prisoners made me want to puke. What the fuck had I let myself in for? I was worried about how Jo was in the women's section of the detention centre, but I felt helpless. There was nothing I could do.

Sleeping on the floor at around 5am, everybody had to get up whilst breakfast was served, a tin of watery soup that tasted vile. You had to clean your space on the floor, and everything was rolled up. The noise and heat were claustrophobic, but there was nothing you could do about any of it. I had been expecting to land in Thailand and have some fun, and 24 hours later we were now paying the consequences of skipping bail the year before. Looking around the detention centre everywhere I looked I would be looking directly at somebody; although I tried not to it was impossible, there were just too many people crammed into the room. The only relief was to close your eyes to try and shut it out. The first couple of days felt like an eternity, not having a clue what was to be our fate; when you are locked up in the UK you had some kind of idea of what was going on, but here I was clueless.

Three days later somebody came from the British Embassy, and then I set eyes on Jo for the first time since we had arrived. I felt really bad seeing her, but glad to see that she was holding up. She had been in the women's section with the babies of some of the prisoners and was having a hard time with the conditions herself. The guy from the Embassy explained we were to be returned to the south of Thailand to be dealt with by the courts in Surat Thani for jumping bail and possession of weed. I asked when this was going to happen, and she said the papers were being drawn up so hopefully sometime next week. I felt a bit better having some kind of idea about what was going to happen, although the thought of being stuck in here for another week was doing my head in. I loved Thailand, but this was a side of it I wouldn't wish on my worst enemy.

Jo really was a strong girl. Born in Manchester and brought up by her Irish parents along with her brothers and sister in a loving home, she had shown an amazing aptitude for sport, becoming a second dan black belt in Shotokan Karate by the time she was 17 years old, which shows how her mind worked. She was a determined woman and when she set her mind on things, she got them done. Like a lot of kids who take up the sport at an early age and dedicate themselves to it with rigorous training sessions, she began to rebel against it all. She had moved to St Ives, Cornwall, when she was 18, and started working in the catering industry, doing silver service waitress work around the many hotels and restaurants in St Ives that catered for the summertime invasion of tourists descending there from all over the UK and beyond, before she became involved in drug dealing, which she was doing when I met her. She was a tough girl, and we had got on really well.

Now, a couple of years later, we were both separated in different parts of the detention centre in Thailand, what a fuck up. She told me how shite the conditions were on her section, but she was coping the best she could. There was nothing either of us could do but sit it out and wait until we were transported back to Surat Thani, in the south of Thailand, to face the music and the courts back there.

The Thai warders were brutal. The place was full of foreign nationals, mainly from Pakistan, Indonesia, Vietnam, Sri Lanka and surrounding South East Asian countries, and my Russian neighbour and I were the only Europeans in there that I had seen. I didn't really eat much in that first week. I had tried to eat the food but just couldn't, and I was starving.

We got a surprise visit from my brother Anthony, my cousin Darren, and my dad, who had flown out after being contacted by the British Embassy about our situation. They had turned up to try and visit us, but the warders refused to let them in, saying, 'No money, no visit', so they had to bribe the warders to be allowed in to visit me by giving them money. I felt ashamed when I saw my dad. We were separated by a corridor; I was behind the barred cages and we had to shout loudly to be heard above the voices of all the other detainees. It boosted my morale when I saw the family, but I was deeply ashamed for them to see me in this situation, especially my dad. Things were a ball ache for them: they were in a foreign country and had had to find the prison, and go through a load of hassle to get to see us for barely five minutes after travelling thousands of miles from the UK.

I had great trouble hearing them. I kind of resorted to sign language by giving the thumbs up to let them know I was okay. I could see they had brought me some food in the plastic bags they were holding up, letting me know they would do their best to help and to be on hand. I shouted to them that at some point we were going to be transported back to Surat Thani, which was about 12 hours away from Bangkok, and felt it was too much for my dad to be chasing all over this country. I told them to find some kind of hotel and to try and enjoy their stay, although I could tell my dad was not enjoying seeing us both in this situation one little bit. The visit was over far too quickly, and then we were both taken back to our dens of iniquity. A few hours later a bag of food was brought to me, containing dried noodles, coffee, rice with chicken in a plastic container, and toiletries, which the family had brought and left behind. I could see the other detainees at all times clocking what I had.

The noise and the heat were mind-boggling. People were in very desperate situations. Some spoke English and some I had to communicate with by pointing and such like, although I knew some Thai. All of the prisoners were foreign nationals and not from Thailand, and it felt weird, to say the least.

One night I heard somebody screaming loudly, and a fight had broken out between some of the other prisoners who looked Vietnamese. One had rammed a chopstick into the poor guy's eye socket, fuck knows what it had been over but he was howling and he must have been in terrible pain, judging by how loud he was screaming, and it wasn't long before the Thai guards came running in and broke it all up by beating the prisoners with their batons. A few of them were dragged out by their hair. The poor guy must have been taken to the hospital, but I never got to find out why it happened. I'm sure the guy must have lost the sight in one eye. The following morning, I was taken into the office. I was met by two policemen, and Jo was brought in too. We were told we were to be driven to Surat Thani and placed in prison there, to await our appearance in court on the charges we were being held on.

After an hour or so when the paperwork was done, we were taken in handcuffs to a police car with the two Thai policeman and drove through the detention centre gates and on to the bustling streets of Bangkok. Jo was looking terrible and dishevelled after weeks of sleeping on the floor in those conditions, but we were both relieved to be leaving this place and at least tasting some kind of freedom in the police car on the 12 hour journey across Thailand to Surat Thani. Jo was now 24 years old but she was wise beyond her years and seemed to take things in her stride. I was proud of the way she held herself during that incarceration; many women would have been crying and in one hell of a mess, but not Jo, she always seemed to find a joke in any situation and she did cheer me up, being close to her in the back of that police car on the journey down to Surat Thani. The two Thai policemen were decent guys and they realised we both could speak some Thai; after living and working in Thailand you started to understand the language, and we'd had a few lessons from a Thai friend of ours when we had been running the bar in Lamai.

The policemen pulled over a couple of hours later and took the handcuffs off us, and we all went into a restaurant. The policemen paid for our meal and we were truly grateful. After the meal was finished, we got back into the police car to complete the rest of the journey to Surat Thani. Thailand is such a lush and tropical country, the scenery is amazing, and if we hadn't been on our way to a prison in the south of Thailand, we could almost enjoy the journey and the amazing sights of freedom we were speeding through. After 12 hours we arrived at the main prison in Surat Thani, where we were to be held before our case was heard. We drove through the gates and I can only describe it as like a Japanese prisoner of war camp: there were large buildings of every description and people were walking around in chains. So, this was to be our new home. My heart sank.

The prison was full of mainly Thai, with a couple of foreign prisoners serving sentences ranging from 1 to 50 years for various offences, as I found out later. I was searched by a trustee who was a lady boy, while I had handcuffs behind my back. He proceeded to twist my testicles to make sure nothing was hidden there, which made me jump and made him laugh. There are many lady boys in Thai prisons, and they love the attention they receive from the other inmates. They look like women, but they are very volatile and fight like men. My sexual preferences have always been women, but many western men fell for the charms of these so-called lady boys. I remember one western tourist saying they gave the best ever blowjobs and they really knew how to please a man. Well, it certainly wasn't for me, but I knew it went on all over, and to be honest, it wasn't my business.

We were then processed through the prison and taken to the centre of the yard to what I can only describe as a huge metal anvil, and I was told to place my feet on there. A long steel ankle bracelet was hammered into place around my feet with a small lump hammer. I was wincing in case the guy missed the steel and broke one of my shins - I only had shorts and flip-flops on - but the guy knew what he was doing, luckily for the both of us. We were now shackled, and it was difficult to walk, never mind run. We were then given our prison garments. I was taken to be held on the men's section of the prison camp, and Jo was led away to the women's section.

When I arrived at the cell block, I could see there was no privacy; there were around a hundred people in my sleeping vicinity. It was back to sleeping on the floor but this time I was the only European in this particular cell block. Most of the Thais were acting very crazy and looked very intimidating. I huddled down on the floor that first night, and I spotted a very muscular Thai guy with tattoos all over his body, sweating heavily, doing press-ups.

He had a face that with just a look could kill you - when he stared at you, you really did feel that. He carried on doing his press-ups slowly and methodically, and I tried to avert my eyes from looking, but after a few hundred, I felt like I was compelled to watch. He was muttering in Thai 'Farang Mai dee mack Mark' to his friend, who was lying next to him. Most of the other prisoners were sleeping; it was around 3am. I started to get really paranoid. I was wedged in and could barely breathe and the other prisoners surrounding me made me feel like I was in a sardine can, and the snoring coming from the sleeping Vietnamese guy to my immediate left was doing my box in. I knew nobody, and felt if things became dangerous, I was well and truly in the shit.

Fuck, why had we returned to Thailand after jumping bail and fleeing the country the year previously? I wanted to kick myself; it had been all my idea, taking far too much smack and living in a delusional world of drugs and travel, never thinking beyond the next buzz or adrenaline hit. And now we really were paying the price for my foolishness. The Thai prison warders had no pity whatsoever, especially with the Burmese, Indonesians, Cambodians, and those from other surrounding Asian countries: they were treated like dogs and the thin bamboo canes the guards carried, along with their batons, would make a hissing noise when they struck out with them on anybody they felt deserved it. I felt like I was in Babylon trying to understand the gaggle of languages; my Thai was limited to barroom talk, but nobody was saying 'I love you long-time', or 'You want cock sucky?', or at least I hoped not in this male-dominated side of the prison I was in, with the occasional ladyboys strutting about the place sticking their asses out, knowing full well that most of the prisoners wanted to have sex with them in exchange for yabba or the potent Thai weed that everybody seemed to be smoking; they had power and they knew it.

I regretted intensely accepting a spliff from one of them, and now I was out of my head and extremely paranoid. The Thai guy stopped doing his press-ups and started stepping over the sleeping bodies and heading in my direction. The stench was unbearable: my head was almost in the hole in the ground where they took their piss, and I was straining my neck trying to keep my head away from the smell, and now this fucker was heading my way and I sure as shit knew he wasn't coming over to be friendly. I could barely keep the Thai style fisherman's pants to stay up never mind getting in a fracas with this fucker, who had no clue about me, apart from the fact he probably took an instant dislike to me; it was so dark and gloomy and I started to hope it was all a dream, and when he stood over me and pulled his cock out, I realised it was not. Then he started pissing and the sudden realisation hit me, he was just taking a piss - thank fuck.

Rats were scurrying about all over the place searching for food, the mosquitoes were intolerable, and I was badly bitten during the night. After a terrible sleep, we were all woken very early in the morning and herded out into the centre of the prison, where all the prisoners were made to crouch down in the Asian way, whilst a head count was made, to make sure nobody had escaped in the night, I presumed. At the same time, the Thai flag was being raised to the sound of the Thai anthem booming around the prison. It was a very surreal experience; my legs were shaking in the early morning sun awaiting the head count to be over. It was an unusual crouching position for a westerner, and with over 1000 prisoners it took some time for the count to be over.

We were scheduled to go to court the next day, which was fine by me: the quicker it was dealt with the better, at least we would know our fate. The rest of the day was a sight. Some of the prisoners were shackled up to the walls; I found out these were the drug addicts going through cold turkey. It felt like I was in the Middle Ages and the thought of a long sentence in this place really wasn't worth contemplating. I met an Indonesian guy who had spent three years there; he had been caught with stolen travellers' cheques and sentenced to five years. He was due out in a few months' time, and I could tell his mental health was suffering: he seemed to be talking to himself constantly. He spoke some English, but it was difficult to make a conversation with him because his mind seemed to be elsewhere. The rest of the day dragged by slowly, and I kept wondering how things were going for Jo, but I would see her in the morning on the way to court. There was some kind of hierarchy in the prison with the Thai guys being on the top and the foreigners being at the bottom. It was predominately Thai prisoners, with quite a lot of Vietnamese and Malaysians, and there were a lot of prisoners who were in there for drug offences.

In the morning I saw Jo before we boarded the coach to take us to the courthouse in Surat Thani. I was shocked by her appearance: one of her eyes was very red and it looked like conjunctivitis. It had come on during the last couple of days and she hadn't bothered to seek medical advice, knowing our case was to be heard that day, she didn't want to delay it any longer. We were both dressed in the Thai style prison garb of light brown fisherman's pants and smock top with no pockets, our feet were in chains and we were handcuffed as we stepped up onto the coach. It was quite difficult shuffling along; the heat was intense but for some reason my spirit was soaring and if nothing else we were getting a day out of here.

The journey to the courthouse took about twenty minutes, and as we stepped off the coach to be taken down to the cells below, I heard a voice shouting, 'Tommy!' I looked around and saw my brother Anthony with my cousin, Darren. He shouted again, 'You look like Papillion'; he was only joking and probably trying to raise my spirits, even though I never thought it was funny at the time. I gave him the two-fingered salute, but I was glad to see him. They had made the journey down to Surat Thani without my father, who Anthony had persuaded to fly back to the UK. Anthony had sorted a lawyer out for us, who came to see us in the cells below. I asked the Thai lawyer in English what he thought our sentence would be, and he said that for jumping bail we possibly could get thee months in jail, and for the weed charge another three months, and once our sentence was completed, we would then be deported back to the UK. That made me feel slightly better, but the conditions were so inhumane I knew it wasn't going to be an easy ride, and after seeing the state of Jo's eye that morning I was filled with trepidation when they brought us up to the courtroom to face our charges, standing in the dock next to her.

The prosecution read out the charges, all in Thai, and it was difficult to follow the legal jargon. Then our lawyer spoke in our defence; he said we had been naive in fleeing the country, but we had re-entered Thailand of our own accord to come back and face the music. He also said the laws in the UK were very different from those here in Thailand,

and that we deserved a chance as it was our first offence in Thailand. After he finished the judge retired to the back room to consider his verdict. I spoke briefly to Jo; we both had our fingers crossed that the sentence wouldn't be too harsh.

Twenty minutes later the judge returned to let us know our sentence; my heart was pumping, wondering what would happen. I really wasn't sure how this was going to pan out and the thought of going back to that prison was not a happy one. The judge had decided that since we had returned to Thailand voluntarily he would give us a chance, and we were both fined something like a 100 pounds each for jumping bail, and on the second charge of being in possession of weed we were jailed for 28 days, but seeing as we had been in custody for the time spent in Bangkok our sentence was over, and we would be sent back to the Immigration Centre in Bangkok, where we would stay until a flight back to the UK became available. Wow, I couldn't believe our luck - maybe the judge felt sorry for Jo after seeing her eye, but whatever it was we were both elated that we were not going back to the prison in Surat Thani. We had had a brief taste of that place and we were in no hurry to go back there ever again.

We were taken back down to the cells below. Our Anthony and Darren sorted out the fines we owed and came to see us both in the cells below, and we were all buzzing. I told Anthony to go and enjoy his holiday as it was pointless them coming back to Bangkok after all the running about and stress we had caused him. When they left, I was glad it was all over and done with, but we were still in custody, and we would be going back to Bangkok with the prospect of being sent back to the UK in the near future.

Thai prisons are shitholes. They call them monkey houses, and they are. I wouldn't put my dog in there. Full of lady-boys, the food is shit, the place stinks and they rob you blind - a bit like Widnes, the next town to Warrington. An hour or so later we were placed in a police car and driven back to Bangkok, arriving at the detention centre late that night. This had been a nightmare to deal with, and although going back to the UK we would be free, our minds were still on global travel. Two days later we were taken back to Don Muang Airport and placed on a British Airways flight back to London. We were now officially free.

'Freedom is just another word for nothing left to lose.' Janis Joplin

Chapter 22
Manchester

After a few days in Manchester we decided we wanted to carry on travelling, and so we hit the nearest travel agents and booked our flights out of Manchester and flew to Bali. We had the wanderlust bad, and so it was that the adventure carried on, and after a few weeks we headed on over to Australia again.

We were making money fast while having fun in the sun. I had friends all over Australia. My good Irish mate Peter Kennedy from Dublin was a top man who had helped me out many years before when I was on my arse in Sydney. He lived in Manly, a suburb of Sydney, a great spot. We quickly found a flat and bought a car. The party was back on. Yes!

Sydney is a top city surrounded by beaches, full of great pubs and a top nightlife. I saw the Prodigy in a small club there one night. We went to parties all over Sydney, and one night we scored some smack from a hooker in Kings Cross. Jo waited outside whilst I went up and took a shot in the arm. I remember thinking, *Wow, this shit is good.* I had overdosed in the room upstairs where the girls were plying their trade, and they dragged me down the stairs and left me on the street; they probably didn't want the police involved. Luckily for me, Jo spotted me and brought me round. A close call.

We travelled all over Australia, and it became like a second home. We were flying in and out on a regular basis. Sometimes we would fly to the UK in the summer months; we were continually on the move. It suited us both, life was good, we were living in the fast lane and loving every minute of it.

My brother Anthony, his first wife Cath, and his two kids, Anthony Jnr and Sarah, came over to Australia for a holiday and stayed for a few months, renting a flat overlooking Manly Beach. Our kid was ringing the change in Australia and was cleaning up, making $800-$1000 Aussie dollars a day; nobody was doing it out there. Gradually teams started to come out from the UK lured by the easy pickings they had heard about in Australia; Sydney, Melbourne, Perth, Adelaide, Hobart, Brisbane, flying or driving all over. The teams would fly in and graft for eight weeks, taking home ten to twenty thousand pounds. Not bad money; plus they were living like kings, staying in top hotels, eating great food and pulling lots of Aussie women. It sure beat London or the north west of England, especially in the winter times.

Eventually, Cath and the kids went home, and our Anthony stayed for another six months. He loved it and loved the lifestyle; he was getting bored in England. We were all living like there was no tomorrow, but it would catch up at some point. I had thousands in the bank. Jo had her own money. My head was spinning with all the travelling. We were catching planes like they were buses, driving brand new cars which we hired to go grafting, and this went on for years. We used to go to New Zealand on visa runs, drinking and doing drugs.

One of the times we went back to the UK, Jo and I went to Creamfields with my niece Donna. We were watching Primal Scream. I was coming up on an E. I remember looking up at the stage and seeing the manager standing in the wings, and saying to myself, *That will be me one day, managing a rock band*. I swear to god I never knew why I said that, it just came out of the blue. I've spent a lifetime going out. I was around the Northern Soul scene, the Glam Rock scene, the Rave scene: I just love music.

Sometime around '98 our kid, Jo and I were driving down the Melbourne coast and grafting on opposite sides of the street. We were arrested by the police: one of the shopkeepers had rung and complained about being conned. They let me go as they couldn't prove it but charged our Anthony and Jo with deception. They were taken to court, fined and deported back to England with the headline: 'Backpackers Sent Back to Blighty'. They were lucky; we had taken some serious money out of Australia over the years. I headed back to the UK to meet them, and had a few days in Manilla on my own on the way back; that is one wild city. I smoked a bit of crack with the locals; my penchant for drugs had never left me.

When Jo landed back from Australia, I met her at Heathrow. After a few days, we decided to go travelling again, but not before I did some more smack at my dad's house just after he went out. I heard banging on the door, and I went downstairs to answer it and collapsed. It was my father, who had forgotten his key. Jo let him in, they rang the ambulance and I woke up in hospital. Another lucky escape! My dad was distraught and thought I was on a death wish. I didn't care.

A few days later we headed out to India, moving across India down to Trivandrum and on to Sri Lanka. Places were becoming all a bit of a blur, and I was taking it all for granted. We went back to India and hired a motorbike. I should have let Jo ride, but stupidly I got on and crashed. I ended up in hospital yet again with a chunk out of my leg, and Jo was burned by the exhaust pipe. That was it, I have never ridden a bike since.

'A man who leaves home to mend himself and others is a philosopher, but he who goes from country to country, guided by the blind impulses of curiosity, is a vagabond.' Oliver Goldsmith

Chapter 23
Back to Thailand

We loved Thailand and once again decided we wanted to go back. We had served our time. We flew into Singapore and had a few beers in the famous Raffles Hotel. We travelled overland to Kuala Lumpur in Malaysia - I love that city - and then on back down to Thailand where we arrived in time for Christmas. We soon settled back into life on the beach in Lamai, going to the full moon parties when we could be bothered.

I bumped into old friends, one from Eastbourne Tiler, Ben Surridge, who I had helped a few years earlier; he was always up for a laugh. I bumped into Rike again from Germany, who had a South African boyfriend called Rudi. He was a great singer and she asked me to manage and promote him when I came back to Europe. Well, why not?

Rike was from a small village in Germany called Wollmerschied. Her husband Peter had died a few years before and Rike had come to Thailand with her three children, Janny, Marios and her daughter, the first time I met them in 1996. Rike told me about her husband Peter and we would talk for hours. She was coming to terms with his death. Rike was very spiritual and she told me her husband Peter had been a spiritual mover back in Germany. This was all new to me but there was something about Rike that rang true - she had an aura of calmness and was highly intelligent. We had hit it off; she had a great sense of humour and was always laughing, it was infectious. We were platonic friends, and over the next three years we got to know each other on various trips she made back to Thailand. Rike was in her 40s and had lived in India for a couple of years in the 70s, and she had also been an active member of Greenpeace; she was great fun to be around.

When we met again in 1999, she seemed in a really happy place, and she told me she had met a South African guy called Rudi who was a rock singer back in South Africa. During her eight week stay in Koh Samui, she started to suggest that I should be the manager of her boyfriend Rudi, who up to this point I had never met. She gave me a demo of three of his songs. One of the songs was called 'I Love Myself'; they were very uplifting and very spiritual rock songs. Rike was quite a small and slightly built lady but I started to believe in her; there was just something about her, I couldn't quite put my finger on it. We started to go to the Rock Bar in Koh Samui, and the secret garden party in Maenam beach, on the other side of the island where they had Sunday live music sessions. Singers would come and perform from all over the island, and it was reputed Mick Jagger from the Rolling Stones had performed there one time.

The Sunday sessions were great fun and I started to learn a little bit about the music business on this beautiful island in the south of Thailand. Up to this point my life - although I was having great fun - had no real sense of direction. I had been jumping around the globe with no real plan in mind other than to have fun and keep on travelling.

She started to instil in me a sense of fulfilment and over the coming weeks I started to believe in myself, and this was to be my destiny: to enter the music business. I had read the book *The Celestine Prophecies*, which had come out in 1993, written by James Redfield, about an ancient manuscript that had been found in Peru with nine spiritual insights, and I realised my mind was now opening to the spiritual side of my life. There were so many coincidences happening that I knew I was starting to meet the people I was supposed to meet and really there were no such things as coincidences: I was meant to meet the people I was meeting. It may seem crazy, but I really felt that all the things that were beginning to happen to me were all connected, and I was now finding my path in life at long last after years of being a nomad with no real sense of purpose.

Lying on the Elephant Rock in Lamai I started to feel the vibrations of the ancient rocks that had been there for millions of years, and when I closed my eyes I was seeing visions of faces; colours were blazing through my mind like I was in outer space, vivid bright colours of every hue and colour; it was so relaxing and thought-provoking I couldn't explain it. Rike had awoken me to the ideas of a truly spiritual world.

People may think I was crazy, but I started to accept what was happening to me and really embraced it all. I had to give up my life of crime and start to help people. I had so many flaws myself and I had done so many things I was truly ashamed of, but I knew I had to change somehow, or I would become somebody I was never meant to be.

Rike introduced me to the Bach Flower Remedies, a way of healing people discovered by a Doctor Bach in the 1920s in England. There are 38 bottles, and they help to restore the balance between mind and body by casting out all the negative emotions like fear, hatred, worry and indecision that interfere with the equilibrium of the being as a whole.

She told me I should walk straighter, and hold my shoulders back: my shoulders are rounded, perhaps with the shame I have carried most of my life. She gave me exercises to do to get rid of the shit that was in my mind and my body, and she told me to look out for places and gardens in the future. She told me to wrap an imaginary belt around myself to protect me when I felt any fear, and she also told me not to forget to unlock it when I took it off. It was quite hard to take it all in at that time but it started to seep into my subconscious over the years. My mind had never been opened to these possibilities years before, but I knew somewhere I had come from gypsies back in Ireland hundreds of years before, travelling people who knew things, things you only learned by moving around and not staying in one place.

Things are hard to explain to people with scientific minds, but we are all connected in some strange magical way. The time came for Rike to leave the island and we hugged the morning she left for the ferry. As I watched her leaving, I could see a brilliant white light that seemed to be glowing all around her; was the sun playing with my mind, was I imagining it? I rubbed my eyes and once again watched as she headed to the small minibus to take her back to the ferry in Nathon and on to the mainland to make the long journey back to Bangkok for her flight to Germany.

Rike had left me with an exciting challenge ahead of me. I really had no clue about what I was letting myself in for, but for sure I knew it was not going to be boring.

I started to explore the island more and more, going to all and any live music events that were going on, meeting musicians. I carried Rudi's three songs with me on his CD everywhere, and I pestered DJs to play it, hanging around the DJ booth all night at The Reggae Bar in Chaweng, anywhere I could find DJs; but it was virtually impossible, nobody would play it. I kept searching for contacts on the island who could somehow be connected to the music business. I knew people came from all over the world to relax on the beaches of Samui, and I heard one day that the internationally known singer Sade's manager, Roger Davies, was staying in one of the big hotels in Chaweng. I kept going there trying to speak with him; I really had no clue about what I was going to say to him but I thought he could give me some advice. Little did I know.

Every time I went there, he was sleeping on a lounge chair by the pool. I wasn't going to give up: I kept asking the waiters and they kept saying he was very tired. I truly understand now, but in those days, I was so naïve, and after 3 or 4 days of trying I finally got to speak with him. I said my name was Tommy and started to explain I was joining the music business as a rock manager and had no real experience, and could he enlighten me. He looked at me and said with a smile, 'You have to find your own way in this business, and it is all about connections.' He was probably used to strangers asking him questions; I felt awkward standing around asking him questions though, while he was trying to relax on holiday. So I decided to say thanks and left him with a bemused smile on his face.

I spent weeks walking up and down the beach clutching Rudi's CD, introducing myself to random strangers who were lying on the beach, trying to find contacts for the journey I had ahead of me; I was a man on a mission and I had so much energy it was the only thing I could think of day and night. I was obsessed with making the right connections.

One morning as I was walking along the beach I introduced myself to a couple of black guys who were lounging around, and I started to tell them the story of what I was up to, when one of the black guys said his name was Mentona and that he was a reggae singer from Liberia, West Africa, and that he was recording some songs in a small studio on the island near Chaweng Beach. I thought this must be some kind of sign, and he started to say he might be looking for a manager also in the future when the songs were recorded.

We started to hang out and I went with him to the small studio in Chaweng run by an Italian guy called Roberto. Mentona's his real name was John Gregory Karkor, and he was around 21 when I met him. He told me he had fled his homeland in Liberia, and he was also on a mission to get his music out to the world. Slowly he started to record the songs and then I had my first real sign of the musical world and the way that musicians operate. He said if I would agree to pay for his recording time, he would sign a management agreement for 3 years, and when I got back to London, I could chase up contacts to get his music to the right ears and make things happen.

So, after a few weeks we drew up a 3-year management contract, and we went into a local tailor on the island and we both dressed up in suits, and laid the contract out on the tailor's desk, and he signed the contract. We had the tailor take photographs of us. I paid the tailor and then left his shop and we headed to the local moneychanger and I cashed up a thousand pounds in travellers' cheques, and paid for his recording times. I gave Mentona some money; he had decided to go to Bangkok and would get promotional copies of his album and promotional photographs for me to take back to London when my time came to leave. So here I was: I now had two artistes on my books and still no real idea what I was up to or going to do.

Jo had gone back to England a couple of months before me and set about finding us a place to live for when I arrived back in the UK. So I carried on networking on the island while Mentona was in Bangkok, getting the promotional materials. I really never wanted to leave Koh Samui but now I was a man on a mission. It was 1999 and it was heading into the millennium. New Year, New Man. Finally, the time was coming to leave: Mentona had come back from Bangkok with all the promotional material and we had decided to set up the management company and called it ZodoA Management after studios called ZodoA back in his home country of Liberia. I prepared myself for the return trip to England and spent the next few days relaxing on the beach in Koh Samui vowing I would be back one day for good; the island felt like home I loved the place so much. I had truly decided to give up ringing the change and on my return to England I would set out on my mission in the music business. Little did I know what I was letting myself in for.

I was 39 years old and I needed a change in my life. Jo had got restless and had already been back in the UK a few months before me. After years on the road, I think she wanted to start studying and do something with her life. We had been arrested in Sweden, Thailand and Australia, and she wanted more out of life.

The father of my Thai mate, Kat, from Nathon, Si Tamarat, had a concrete business delivering concrete around Thailand. He wanted to set me up in business: he knew I could speak Thai and I was good with people. He wanted to buy some speedboats for me to take tourists around and entertain them, and we would make good money. I said no, and he said, 'Tommy, the music business is very hard.' Almost 20 years later, I have to agree.

'Long distance no subsistence'

Chapter 24
Dunstable

When I landed at Heathrow Jo told me she had found a place to live in a small town, Dunstable, outside Luton, around 35 miles north of London. The flat was very nice, but I wanted to be in London. Jo had got herself a job in a bar in the town, and I carried on with my mission, driving to London every day looking for contacts, backwards and forwards going to gigs, chasing up contacts, spending money hand over fist. Jo and I were drifting apart; she was getting bored with me and I was not sure how long she was going to put up with my antics. She never could understand why I was doing what I was doing; she thought it was for teenagers, and we started drifting apart. We never went out together as I was always in London or she was always at work, and we argued a lot; we had been together for seven years but the next few months became hard on both of us, and I had my head was well and truly buried in the sand. I just carried on pretending nothing was wrong.

Jo was applying to colleges to do some more studying, and we were becoming more like brother and sister, and not good ones at that. I started putting on gigs at the Rifleman's in Hounslow, and it was costing me money; I was ringing up record companies, chasing up all kinds of people, spending money left right and centre, my savings depleting rapidly. I really never knew what I was doing half the time, I was winging it and learning as I was going along. I spent my 40th birthday picking bands up and driving to Hounslow to put shows on with them, on my birthday; even my dad and family were beginning to wonder why I had made this sudden change in my life. Maybe it was a mid-life crisis, but I never listened to anybody; I just carried on regardless taking no heed of anybody; I was in it for the long haul.

The deeper it got, the more I was determined not to fail, but I let go of my money - it was slipping through my fingers. I would soon end up broke, and with no job. I was chasing my dream and the excitement of it all; I was lost in the whole caper and couldn't yet see the reality of how hard the music business could be with no money and no contacts. I was getting emails from Mentona in Thailand, and phone calls from Rike and Rudi in Germany, asking how things were going. I was feeling the pressure from everywhere and we were now approaching the millennium. Jo got pissed off with my obsession and on New Year's

Eve 1999 as we brought in the millennium watching the fireworks on Westminster Bridge, Jo told me our relationship was over. We had bought a house from my brother a few years earlier, which I sold to a mate. I gave Jo her cut and we split.

After seven years with Jo and not having a clue about my next move, I moved into a flat in North Kensington in one of the tower blocks, Markland House, with my old mate Rob Taylor. I was blowing all the money I had left on bands. I brought Rudi over from South Africa and had him playing around the UK. I had started to believe in karma, and I gave up my life of crime. I started networking around Notting Hill and Ladbroke Grove, constantly searching for the next big thing. I had even given up drinking, thinking people would take me more seriously if I was sober. I was putting gigs on all over West London, meeting more and more musicians.

Mentona was constantly emailing me to send him money via Western Union, to pay for his food and lodgings in Thailand, and I was sending him money from the sale of the house, but it was never enough. Like most musicians he could only think of himself: I was his investor and he was determined not to let me go. As the months flew by, I was in real danger once again of ending up broke. I took a job with a company called Stage Miracles as a production runner; the money was crap, but I got to see all the big gigs at various London stadiums. I met a Russian guy called Andre, who was doing security at one of the Madonna shows, when she was playing at the Earls Court Arena in 2001 on her Drowned World Tour, and we became friends. He had not been long in the country and he had aspirations to work for the council in the next few years. We started hanging out. I had bought a car on hire purchase, and Andre loved driving, so he used to come and drive me all over London.

'Without music life would be a mistake.' Friedrich Nietzsche

Chapter 25
Rasta Man

Around this time, I had started managing a band called NRG Fly who were local to the Notting Hill area; they were a wild bunch. Andy the lead singer was from Cheltenham, a cheeky fucker who loved taking the piss and causing havoc everywhere he went. Dave, on guitar, was from South London; he had a crack and smack problem, and had a vicious wit that he would mercilessly unleash on me or anybody in earshot. But for some reason I liked Dave: he was a straight shooter and I found him amusing. Then there was Andrew, who they nicknamed Dandi; he was London-Irish and could recite Shakespeare very eloquently and had a great sense of humour. They had a weaselly-looking Scottish drummer who they called Jock. I started booking gigs around London with them, but they were a freaking nightmare to deal with. Dandi was the only one not taking drugs. They played great rock and roll, and it was always a good laugh. We got booked to play a wedding once in London Bridge and the bride ran out crying when they started playing, as she was expecting a soul band, and we all got thrown out and told to fuck off by the bride's father. The mate who had booked us hadn't told her what the band was like. Why I was managing them on top of everything else, I will never know.

Having pressure bearing down on me, mainly financial, I was constantly looking for ways to make money, and through pushing Mentona's reggae album I met a Jamaican producer called Gilly who had arrived in London. He had a compilation album of various unknown Jamaican reggae artists on an album called *Better Days are Coming*. Gilly was quite a mysterious character and he always seemed to have money on him, and he suggested I set up a record label, and the first release on ZodoA records would be the album. Having listened to the album I thought, *Hell, why not?* We started meeting up regularly and Gilly started to introduce me around to his Jamaican connections in London. I met Carl Palmer, from Jet Star Records in Park Royal, a legendary character who had the largest distribution company in the world of reggae music. We had a thousand copies of the album pressed up and went on a tour of all the reggae record shops in London, including Blacker Dread's shop in Brixton, and started to leave fifty copies in each shop, driving round in my car and opening the boot and leaving the records on a sale or return basis.

I also met David Roddigan, the biggest reggae DJ in the UK, who ran a night at the Subterrania, a venue under the Westway in Ladbroke Grove, and I gave him a copy of the album; without promotion the album was going nowhere. I also started going around the pubs and clubs of London selling the album for a tenner to various people I met. We started venturing outside of London, even gatecrashed a wedding in Luton and sold the bride and groom a copy of *Better Days are Coming* - they fell for my spiel - I mean, that is what you wanted to hear, surely, when you have just got married, Better Days are Coming! But all of this was hard work that went on for months. I had haemorrhaged all of my money and was on the point of being destitute.

When Gilly one day suggested, 'How would you like to go to Jamaica, man?' I was very interested indeed. He started to explain that I would have to bring some weed back. 'Some good sinsemilla, the herb for the healing of the nation,' he laughed. Well, I thought about it over the next few days, and where my head was, I will never know, but I knew for sure I wanted the money, so I rang Gilly and told him I was interested. He told me to come and meet him outside Brixton tube station the next day. That night my head was all over the place: what the fuck was I doing? But I just thought it was a shit or bust trip for me. I drove over to Brixton the next day and met Gilly.

We went to a coffee shop on Coldharbour Lane and he explained, 'You will be met in Kingston and will stay in the Hilton Hotel in Jamaica.' All my flights would be paid for and I would be paid five thousand English pounds; he would give me a thousand pounds today upfront if I agreed. He said it would be a breeze: his friends worked in customs and they would let me through, no problem; he said nobody would suspect me, a white guy on his own in Jamaica. I thought it over. I badly wanted the cash, I knew I would say yes, so I agreed. We left the coffee shop and it was pissing down outside so I pulled the hood over my head and he took me to the local travel agents, and we then booked a 7-day return flight to the sunny Caribbean. Outside the travel agents he passed me a white envelope, stuffed with cash I assumed, and we then left each other. I was due to fly to Kingston in five days' time. I told nobody. 'I will be in touch,' were his parting words.

When I got back to the car, I opened the envelope and counted fifty brand new twenty pound notes, the agreed upfront one thousand quid. Over the next few days I liaised with Gilly by phone, and he told me not to worry, Jah would bless me and all would be fine. I bought some new clothes and I was looking forward to going to Jamaica, a country I had heard so much about but had never visited. Finally, the day arrived, and I took the tube to Heathrow airport and checked myself into the British Airways flight direct to Kingston. A couple of hours later I was aboard the 9-hour flight. I had a few drinks; I wasn't nervous at all, after all, I was going on holiday and had no drugs on me entering Jamaica. I finished off the meals that were brought around and then fell fast asleep, waking up for breakfast an hour before we landed. Eventually, the plane landed, and we all trooped off the plane with the heat blasting into my face as we stepped out into the Jamaican sunshine, and it felt good: London was grey and drizzly before I left.

 I picked up my suitcase on the carousel and passed through customs without a hitch. Coming out of the airport a gorgeous Jamaican girl approached me and asked me if my name was Tommy. 'Yes,' I replied; I had not been expecting a girl although Gilly had said I would be met by somebody, but immediately I felt good in her presence and things were definitely looking up. She said her name was Alvita and she was a good friend of Gilly's and, 'Welcome to Jamaica.' I guessed she was around thirty; she had brilliant white teeth that really stood out with the blackness of her face.

 I followed her outside the airport, and she was laughing, and joking; I felt she was flirting with me or just trying to make me less nervous. She led me to a parked car and inside were two Jamaican guys in the front seats. Alvita opened the boot and told me to put my case in there, which I did. We both got in the back seat, the car pulled away and we made our way out of the airport. The driver said nothing, but the guy sat next to him introduced himself as we were driving along: he said his name was Akoni and welcomed me to Jamaica. He was quite a muscular-looking guy and I figured he was around fortyish. I thought they are giving me blag names in case things went wrong. I had no clue what the score was but the sudden realisation of what I was letting myself in for started hitting me. I was in a strange country, knew nobody and I was going to be smuggling drugs out of this island paradise; if I got caught, I would be fucked. Jesus, I needed a drink.

 There was something about Akoni; he spoke gruffly and had an air of menace about him, but I knew nothing would happen to me by their hands, it was in their interest that I got their drugs through and back to England, so I started to relax. We were just chatting about Jamaica and finally we pulled up outside the Hilton Hotel on Knutsford Boulevard in downtown Kingston. Alvita kissed me on the cheek and they said my room was booked and I would be on my own until the final day. I would have a great time and not to worry about the hotel bill, it was all paid for, and I could use room service for anything I wanted. She then passed me a mobile phone and told me to keep it switched on and gave me a mobile charger to charge the phone.

I got out of the car, picked my suitcase up, and watched them drive off before entering the hotel and checking myself in. It was around 10am. I took the lift to the 8th floor. The room was very nice. I took a shower, combed my hair, put a light blue shirt and shorts on and headed downstairs to find the bar. I ordered a double whiskey to calm my nerves and went out to the pool area to explore my surroundings. The heat was suffocating as it was the height of summer and I came back in, found the restaurant and decided to eat and wait for the sun to go down. I had thoughts of Rike: was this the spiritual path I was on? I pushed it to the back of my mind. I ordered from the menu some nice Jamaican Jerk chicken and rice; I was famished. I wolfed it down, ordered a beer and my mind started to wonder about the job ahead. What if I got caught? What if I got murdered? What if something went drastically wrong? I could end up rotting in a Jamaican prison, or even if I got through to England I could get caught in Heathrow and jailed in England.

Aw fuck it, I thought, no sense worrying at this stage, I have just arrived. I knew for sure I was not going to back out, it just wasn't in my nature.

'I won't back down.' Tom Petty and the Heartbreakers

Chapter 26
Kingston

I took a taxi around Kingston the next morning. The taxi driver was telling me it could be dangerous if you are alone and went into the wrong part of the city. I found Kingston to be quite small, but we drove around, and he took me to the Bob Marley Museum, where I wandered around looking at the relics of Bob's life, spent a pleasant hour and stepped back out into the blazing heat. The weather was so hot people were walking around with umbrellas for shade. We drove through Trenchtown; he was explaining the history of Kingston, and I found him quite knowledgeable on the city. After a few hours he dropped me back at the hotel, and I paid him; he gave me his card and said if I needed a lift anytime to give him a call.

The next few days I caught up on a lot of reading and just relaxed by the hotel pool, watching the comings and goings of the American tourists who seemed to dominate the hotel. They had a small disco at the hotel at nights, and I would drop in for a few beers, but to tell you the truth I was just waiting for the time to come when I would be taking my chances at the airport with a suitcase full of drugs. My fingers were well and truly crossed that all would go to plan and I would arrive safely back in the UK in a few days' time. I lived really well at the hotel, living like a king; fuck it if I got caught. I felt a bit like the condemned man, so I was going to make the most of it. I noticed there were hookers hanging around at night: with their short skirts and made up faces, they stuck out a mile. Well, we all had to make a living and who was I to look down on anybody? On the final night I got a call from Alvita and she told me that they would meet me in the morning and drive me to the airport.

I slept fitfully that night: my mind was on overdrive about what I had to do the next day. The night went slowly by, and suddenly it was morning. I showered, changed my clothes, packed my suitcase, and went down to the foyer, where the bill had already been paid. I walked outside and Alvita was waiting. She beckoned me to the car and once again Akoni and the driver were in the front. I placed my suitcase in the back and noticed another suitcase. I knew this was mine to be taken through customs. I got in the car, and Alvita was all smiles: 'Hope you had a good time in Jamaica, Tommy?' 'Yes, thanks.' I could see Akoni was watching me in the mirror, and I tried not to look nervous, and to give off an air of confidence.

We arrived at the airport thirty minutes later. Alvita stepped out and gave me the two suitcases, kissed me and said, 'All will be fine. See you again baby' and pushed her breasts against me. Wow, she was a stunner and she knew it. They drove off and left me, and I entered the airport. My heart was racing, and I was shitting it on the inside, but outwardly I was calm and composed as I made my way towards the check-in desk. There were a few people in front of me; at last it was my time and I gave my passport in to the girl on the desk, and she checked in my luggage, and gave me my passport and boarding pass. Wow, so far so good. I made my way to the gate to wait for the next couple of hours for my British Airways flight to take me back to Heathrow.

I noticed customs officers walking around the airport, but I was telling myself it would be fine, I would soon be on the plane and flying out of there.

I had a couple of beers to calm my nerves and at last the time came for me to board the flight. I settled back into my seat as we flew out of Jamaica and headed into the skies; so far, so good. Now I had to worry about getting through customs at Heathrow. The hours passed very slowly. I was gearing myself up for the landing and taking the suitcases through Heathrow. We landed about 5am in London, and once again I collected my suitcases and made my way through the 'Nothing to Declare' gates. Fuck, my heart was in my mouth. A customs officer stepped out and pulled over a woman in front of me, Jeez, I nearly fainted, I thought they had me. I carried on walking, passing through the gates and into the lounge... Fuck, I was elated, I had done it, thank god all was well! A chubby-looking Jamaican girl came over and said, 'Hi Tommy, Gilly is waiting outside', and I followed her to the carpark. Gilly was in the car, all smiles. 'Good man,' he said, and we both started laughing. I got in the front with Gilly and he gunned the engine and we made our way to South London.

Arriving in Brixton Gilly gave me another white envelope. We all got out of the car, I took my suitcase and Gilly took the other one. We gave each other the knuckles to knuckles, the Jamaican greeting, and I made my way to the local cab rank and got a cab back to West London.

I really appreciated the sense of freedom as the taxi snaked its way over Westminster Bridge in the early morning light, arriving back just in time before the rush hour started. I let myself into the flat, and counted four thousand quid in fifty pound notes - it felt good to have some money on me. I was exhausted as the stress of it all hit me, and I went straight to bed and slept like a baby.

Later I awoke to the phone ringing. It was Gilly. He said, 'Anytime you want to do it again, Tommy, we will be ready.' Once again I thought of Rike and the spiritual path I was on. I hesitated and said, 'No, once was enough.' He laughed and said, 'Okay man,' and the phone went dead.

'Don't run from the lion because you will meet the crocodile, better run through the lion or die trying.'

Chapter 27
Back to Jamaica

Within six weeks the money was drying up, so I got on the phone to Gilly and said, 'Let's do it again.'

A few days later I was back in Brixton, and Gilly said I would be flying into Montego Bay this time. I had just blown four thousand quid on fancy restaurants and new clothes and sent a further thousand pounds to Mentona in Thailand, and I sure wanted the money. Gilly explained I would be taking back five kilos this time and £10,000 in cash, but he would pay me £8000 for this trip. 'Yes man, no worries.' I was getting cocky. We once again went to the travel agents in Brixton and he booked the return flight to Montego Bay.

Over the next few days I was speaking with Rike in Germany about Rudi. He was getting impatient as nothing was happening. I lied to Rike and said I was sorting things out and not to worry. I never mentioned anything about Jamaica. How could I? I felt guilty, but told myself this was part of my journey, I was meeting the people I was meant to be meeting. I was also looking to make contacts in the reggae world to see if I could make things happen for Mentona. The rock band NRG Fly were falling apart and taking far too many drugs, and I had to get an injection of cash, get them in the studios and show my faith in them: I really needed the money and I thought it was going to be easy.

In the late summer of 2001, I flew out once again to Jamaica. Gilly had given me two grand in cash the day before and told me I would be staying with his friends in Mobay, instead of at a hotel. I did wonder why; but perhaps he was having a cost-cutting exercise: after all, he was a businessman. I landed in Montego Bay ten hours later, cleared customs, went outside and waited for Gilly's contact. Not long after, a Jamaican guy with a yellow shirt introduced himself to me. I guessed he was in his late thirties; he looked like a gangster and gave me a strange feeling that something wasn't quite right. But I shook the feeling off as I got in the car with him and he drove us to the suburb of Ironshore. He told me his name was Delroy, and I would be looked after for the week by some friends of his, and the weed would be delivered to me in due course. We arrived at a large house and he took me inside, where there was a man and a woman; the woman looked nervous but the man she was with was smiling. He said his name was Gary and he would show me my room at the back of the house. Delroy left quietly. The room was very clean, and he left me to it. I unpacked my cases, and had a lie down for a few hours to catch up on some sleep. I awoke a few hours later and could hear the radio. I was feeling a bit strange in somebody's house, but I decided to go out and start chatting with them. The woman introduced herself to me and said her name was Amelia, and she seemed less nervous and said to make myself at home, and she would be doing the cooking and hoped I would enjoy my stay. Gary was laughing and joking with her and I surmised they were married or at least partners.

Over the next few days Gary took me around Montego Bay and showed me the sights and beaches, and we would go back and eat with Amelia, who prepared some great Jamaican dishes; they became quite friendly with me during the course of the week, but at the back of my mind I was really thinking about the trip and wasn't really concentrating on the conversations they were having. I assumed they knew what was going on. Then I heard the door knock one day, and it was Delroy; Amelia went and answered the door and told me Delroy wanted to speak with me. I went outside and Delroy said, 'There is a change of plan, you will be flying out tonight from Kingston.' This was a four hour drive from Montego Bay. He told me to go and pack my case.

I thought *What the fuck?* But to be honest I was getting bored hanging around the house and wanted to get this trip over and done with. I got in the car with Delroy ten minutes later and bid Amelia and Gary goodbye. On the four hour journey back to Kingston Delroy started to become aggressive in the car: 'Don't think about ripping me off, I will have you killed if anything goes missing.' I knew what he meant: it was known sometimes on arrival that drug mules would just fuck off with the drugs and not meet with their contacts at the other end. I assured him that would not happen in my case.

Arriving at the airport, I was glad to get out of the car. He passed me the suitcase and glared at me. I just thought, *Fuck you*. He got back in the car and drove off; he had upset my equilibrium, even though I was nervous enough as it was.

The plans had changed, and I couldn't understand why. Now, I knew I had five kilos of weed in the suitcase and £10,000 in cash and this was going to bang me in the shit if I got collared, what the fuck was I doing? It was way too late to go back on it now. I made my way to the check-in desk, and there seemed to be loads of police and customs officers around. My stomach was churning like fuck and I felt slightly nauseous. I noticed the customs officers were pulling people out of the queue and opening their suitcases, and I truly had that sinking feeling in my stomach that somebody was going to pull me, and sure enough a few minutes later I heard a voice: 'Are you flying to the UK?' I looked and noticed it was a huge fat woman in uniform; my mouth was as dry as fuck, but I forced a smile and said, 'Yes.' She told me to step out of the queue, took me to a table, and said, 'Did you pack these cases?' I said 'Yes.'

She opened the first suitcase, with just my clothes in; my mind was screaming please let me go now and leave the other case alone. Then she opened the other suitcase and inside were a load of clothes, and for a brief moment I was so relieved, until she pulled the clothes out and revealed the tightly packed weed underneath it all. She then radioed through and two police guys came, and all three of them escorted me to a back room in the airport. Oh man, I was well and truly fucked now. I was thinking about Rike and the spiritual path I was on; what had made me so foolish to do this? Mentona would be wondering what was happening to me, the band NRG Fly back in London were all depending on me, all these things were flashing through my mind, my dad and my family. I had told nobody I was even here; I was fucking gutted and I wanted to kick myself so frigging badly - this really was not looking good. My plane was due to be leaving in a few hours and my heart and mind were desperately clinging to the idea that this was all a joke and it would be sorted, and that I would be getting on the plane and flying back to England.

They opened all the packages one by one, packed tightly with weed, then they opened one of the packages and I saw a white powder; *oh shit I hope that is not cocaine*. The customs officer looked at me and smiled as if to say you are well and truly in the shit. They found the money, ten grand in cash, and laid it all out on a table in front of me; fuck, I felt like Pablo Escobar the way they were all grinning at me and congratulating each other. The fat lady left me with the two policeman, and they started questioning me: how had I come by the money? Who had given me the drugs? Who was my contact in Jamaica? I knew for sure I had no hope: even though Delroy had been threatening me there was no purpose in me dropping him and Gilly in it, I knew for sure this wasn't England and I knew I was going to jail in Jamaica, and they would have me killed.

I had never been a grass, but my arse was going. Fuck, how long would I get? I had no idea what a Jamaican prison would be like, but I had a feeling I wasn't going to like it.

I told them it was all mine and I bought it in Kingston off a Rasta, but I never knew his name; they both laughed, they knew I was bullshitting, but what else could I do or say? 'Come on white man, you think we are stupid?' He gave me a slap around the face. 'That fucking hurt,' I said rubbing my cheek. 'Come on then, give me the names...' This went on for a couple of hours. Then the taller policemen said, 'Look, white boy, we can do a deal,' and told me they would keep the weed and the 10,000 grand in cash, and I would only be charged with the kilo of cocaine, to keep my mouth shut and my sentence would be lighter. I had no fucking choice really, and readily agreed.

This goes on all the time with the Jamaican police and customs officers, I found out later; they all work in cahoots. At the end of the day, I knew I would get a few years knocked off my sentence, and I would have to deal with the consequences at a later date with Delroy the gangster whose money I had just given to the policemen. Bollocks, my luck had well and truly run out and now I had to face god knows how long in the Jamaican penal system.

They left me alone in the room for a few minutes while I pondered what lay ahead. I was fuming. I had no idea about the coke, the bastards. I had no choice. Well, this was where my spiritual path was leading me, was it? My thoughts were of Rike back in Germany. They led me out of the airport in handcuffs, placed me in the police car and took me to jail, Rema Remand Centre, near Trenchtown in Kingston. Late that night when we arrived, the policeman said, 'Have you ever been to jail before, white man?' I lied and said no. He laughed and said 'Bumbaclart!' They both drew their guns out when we got outside the car and walked me towards the remand centre. I could hear gunshots going off in the distance, and my blood ran cold; what was I getting into?

Inside the remand centre was like Bedlam. Hundreds of prisoners started yelling, 'You are going to die in here white pussyhole', and I felt like I really was; the noise was deafening, and the guards started processing me and asking me questions, and my mind was all over the place - at any minute I was going to be placed in one of these dark cells with god knows who. I was on my own without a friend in the world. Anybody who knows Jamaica will know how fearsome the Yardies really are, and I was fresh meat, a white man who had appeared in the middle of the night; the abuse they were shouting at me was terrifying and I had no clue about this place whatsoever, there was not one kind face or word said to me, I was being treated lower than a dog and the guards were laughing at me: they could see I was fucking on edge, big time.

They processed me then roughly grabbed me and walked me along a corridor; passing each cell, the threats were coming thick and fast, and the air of violence was so palpable, I was so tired and feeling like the end of the world was really here, maybe I was in hell and I had died, and this was my karma for eternity for my past deeds. I wanted to run away and get the fuck out of there immediately, but that was just a dream, I was going nowhere, surrounded by guards and cells, the enormity of what I had done closed in on me in the most horrible way you could imagine. The smell was vomit inducing and with each step we took to the cell I was going to be placed in I became more alert. What would lie behind the doors waiting for me? It was not going to be long before I found out. I was covered in sweat; it was so hot and humid I could smell myself mixed in with the fear and the horrible reality this was not a dream; it was almost too much to bear and my spirit felt totally crushed. I could not believe I had been so stupid.

Surely this was not the spiritual path I had chosen; or was it? This was not the tourist brochure of white sandy beaches and smiling faces that most people think of when they dream of Jamaica, this was the most brutal and horrifying place you would never wish on your worst enemy. I had only been here five minutes and I knew nothing of Jamaica really, I was a total stranger to these shores and at any second they were going to place me behind one of these cell doors and I was going to find out with horrifying clarity how I was to be treated in this third world cesspit. Some of the Jamaican prisoners seemed to hate the white man with a blood-curdling vengeance and I was going to be made to feel the wrath of their bitterness with no mercy given whatsoever, period. I truly was a prisoner, and, in that moment, I could see no light at the end of the tunnel, only dark imaginings that kept running through my mind. When they opened one of the cell doors, I took a sharp intake of breath and steeled myself for what was in store for me and lay ahead.

'When the going gets tough, the tough get going.' Billy Ocean

Chapter 28
Trenchtown - Rema Remand Centre 2001

They opened the cell door and pushed me in. The cell was fucking crazy. All five of the Jamaicans in there were in for murder, they told me that night. There was no room to move or even to breathe. This really was the end of the line for me. I knew for sure I wasn't going anywhere for god knows how many years. I knew I had to stand my ground, or I would really be pushed around. They started goading me, calling me a white pussy, and telling me I wouldn't get out alive, and that when I got sentenced, I would be sent to the General Penitentiary, the maximum-security jail, where I would be killed within a few weeks. But I was having none of it.

I thought, *They are testing me*. All five of them pulled homemade knives on me, and put them near my body. I thought, *Shit, this is getting dangerous*. Then they all started laughing and put the knives away. In the cell opposite, this guy kept shouting that he was going to kill me. In the morning I was getting seriously worried about my life. I don't know how I slept that night, but somehow, I did. I was in shock, and in the morning, I heard screams and shouting. The guy opposite, who had threatened to kill me, was stabbed to death that morning by some Yardies who had had some beef with him for months. He was only 19.

Perhaps they saved my life but fuck me! I had only been there one day and already I'd had knives pulled on me and heard a murder. I was not sure about anything, but the one thing I did know, I had to survive. The cell was terrible: no lights, a hole in the floor for the toilet, no toilet paper, no room to move. I was sleeping on the concrete floor with nothing, and with five murderers for the company.

Not one person knew where I was. I had told nobody as usual, and I had nothing left but my sense of humour. I really started to think I was in some wild movie. They were asking me what I thought about slavery. I could only reply that it had fuck all to do with me. Weeks went by, sleeping on the floor, back and forth to court, taking showers by pouring bottles of tap water over your body. Using the toilet was a nightmare, emptying your bowels in a cell full of people, to a hole in the floor, everybody shouting, 'You stink, white man!' I tried to hold it in for weeks but in the end, I didn't give a fuck, I had to relieve myself.

Finally, in October 2001, I was to be sentenced.

'Book learning a nuh intelligence.' Jamaican Proverb

Chapter 29
General Penitentiary

I arrived at the Halfway Tree Court and was held in the cells. Finally, they brought me up in the dock and my case was read out. I had lost a stone in weight over the last few weeks. The judge listened to my solicitor, then he considered his sentence in a back room and came back out. I was told to stand up. The judge took a long look at me and then he said, 'You are sentenced to two years hard labour for drug trafficking, and a fine of $300,000 Jamaican dollars or a further six months if the fine is not paid.' My head was spinning; hard labour - what the fuck? At least I now knew where I stood. I would be out in just under two years, much better than twenty years. Mind you, a week in a Jamaican prison felt like a month in an English one.

They drove me to the General Penitentiary in Kingston, built on a former slave colony. It was the most dangerous jail in the whole of the Caribbean. I really wasn't looking forward to it, but I had to get through and survive it somehow. Six inmates in a cell again. The General Penitentiary was where the most dangerous Yardies (Jamaicans) were held, over 2000 of them. I was just one of only two white men there when I arrived in October 2001.

The Penitentiary was situated not far from the airport. After a few days, they moved me over to the hospital wing of the prison. It looked the same as the rest of the prison. I had no light, no blanket, no bed, nothing. I had to sleep on a concrete floor with a plastic bottle for a pillow for over two months, but I felt blessed I had the cell to myself. It was deemed too dangerous to leave me in a cell with five Jamaicans, I was getting so many threats.

The British Embassy had finally got in touch, and it wouldn't look good if the white man got killed. Thank god for that! They tried to bully me all the time, but I knew I could show no fear, otherwise I would be dead meat. I kept myself to myself for the first couple of months, weighing up the situation and keeping my mouth shut. Finally, I heard from the embassy and the Prisoners Abroad Organisation set up to help prisoners held captive overseas. I received money, so I bought a mattress, got a bulb and a pillow; everything had to be bought here. Sometimes I would look around the prison and it felt like Belsen. Some of the prisoners who had no money were just skin and bones. The food was really disgusting, and I starved for months until I got money coming through.

Back in the UK, my family were worried. I had just disappeared off the face of the earth. I didn't want to worry my father, but I finally asked the Embassy to let them know. My dad and family started to send me money, which had to go through a warder; he took his cut but at least I was surviving, getting one cooked meal a day. The cell was like an old cowboy cell with bars you could see through. In the summer heat it was stifling, and during the rainy season the rain would lash in my cell and I would be freezing. Being near the hospital I would see dead bodies being dragged by their feet, another senseless killing over nothing.

One of the cells had a red skull and crossbones above it with 'Very dangerous inmate' painted above it. I decided there and then I would keep well away from this guy. Some of the inmates had been there 20, 30, 40 years. It was a very dangerous place to be, not for the faint-hearted. In the cell next to me was Waynesworth Aljoe, who used to play his guitar. He had killed his grandparents with a machete when he was 17. He was then 45, but he really was a nice man. He got me to join the prison band, The Bloom of Light, which was made up of lifers. I started to play the bongos and became the prison secretary for the band.

This was a third world prison and some of them could not read or write, through no fault of their own. I started to write a diary. I had to be careful what I wrote, and kept it light in case it was discovered. I'm looking at it now. I realised I really was on my own, and I had to be careful - in prison you are going nowhere, and you can't get away from anybody, you are stuck.

Over 200 people were held on death row in 2002 in Jamaica. Up until 1993, it housed the highest number of death row prisoners in the world. This changed in November 1993 when the Judicial Committee of the UK Privy Council reviewed the case of Earl Pratt and Ivan Morgan and ruled the excessive delay prior to execution was cruel and inhuman treatment. The result was the commutation of the death sentence for Pratt and Morgan, and a recommendation for the commutation of over 100 other prisoners who had been on death row for over 5 years. Luckily for them the last hanging had been in 1998.

'If you never heal from what hurt you, you'll bleed on people who never hurt you.'

Chapter 30
Dynamite

I heard a massive explosion one day; it almost gave me a heart attack, the noise was deafening. I had been talking to Moses, one of the Rastas; he was doing life for murder at the time. Concrete and masonry were flying all over. Someone had stuck dynamite in the walls trying to escape but never succeeded. There were two walls, and the first wall had a big hole, but the second wall had no hole. I laughed; the warders were going crazy and locked us all down.

Some of the Jamaicans would try intimidation tactics on me. One of them was six foot and hated me for some reason. He was always trying it on. One day I felt a whoosh of air, and a house brick whizzed past my head. Lucky for me it missed, or I would have been either dead or seriously brain damaged. I nicknamed him The Twat. I looked down; he was laughing with an evil look in his eye.

I received a postcard from my friend Rike in Germany telling me not to mix with the wrong people. It made me laugh: it was a picture of the devil dancing with someone on the postcard. I thought of The Twat.

I was reading four or five books a week. I spent too much time in my cell, and books helped me escape. I love reading about everything. I could hear Aljoe playing his guitar late at night. Most of the time I was starving but I kept my wits about me. We were locked down every day at 3:30pm until the next morning. Me, who loved going out at night - what a life!

I was rehearsing a lot with the Bloom of Light when I met dub poet Dennis Leppo Lobban who had been in there since 1987 for a triple murder, including that of reggae superstar Peter Tosh of The Wailers. Leppo had spent seven years on death row before it was commuted to life, and he was the most infamous prisoner in there. He wanted me to be his manager. He had some good poems. He said he was innocent.

I used to write letters for some of the prisoners who couldn't write; it always feels good to help people and I had plenty of time on my hands. There had been a strike on for a few months, and the prison was being run by soldiers, and there were gun towers. I wasn't going anywhere, I just wanted to serve my sentence, keep my nose clean and get out of this hellhole. In prison minor arguments can magnify: men were doing life sentences and could be extremely dangerous, and I had to be on my guard at all times. Things were very volatile, to say the least, and when the trouble started you felt the atmosphere in the prison. Finally, the soldiers left, and the striking wardens returned. Things never changed.

In the General Penitentiary, you washed your clothes by hand under a tap and you took showers under a hosepipe. Because of homophobia, everyone left their underwear on when they took a shower. If they thought you were a batty man, you could easily be killed. There were separate wings for the gays, and they were not allowed to mingle with the rest of the prison population. During the riots of 1997, sixteen batty men were dragged from their cells and beaten and stabbed to death by the rioting prisoners.

I started to exercise in my own cell in the mornings, doing 100 press-ups and sit-ups. There was a small gym outside which I used, but the equipment wasn't much good. It was better than nothing and I started to get to know people. There were a few Columbians in there who had been caught with a boatload of cocaine and were serving twenty years. They couldn't speak English, which made it difficult to communicate. By looking at their faces I could tell they weren't happy, twenty years in this shithole was no walk in the park. You would quite often hear gunshots around the prison.

Parcels of weed would be thrown over the walls to be distributed and sold within the prison. I started smoking lots of Jamaican sinsemilla, and crack cocaine was on sale too, but I decided this was the last place I would want to do that. I started getting letters from home. My brother Anthony and his second wife Paula had just lost their baby. It made me really sad. Old friends were sending me books and I read all the time; there was a prison library full of dusty old books, but it was better than nothing.

The Twat used to come calling late at night when I was locked down and couldn't go anywhere. He would roam the prison for a few hours. He had a job as a trustee.

He would try to torment me, always telling me I would be killed in there soon. I had seen enough dead bodies in there to know it was always a possibility.

I hatched a plan to get rid of him completely. I decided I would confront him very soon; I had had enough, this had been going on for months now, and I had to put a stop to him. He had been trying to make my life a misery since I got here. I knew he was only serving a small sentence and was due out in the next year.

The next time I saw him I was in line for my food, usually a cup of rice welded together with some watery chicken neck. Lots of the prisoners had homemade shanks hidden all over the prison, and when a fight was about to start, they would collect them and use them. When he passed by me, he started calling me a white pussyhole. I threw the hot watery chicken neck straight in his face and he yelped and jumped back. He was six feet tall and 10 or 15 years younger than me. I had the element of surprise, but I had to move fast. I ran towards him and butted him in the face really hard, and felt his nose break; there was blood everywhere. The other prisoners were laughing and cheering, as nobody liked The Twat and it was quite amusing for them. It broke up the monotony of prison life.

The wardens were on the scene in a flash and dragged us both back to our cells. They slapped me around a bit, nothing too heavy, as they knew the British Embassy would demand to know what had happened. We were kept apart, and The Twat was shipped out to St Katherine's a few days later. He had been issuing death threats to me and they did it for my safety. I'm not really a fighter, but fear can make me crazy and I had to do him for myself. A lot of the Yardies started to show me a bit more respect. All is fair in love and war.

A few weeks later I had enough money to buy myself a small radio. I started listening to the radio stations including the BBC World Service; this was keeping me informed of world events. Months went by, always some kind of trouble going on in the prison, fights were going on all the time. The warders would draw their batons and beat prisoners with no mercy, hitting them on their kneecaps, elbows and skulls. I was getting immune to the violence; I had witnessed so much. I was determined not to get in any more trouble.

I carried on rehearsing with the prison band, the Bloom of Light, playing the bongos. Occasionally we would play live gigs for visiting dignitaries. It got me out of the cell. I was writing songs and giving them to the singers in the prison to sing. Some of them were brilliant. I often wonder what happened to them. I was sometimes stage managing 20 or 30 singers, getting them off and on stage. They would do one song, then I had to get them off and get the next one on.

After about a year the whole prison knew me. I stuck out like a sore thumb. I started to understand patois and had a good laugh. The Jamaicans are a lot like the Irish, they love having the crack and are always shouting at each other in a good-humoured way. I heard that in the slave trade days, all the slaves who were causing the most trouble to the slave traders would be dropped onto the island of Jamaica, so Jamaica was made up of rebels from the very beginning.

The guards walked around with their batons gleaming, ever ready to beat and pulverise, made from the hardest wood in Jamaica, carved from the Lignum Vitae, loosely referred to as the 'Ironwood', almost like an extension of their 'manhood'. Woe betide any prisoner that stepped out of line: the rod of correction would be drawn out like a bolt of lightning and the offending prisoner would be beaten without mercy; the screams would drive the guard on, almost like a lover waiting to give their partner an orgasm, the blood-curdling cries could be heard around the prison, wood on bone, the sound was a terrifying warning not to cross the path of the guards. Many walked around with the batons nestled in their leather holders around their waists, and some walked around with the baton slapping it into their hand and glaring at any passing prisoner they wished to intimidate, much like the SS in World War Two. It gave them a feeling of extraordinary power. Cruel and inhumane treatment was the norm for these bloodthirsty savages who were paid to oversee the prisoners, and if you had no protection and you were not connected in any way, you could be sure you would be targeted relentlessly by the guards, who would take out their petty frustrations on you without a moment's hesitation. The batons were their rods of correction for keeping the prisoners in line.

'In order to exist man must rebel' Albert Camus

Chapter 31
An Uneasy Feeling, Jamaica

I was feeling a bit wary after The Twat got shipped out of the prison. I always kept an eye out in case of repercussions; the violence in this place could ignite at any moment and you always had to have your wits about you at all times. Life was very cheap, and people would get murdered willy-nilly over the most trivial of things that you could think of. It was not a good feeling and at times my paranoia would creep up on me when I walked past a group of prisoners. I would be expecting a knife to be pulled out and somebody to rush me and carve me up. The mind can play games with you when you are surrounded by real-life murderers, and indeed my paranoia kept me on my guard even if it was something I had no control over.

Sometimes a little bit of paranoia was quite healthy for me, it helped my heightened senses to be on full alert. The food would come around three times a day, and usually trouble could flare up around mealtimes. I was ever watchful who was close by to me, my life depended on it. Berry was a few cells down from me; he was a huge fat guy who was doing life for the murder of his wife. He had been in the penitentiary for the last ten years, and he was also a trustee; he did a lot of grovelling around the guards. He was always trying to garner their favour; he was one of those prisoners who truly believed he was above everybody else. He came from an elite Jamaican family and he always had the best food in his cell, he knew everybody's business and he made it his business to find out. Outwardly he was quite jolly looking, and he had been well educated; he had little piggy eyes and a smirk that would make your blood run cold. He used to give me newspapers to read, and occasionally he would give me food that he cooked in his cell for money. He pretended to be your friend.

The food in the GP really was terrible, but he always made the best food, and indeed he looked a picture of health compared to a lot of the other prisoners. Hunger was something he never knew about, and a lot of the other prisoners resented him. The problem is when you are in prison and your neighbours are in for horrific crimes, it's impossible to try and stay out of their way: you have nowhere to go and you have to face them daily. In prisons in the UK you would be separated from child molesters, rapists and such like, but here in Jamaica, they all mixed freely. I never asked people what they were in for, but you always heard the rumours from other prisoners about certain people who were on your section.

I had never seen so much violence in my life. I tried to make myself inconspicuous when walking around the prison, but it was virtually impossible. I stuck out like a sore thumb, and everywhere I went I could feel eyes burning into me. Some people presumed because I was white, I must be rich, which made me laugh: who in their right mind would be smuggling drugs out of Jamaica? Indeed, if somebody had shown me the conditions I would be living under if I was ever caught, I would never have done it in a million years. Hindsight, what a wonderful thing. In the mornings after the cells were opened, you would all rush down to the yard below to take a shower, which was a hosepipe attached to the wall, with people screaming at you to hurry up and finish. It was never a long leisurely process, but you would be caked in sweat and mosquito bites and you had to get the night's grime off you. You also had to empty your slop bucket full of urine and shit - you can imagine the smell - and in the heat it was almost too much to bear.

At times I really thought I was going mad and wondered how I was going to survive under these animalistic conditions. There were gun towers all around the prison keeping an ever-watchful eye on the prisoners below in case of escape, and when violence erupted the guards wouldn't hesitate to shoot and kill. Living under these conditions truly tested your mental strength. It was a relief when your cell door was opened and you could step outside, but every single time that cell door was opened you really had to have your guard up, because you knew you were in a vulnerable position. Petty jealousy festered in prisoners' minds, maybe you had something they wanted, the way you looked, the way you dressed, what you had in your cell, anything could set them off, and you could easily be killed in a fit of jealousy. If I had not been there to endure these conditions, I would never have believed them to be true. The General Penitentiary was renowned all over Jamaica and the Caribbean Islands as being the most dangerous maximum-security unit, and anybody entering these gates would be lucky to survive. If you had no connections and no money you could easily starve to death or be cut to pieces in a nanosecond.

This particular morning started out with the usual shouting and screaming between fellow inmates. The Jamaican style is very blunt, they don't talk, they shout at each other, and everybody has an opinion on everybody else, and with the first sign of weakness, you would be set upon by everybody, verbally or physically. You had to be strong and show no fear; even if you felt it deep inside your mind, outwardly you never showed it. Berry used to give the medication to the other prisoners to keep them calm; some of these inmates were so psychotic they had to have medication to keep them under control, and you cannot imagine how it felt living under these conditions daily for years on end. The guy below my cell who had the red skull and crossbones and 'very dangerous inmate' emblazoned over his cell door was never allowed to mix with other inmates; he was reputed to be a serial killer and had been in the prison for over 30 years. Every time I had to pass his cell door I would try and look the other way, but sometimes my curiosity would get the better of me and I would take a look. These were not heavy cell doors; you could see behind the bars, and I still have nightmares. He was the most dangerous looking individual I have ever had the misfortune to clap eyes on. He was a real-life Hannibal Lecter, and he was living underneath my cell. You would try to block it from your mind, but it was always there.

He was around 6ft 2in tall, very skinny, with long hair and a beard. He would rattle his cell door when anybody walked by. Although I knew I would never have to mix with him - he was always locked down when the other prisoners were outside - he really gave me the creeps. Sometimes it would be hard to comprehend when he shouted, shrieking at you in a broad Jamaican patois that he would end your life at the first opportunity; it would unnerve me, and I would swiftly pass by his cell like a man on a mission. Berry had the job of entering his cell in the mornings to give him his medication, and this particular morning I heard a blood-curdling scream like a woman was being attacked, and then I recognised it was Berry's voice, a very high-pitched scream. The madman had attacked Berry in his cell and was trying to strangle him to death. Luckily for Berry, the guards had taken out their batons and had rushed in to help and beat the madman to a bloody pulp.

I saw Berry thirty minutes later and he was in so much shock that he looked like he would collapse through fear. A lot of the other inmates were laughing at Berry and thought his near-death ordeal was a huge joke. Secretly it made me smile, and it took the smirk off Berry's face at least for the next week or so. These were the kind of people who I had to endure and who were my neighbours.

Anything was welcome to break up the monotony of the day; even a killing became a form of entertainment and the prison would be awash with the news of the latest murder or stabbing - it gave the inmates something to talk about. This was the reality of the General Penitentiary. Things were getting wilder and threats were coming my way constantly, I was the rich white guy who thought he was somebody special, in the eyes of some of the prisoners. They had no understanding of me whatsoever, how could I explain who I was? Some white man who came from a town called Warrington, who just loved to travel, and had spent his whole life ducking in and out of trouble in some form or other. I had no protection from anybody: there was no fucker to try and explain my situation to. The British Embassy came every few months, and they knew the score about the conditions, but they could do nothing about it except relay messages from home and bring money that was sent from Prisoners Abroad.

I saw so many savage beatings given by the guards I was terrified of their long wooden batons, and when they lashed out with them you could hear the hard wood hitting the bones of some unlucky prisoner. They pulled no punches, and it was horrifying to watch: they swung them like baseball bats and really went for the shins, the elbows, and the back of the head to cause excruciating pain. The offending prisoner would beg them to stop but they would carry on with their grim work until the prisoner lay unconscious at their feet, and if they were lucky would still be alive. I could never work out how they got away with it but get away with it they did.

Music was my escape in prison. A huge Cuban guy called Pedro, who had lived in America, was doing fifteen years for drug smuggling, and he was a fantastic percussionist and had played all over Latin America, Cuba and the Caribbean. He taught me how to play the bongos, which was my way into the Bloom of Light, the prison band. Pedro was a funny guy; he had quite a few scars where he had been shot and stabbed, and he was fearless, and even the most hardcore Jamaicans left him alone. He had great stories of growing up in Cuba under Fidel Castro, and he told me he owed Fidel big time when Fidel cleared his prisons and sent them on to America. He was one of the prisoners who joined the Cuban exodus to Miami, and he laughed loudly when he told me that story. We would chat about various things; he was very knowledgeable about the cocaine trade, the routes and landing spots on the Jamaican coastline. He had spent his whole life in the drug trade, alongside his skill as a musician. He told me I must go to Cuba and sample the Cuban women who were the hottest women on the planet. When you're in prison these are the kind of stories you want to hear - maybe one day I will get there.

There were many characters in the prison band, and I had more in common with them than any of the other inmates.

I awoke in the night and saw a couple of rats scurrying across the cell floor. It must have been about 2am, the prison was quiet, and I could hear one of the guards walking along the section of the prison I was located in, his feet getting louder, coming closer to my cell door. I pretended to be asleep as he passed by after checking there was somebody in my cell. I turned on my light, which was a bulb that I had rigged up after the first few months with no light; it was bliss, enabling me to read under the light in my squalid cell after months of being in total darkness. I found reading to really lift my spirits: it helped me to forget about where I was, and escape from my own thoughts, which could be my own worst enemy at times, conjuring up the most violent scenarios. Sometimes I felt so alone and constant danger was always around me, and the books helped me to calm my mind and focus on something else other than the situation I was in.

I had loosened one of the brick joints to the adjoining cell of my next-door neighbour Aljoe, and we would pass things through to each other which we could barely squeeze through, cigarettes, matches; it was a huge risk we were taking if we were caught, but we kept it covered with Blu-tack and grime. We could easily be beaten and thrown in the hole, but it was worth the risk. Aljoe sold me cigarettes, and many times in the night he would pass them through to me; it was a strange thing, my best friend in the prison was a double murderer. Aljoe was a guitar player and he could play the guitar like nobody else in the prison. He would play the guitar constantly for hours on end and I never minded; it was so good that when he stopped a kind of sadness would come over me. He was a very quiet man and very studious with the guitar, and I often wondered how he lived with the fact that he had killed both his grandparents in a psychotic rage when he was just 17 years old.

He had been in the penitentiary for almost 30 years and yet I had never seen him raise his voice in anger or cause any problems with anybody whatsoever. Sometimes we would chat for hours and he would open up about his past but in the main he would just focus on talking about music. He was a fanatic and knew everything about the old American blues players and reggae stars of the day. He wasn't an intimidating looking man, but he had a quiet strength about him, and nothing seemed to bother him, he was purely all about the music. With his guitar and a very small amp, that was his whole world. He never had any visits as his family had disowned him after his terrible crime. He could have starved to death in prison, which is why he started to sell cigarettes to survive. I knew he was on medication by the look of his eyes sometimes, but the medication seemed to keep him happy and I never once felt threatened by him in any way.

    I looked around my cell after all these months sleeping in total darkness on a concrete floor, with only a plastic bottle for a pillow, no light, no bedding, no cutlery. I had been eating my food with an old empty tube of toothpaste, fashioning it into some kind of spoon, something I thought up myself; it stopped my hands from getting burnt or scalded, especially by the porridge we would get occasionally. But now I had a foam mattress, a pillow, a bulb - it had taken many months to secure these after money changed hands. The Jamaican penal system gave you nothing, you really had to fend for yourself, and if you didn't have money you were in deep shit. I looked at the small pile of books and it helped me to feel slightly human. I had recently finished reading George Orwell's *Down and out in Paris and London*. He was such a descriptive writer and I could truly empathise with his situations when he had worked on menial jobs to survive on the streets of London and Paris in the 1930s. Eric Blair, AKA George Orwell, had lived briefly on the Portobello Road in London's Notting Hill, and there was a blue plaque on the wall of the house that he had lived in to commemorate that fact.

    I thought of my father, who had recently had a heart attack. I was helpless to do anything about it. I had caused him so much grief over the years in one way or the other, but he had never let me down, even in my lowest moments, and there had been many incidents over the years. When I had hit rock bottom and had nobody to turn to, he was there; he was a good man and I often wondered what he had done to be landed with a son like me. Alone in the cell at night, my mind would wander all over the place; not only did I have to survive this prison sentence, but indeed if I did what was to become of me? That was on my mind constantly; it certainly wasn't easy being me, I really found it hard to settle down, in fact, to settle anywhere. My father deserved so much better, but he was stuck with me. The dim light of my electric bulb would cast shadows around my cell, and it felt quite eerie, but I felt more comfortable being locked up in the evenings away from the other prisoners, you knew you were safe for that night at least.

Then I heard a quiet sobbing; it was Aljoe in his cell. I decided not to say anything. All alone in his cell, the futility of his life and the murderous rage that had engulfed him when he was a teenager, which had made him mutilate and kill his grandparents in cold blood, the guilt must have been too much to bear at times. What could I say to alleviate his pain and anguish? The thought of spending the rest of my life in this hellhole I really could not contemplate. He had endured over three decades under such conditions with no help from anybody, yet he never really complained, and his face would light up whenever we spoke about music; but alone in his cell, he would break down when it all became too much.

The young guys in this prison, some of the members of the Shower Posse, strutted around the prison barking orders at their subordinates. They had the best of everything that money could buy you in Jamaica, they had gold chains around their necks, they had tattoos of Uzi submachine guns emblazoned on their chests, and if you crossed them you really were a dead man. One of them was only 18 years old, and I was told he had killed or executed over 200 people; this may sound mind-boggling to your average person, but I could well believe it. I had met one in Rema on my remand; we had both been taken by police escort to the court in one of the horse-like boxes, standing up locked in together with hardly any room to breathe. He told me stories of kidnapping and torture of many people. He laughed when one of his victims screamed; he would inform on him, he took out a razor-sharp knife, and he told me how he had sliced his tongue off before putting a bullet in his brain for good measure. How could I relate to stories like this? I felt physically sick in close confinement to this psychopath, but I acted like I had heard it all before, what else could I do? As the months went by, I heard so many horror stories, I really did fear for my own safety as I have never done before.

I had been incarcerated in Thailand previous to this, but my life and my sanity had never felt like they did when I was in this Jamaican prison. Thailand had felt like a holiday camp compared to this lunatic asylum I found myself in. There were very few people in this Jamaican prison who had not committed murder. The whole of my sentence I was walking on eggshells: my very being was attuned to staying alive in the world's most dangerous prison, and without a shadow of a doubt, I would rather have spent ten years in an English jail than one year in this barbaric fleapit. I have seen things in that prison which sometimes give me nightmares to this day. How could I explain this to my friends and family? I had the stiff upper lip and never gave the impression that anything was so bad because I never wanted to worry them; I kept things to myself. No wonder Aljoe would break down: he was a gentle soul even if he had murdered his grandparents, he certainly was not a ruthless calculating drug dealing murderer like many I met on that sentence.

There were people in there that would kill you in an instant without a single regret. I had a sixth sense about them and would stay well clear if possible, but it was virtually impossible, I was constantly surrounded by them no matter where I went to in the prison. You really could feel the tension at all times. Admittedly I had been a petty criminal most of my life, who had fallen in love with life on the road and was truly living on the edge for most of it. Never did I think I would end up in this place; it really was like living in your worst nightmare. The heat, the mosquitos, the food, the lack of anything, was nothing compared to the people I was dealing with in here.

The Yardies would casually mention murders they had committed like they were talking about killing a flea; you had to survive in Jamaica and outside it really was like the Wild West. They lived and died by the gun and machete. People think of the beaches and reggae music of Jamaica but in here I heard a whole different story; cocaine was being distributed all over the world from Jamaica, and behind it all a select few became wealthy beyond their wildest dreams. Murder and corruption is everywhere in Jamaica.

Suddenly I froze. Gunshots were being fired within the prison. That snapped me out of my thoughts. I could hear sirens wailing - it must be an escape attempt. There was the sound of running feet all over the prison, and I could hear shouting and more shots being fired. It was difficult to make out what was happening from inside my cell, but I knew for sure somebody was going to die. After what seemed like a few minutes the prison became silent, my guts were churning and I realised I had to go to my bucket and empty my bowels; the smell was horrendous, but I had no control and relieved myself over my plastic bucket. Suddenly realising I had no toilet paper and no way of cleaning myself, I had to lie in my own shit. I lay awake wondering what the fuck had happened for an hour or so, then I fell asleep.

When I awoke that morning, I was going to race to the shower and clean my arse properly.

But then we were told we would not be coming out of our cells for the next 48 hours. Nobody told us why. Fuck, I had wanted to empty my slop bucket, which was full of piss and shite from the night before, and more importantly, I needed a shower under the hosepipe, and had really been looking forward to it. My arse was caked in excrement from the night before, and I was so embarrassed, but I really couldn't say anything, it was so fucking degrading. I had no water in my cell, I couldn't wash my hands, and the chance would not arise for the next 48 hours; I literally was in the shit, big time.

Along came Berry. The fat twat was laughing and joking; he was a trustee and was allowed out of his cell to help to bring the food to the rest of the locked down prisoners. I had no other clothes to change into: I was wearing the same clothes for months with the same pair of flip-flops that had holes in them. I used to wash my clothes daily by hand and they dried very quickly in the Jamaican heat, and now here I was to be locked down unable to move out of my cell for the next two fucking days, with a shitty arse and a bucket full of crap to keep me company. Maybe I should have said something, but what? The prison was on lockdown and they sure weren't going to let me out just to go and clean my arse. I would have been the laughingstock of the jail. When the fat cunt arrived at my cell, he poked his nose through my bars and tried to hand me a round of stale bread, the usual breakfast we had every single day of the sentence. I told him I wasn't feeling hungry; how could I touch food in this condition with my hands? I asked him why the prison was on lockdown and he just smirked and carried on to the next cell; he really was a cock-sucking mother fucker who would kill his own mother to get out of this place and curry favour with the guards.

Rumours were bouncing around about what had been the disturbance from the night before; maybe it was an escape attempt. Some prisoners had bits of broken mirror that they would hold out in their arms and push through the bars to point at an angle to try and see who was walking around. I had no such luxury, I could only see out of my cell what was in front of me, not to the right nor to the left. After another three hours the food was brought around again, mouldy rice and watery vegetables, and once again I told Berry I was not hungry, but in reality, I was starving; I really didn't want to tell this prick about my predicament. Today felt like the hottest day I had ever encountered in my cell; there was no breeze whatsoever and I had nothing to drink, as you got your water from the hosepipe at the end of the prison. I was fucked right off, the day was dragging on and then the final meal came at around 3.30pm, which was usually the time we were all locked down for the night. Berry started asking me why I wasn't eating, and by this time I was starting to feel unwell with the heat, the hunger and the smell; even if it was my own smell, it was beginning to make me want to puke up. The bucket was covered in flies and I just couldn't face touching or eating anything in this condition. I told him I just didn't feel like eating and then he waddled off to the next cell.

That night really was the longest night I have ever endured. I was wondering how I could clean myself properly. It was mostly in my own head, but I was so paranoid I would be found dead in my cell with a shitty arse. I started to think maybe I was losing my mind for real. How I slept that night I will never know. The rest of the prisoners were complaining: they wanted out of their cells big time. The whole prison was on lockdown, nearly 2000 men. Again, the next morning we had another 24 hours to endure. I was determined not to eat anything until the next day. I heard Berry coming to my cell, and by this time I must have looked like a madman and was acting very strangely. Once again I asked Berry what was going on, and why we were on lockdown? He said he didn't know, but I didn't believe the fucker, I was sure he knew. I would have killed him myself if I could have got a shower and cleansed myself; he deserved to die just to get me out of this cell.

I was pacing around my cell for hours on end, willing for the time when they would open up my cell door. I was holding onto my sanity by a slim thread. How the fuck did this happen? I had enough fucking problems just staying alive, and now here I was with hunger pains, another night to endure, and I still didn't know why we were on lockdown. I wanted to tell Aljoe, but I was such a state I couldn't bring myself to tell him; it was almost comical if it hadn't been happening to me. That final night was like hell on earth, the stench was unbearable, I was so out of my mind I thought the whole prison knew about me and my shitty arse problem. In the morning I was like a racehorse waiting at my cell door for the warder to unlock me to rush down to the trough where we emptied our buckets full of slops. When the cell door swung open, I was so happy, I rushed down the stairs and was faced with about 200 guys standing in line probably in the same situation as I was. I had to wait patiently because I had seen so many fights over these troughs.

Finally, my turn came, and I got rid of the filth, and now was able to have a shower. I had my shorts on and jumped under the icy cold tap, cleansed myself vigorously while being watched and shouted at to hurry up, only this time I was in no hurry - I had to clean myself properly with my shorts on and my underpants underneath, but I somehow did a good job. I felt so happy I cannot describe how happy I was, the shitty arse problem had finally been resolved after 48 torturous hours. I took two of my empty plastic bottles and filled them with water to make sure this never happened again, and I stocked up with toilet paper and went back to my cell for my round of bread; I was fucking famished. Finally, two days later I heard the news that one of the Shower Posse had been shot and killed whilst trying to make his escape. How he thought he was going to get out I will never know. There was a big inquiry and it was thought he had outside help from some of his Jamaican friends both inside and outside of the prison. Life went on, and after a few weeks, it became old news.

Walking around the prison you felt like you were in a zoo, or at least I did; eyes followed me around everywhere. I sometimes played football with the Yardies; they were good players, there's a great love of football right across Jamaica. It was also a good way of trying to keep fit in the jail. I had bought a pair of running shoes off Aljoe that he never used, and started to join in with the games. They played hard and gave no quarter, and although I'm not a fan of watching football I had loved playing it at school, and during my various incarcerations growing up in the North West. There were all types who played football. I was usually the oldest on the team: I had gone into the penitentiary when I was 41, and most of the players were in their twenties or early thirties, but I did my best to keep up with them. Several high-ranking members of the Shower Posse played nearly every day, but they didn't really speak with me unless they were shouting at me to pass the ball, and in the Jamaican heat it was exhausting, and the pitch was full of gravel so if you slipped you were guaranteed to do yourself some damage: at the very least you would have grazed legs.

I was usually a target for the younger players to take their frustrations out on. You have to remember a lot of the Jamaicans were not educated, and a lot of them had grown up in Kingston Tivoli Gardens, Trenchtown, Arnett Gardens and Mountain View, where violence was a way of life; even the police didn't like going into those places. I did represent the white oppressor in some of their minds, and racist comments were openly thrown at me. 'White pussyhole' was one of their favourites, but I would just let it ride, I never took it to heart and anyway, what was I going to do? I couldn't fight the whole prison, and if I had tried, I would have been skinned alive or beaten to death. I may have been stupid to end up in here, but I wasn't that stupid.

I had a few friends in the band and they told me to be careful who I was playing football with, but I really did enjoy playing out in the gravel fields and took no notice and carried on playing. The General Penitentiary had a huge wall around it, and there were also two chain link fences on the inside perimeter, and guards watching your every move from the gun towers so escape was virtually impossible. Walking around the different cell blocks could be quite intimidating. I was known personally by a few on my section but in the other cell blocks I was an unknown quantity, and I had to tread carefully. I always liked to explore my surroundings, and in prison, your world was quite small, but I had to go walking, checking the place out daily. You are locked down for 20 hours a day, so any bit of freedom I was out of the cell in a flash, but this was when you were at your most vulnerable. Drugs came in infrequently; they were thrown over the wall in parcels and the minions were ordered to go and collect them, and it was quite a dangerous job being the pickup man, you risked being shot or at the very least being beaten if you were caught. Mobile phones came in via this method, as well as knives and assorted weapons. The mobile phones had to have the sound off, and people were paid to watch for the light flashing on the mobiles to see if they had incoming calls in the cells.

The prison ran on a hierarchy and the prison dons gave the orders to their subordinates on who would fetch and carry for their masters. The monotony of prison life could get to you, and I used to feel sorry for some of the prisoners who had no friends or family, or any influence within these walls - their lives were terrible. Some of them looked like walking corpses, their bones showing through their withered skin; it was heart-wrenching and reminiscent of Hitler's death camps at times. But I had my own troubles getting by in this third world ghetto that was now my home for the next few years. There was no repatriation for UK prisoners to be sent back to England: I had to serve my sentence out in Jamaica and see it through until the bitter end, and first and foremost on my mind was survival and seeing my family once again.

There were many broken stones around this prison which were used as weapons - prisoners would frequently throw them at each other, and when trouble escalated the warders would run in with their batons and quell the problems in an instant. One of the warders really did not like me and would often pull me up and search me for weed around the prison camp when I was on my walkabouts. He would sometimes draw his baton and pretend he was about to hit me. I had seen enough beatings to know how painful it was, and it would make me jump in fear. I only had a t-shirt and shorts and was scared that he would. He would give an evil laugh and told me he had his eye on me, and that at the first sign of anything from me I would get what was coming. I never really understood why he personally took a dislike to me, and I was always glad when his shift was over.

He was around 6ft and always dressed immaculately; his name was Mr Williams and he always made me feel uneasy whenever I saw him. It was a dangerous job for the guards, as inmates held grudges and it was not unusual to hear about a prison guard being murdered on the outside by former inmates, or their friends would have a hit carried out on them from within the prison. In general, I was a peace-loving man and in all my years on the road I had become more and more mellow as the years went by, so to be placed in such a violent hostile environment was a rude awakening, and one I had to deal with in my own way.

The prison cells were small and held up to six inmates; some would sleep in hammocks and people would sleep on the floor below them, and there was hardly any room to breathe for most of them, so it was a sheer luxury to get outside of the cell. Visits came on a Wednesday and you would see prisoners come back from visits laden with fresh fruit, and food and drink in brown paper bags. My mouth would water when I saw them returning to their cells. I was always hungry and I never had or expected any visits so I knew, for the most part, I would be going hungry and thirsty. I have never experienced hunger before in the way I did in the General Penitentiary. I would be in the band's room a lot to practise my bongos and I felt a part of the musical community within the prison; it was an escape from the Yardie mentality of violence and threats that the rest of the prison had. The musicians were a different kettle of fish, although many of them were convicted for horrific murders that were in their past, and they were for the most part non-violent and concentrated on the music above all else. It was good being in the band's room away from the rest of the prison and I would relish my time there. It was quite funny at times being the only white member in the band, and when we did shows inside the prison, I really was the centre of attention for visitors who came to the prison for the shows. They really didn't expect a white man to be up there, and it felt a bit weird at first, but I soon got used to it.

I did get some perks out of being in the band, sometimes getting an extra thirty minutes out of my cell whilst we rehearsed for any upcoming gigs that were planned. I kept myself busy each time I was out of my cell: I would go to the small gym that was outside in the yard, and I was getting fitter and losing weight rapidly, more to do with the food than anything else - I just couldn't stomach it most of the time and constant hunger was my friend throughout. After my accident in the cell I had acquired a few more pairs of shorts and underwear, and each day I would routinely wash everything by hand in the scorching Jamaican heat. It was no easy task, but it was good for the soul to have clean clothes, and although I didn't have much, I had more than some of the poor souls in there.

Some of the gang members would have on brand new clothes, and Hi-Tech trainers, and everything would be done for them by their minions. They ate the best food, which was prepared for them, and their cells would be plentiful with fruit, drinks, loads of weed and drugs and magazines. I was the lowest of the low in the prison hierarchy, a white man who was not from Jamaica, but I knew it wasn't forever and so I kept going, doing my own thing, asking for nothing from anybody. I had the money coming in from Prisoners Abroad, and my family sent me money on a monthly basis. I was far from living like a king, but I was getting by in my own way; money was the key to survival. Back in my cell, I had my routine when they locked us down for the evening from 3.30pm: I would do my exercises, smoke a spliff and read my books under the small bulb I had, late into the night. My eyesight began to suffer through so much reading in that dim light, but it was my only escape and so I persevered, reading constantly everything and anything. We would then be unlocked at 9 in the morning to empty our slop buckets and take our showers, would have the next meal at 11am, and be locked down until 1.30pm, then unlocked till 3.30pm; that was the routine every single day - it was relentless, but I did do a lot of thinking and made my time as useful as I could.

When officials came to the prison to check on living conditions the place would be smartened up. Sometimes a building block housing the prisoners would be painted, and all the clothes people had hanging out to dry would be removed, and certain parts of the prison would be cleaned up. The rats could always be seen where the food was made in the kitchens, and they would try to exterminate them, but there was so many it was just a token gesture. There were sometimes women guards on the shifts and one of them I really fancied; she was about 40 and had a great figure even through the drab prison blue uniforms they wore, or the grey and beige uniforms. She stood out and she knew it, and some of the prisoners would masturbate openly when she walked by, which I thought was disgusting, but she seemed to take it in her stride, and it was always a pleasure to clap eyes on her. That's a big thing in prison when you're surrounded by men all wanting sex, it was a massive turn on when she walked by and it would drive you crazy.

Jamaica is such a homophobic place, one thing I never had to worry about was being raped in the main population, which suited me fine. The openly gay prisoners were never allowed to mix in the main population with the rest of the prisoners; for sure they would be killed. At night when we were locked down the woman guard would patrol the prison sometimes, and she must have felt everybody's eyes on her. It drove me crazy and I did fantasise about fucking her on many occasions, but I knew it could never happen and that was the allure, it was just a fantasy. I really would have paid good money to spend the night with her in my cell though; perhaps it was the uniform, but under these conditions, it really did make you sexually frustrated. I had no girlfriend at this time, and you can imagine how I felt.

I carried on playing football even though it was difficult to get the ball passed to me and the tackles were quite violent, my shins took many a good kicking and lots of the time I was chasing the ball needlessly. Some of these younger men were superbly fit and I probably looked a bit of a joke, but nevertheless I had a go, and I enjoyed playing the game. Then it was announced we would be playing a football game against the guards in a month's time. The Governor had decided that it would be good for the prison morale, and the team were excited that they would be getting a chance to have one up on the guards, and really give them a game. I put my name forward, but they didn't want me to play. I was well pissed off but to be fair I was far from being the best player and at my age I didn't have the stamina to really keep up. But even so, I have a competitive nature and wanted a chance to play.

Letters were coming from various members of the family and I would write back immediately; the boredom of prison life wanted me to be involved in everything and anything that kept me occupied - it was a good thing in my mind, and I enjoyed writing letters. I kept them lighthearted and I didn't want to worry anybody, what was the point? There was nothing they could do anyway. You had to give your letters to one of the guards, who would then post them from outside if you had things you didn't want the office to see; you paid for the privilege but at least you could say what you wanted without it being read by the guards in the office. Aljoe never had letters from anybody: it was such a shame, he really was on his own. Being the guitar player in the prison band gave him some prestige, and he was well-liked by the guards and prisoners alike. He had been in there for so long he was part of the furniture, and I was glad he was held in high regard, as he really was a good man and had a great sense of humour. He tried to teach me guitar, but I was hopeless, and he gave up asking me to try after a few weeks, so I stuck to the bongos and carried on having my lessons with the Cuban guy Pedro.

The prison was getting very humid and hot; it was getting closer to July and there was no breeze, it was almost suffocating at night and I was having trouble sleeping, the heat draining my energy to the point I was continually parched and constantly wanted a drink. I was having dreams of an ice-cold beer, then waking up and realising it was only a dream; it used to do my head in big time. I had my plastic bottles of water, but it was like drinking hot water most of the time. I had never drunk tea or coffee in my life and it was only when I became ill that I did. I had a constant toothache, and my stomach wasn't holding food down, and I had a fever; the combination of all three made me want to die. I had seen the prison dentist in action, and it wasn't good. I'd walked past his place of work. He had a long table in his room, and he was leaning over this huge Jamaican with a pair of pliers; the guy was screaming out loud and I thought there is no way I am going to him - it was imprinted on my memory.

Alone in my cell at night, I was in agony: my face had swelled up to my eye and I must have looked like Quasimodo. The toothache was unbearable - I was literally banging my head on the wall in sheer pain and frustration, and continually pulling on my tooth trying to dislodge the fucker. Trying to sleep was really difficult. I still had another year to go before I was released, and I was feeling really down in my mind. The cell was so hot I felt like I was in a sauna. Some of the inmates had fans in their rooms but I had none, and I was determined to get one when the money came from my father the following month. I was looking around my cell and out into the night through the bars, and I could see the stars and see the faint lights of the airport in the distance, and it was driving me crazy, people flying back to the UK and beyond.

The pain was almost driving me insane: I couldn't think straight, my mind was in overdrive, how could I take much more of this place? I was feverish and felt like I was hallucinating, I wasn't sure about anything or anybody and this went on for hours until somehow I must have fallen asleep, completely exhausted. When I opened my eyes in the morning, by some miracle the pain in my tooth had subsided. I was covered in sweat and still felt feverish but thankful the pain in my tooth had diminished. When the cell door opened, I walked out into the blazing sunshine. Aljoe saw the state of me and asked what was the matter. I told him I felt fucked and had been in pain during the night with my tooth and was feverish. He laughed and said, 'I will get you some coffee.' I hated hot drinks, but I felt like shit and when he brought the coffee, I drank it, and I really enjoyed it. Afterwards, I went down to the trough and emptied my slops, had a shower, returned to my cell and lay down for the rest of the morning. I felt like death warmed up, but the pain had gone.

I stayed in my cell all that day and was continually pulling on the offending tooth until, finally, I loosened it. It came out in my hand in a bloody mess, but I didn't give a fuck; it was gone. When you're in pain and feeling weak you start to feel sorry for yourself; I never thought a toothache could cause me so much pain, but it did, and I had a feeling of joy when the pain went away. That night I slept like a baby - even the mosquitoes couldn't wake me.

The following day I was unexpectedly called out for a visit from the British High Commission, a lady called Kerry Graney who was living in Kingston. She had brought messages from home: my father was fine after his heart attack a few months previously, which was great news. She left me with 50 pounds from Prisoners Abroad, which was a great help; it enabled me to buy a fan for my cell from Berry, and buy some vitamins that were badly needed. I had lost so much weight over the last year my ribs were starting to show. I just had so much trouble trying to eat the prison food that I could only manage a few mouthfuls before I would give it to Aljoe, who would eat anything you gave him.

There were constant power cuts, which were really annoying when I was reading and the bulb would go out, but you just had to live with it: this was a third world prison, and anything could happen. Some nights you would hear drumming going on, and it was the Rastas in their cells playing in sync celebrating some of their festivals in the year; it sounded quite spooky sometimes and made me feel slightly uneasy. One day I asked Aljoe what all the drumming was about in the night, and he said it was in preparation to kill the white man, and laughed at me; he did have a sense of humour and I hoped he was joking!

A few days later one of the Shower Posse members sent a message to my cell about the football game with the warders, via one of their minions. They had decided I could train with them, but I would be in goal. To be honest I really had trouble running around the pitch chasing after the ball: I have been smoking since I was 11 years old. I wasn't sure if I wanted to be the goalie or not, but I said yes, fuck it, why not?

Over the next few weeks I was placed in goal and we trained hard for the upcoming games against the warders. It was hard training with them. Every opportunity they had they would kick the ball hard towards me, and I had no gloves so the ball stung my hands badly when I saved a goal, but I persevered and enjoyed the camaraderie, and the younger players started to show me more respect. Some of them started to bring me fruit and food and I was beginning to put weight back on, and for sure I was getting exercise.

There were constant cell searches, which would be accompanied by the dogs searching for drugs: your cell would be ripped to pieces and left in a mess, and sometimes it could happen twice in one week. The Shower Posse had control over the whole prison, and they had all their drugs and knives stashed in other prisoners' cells; nobody would grass them up for the real fear of losing your life. I was a nobody in the rankings of the prison, and nor indeed did I want to be. There were by now many other, many black, English inmates from all over the UK. There was a young lad from Bristol called Michael who was really sound and had a good head on his shoulders; he was young, in his early twenties, and I liked him - he was always polite and respectful, and he hated this shithole as much as I did. There was Les from Moss Side, Manchester, who had been a ticket tout in the UK and had family in Antigua; he knew people that I knew back in the north west of England and it was good to hear the northern banter. Les had been around and was an old head from the north.

Listening to the news on my small radio you would hear about the latest drug smuggler who had been caught at the airport, and you knew at some point they would arrive in here. It was a frightening experience when they first held you and you were taken to Rema with no clue of what was going to happen to you. I thought back to my first night when I entered Rema on remand, and they led me through the corridors in total darkness. Coming out of each cell was smoke and I found out later it was toilet paper rolled very tightly into a long cord, which the prisoners would light to keep it going on which to light their cigarettes. People would be shouting at you: 'You are going to die in here.' It was really unnerving, and I knew how the new arrivals from the UK would be feeling, especially if they were white. There were always shootings going on outside of the prison and the news reports were full of the latest senseless killings.

A parcel arrived from the UK: my father had sent me underwear, shorts and t-shirts, which I badly needed; I was walking round in the same clothes for the first year and was extremely grateful, especially now I was involved with the football game with the warders. I had felt I was looking like a tramp and the new clothing made me feel like a new man - small things like this really helped to raise my spirits. I was doing stretching exercises in my cell and incorporated them with the daily routine to keep my body in the best shape I could. I have never been one for lying around doing nothing, and once I set my mind on something, I would give it my all. But still, I was in the GP. It was really hard being there, really hard.

We had many visitors come from the University of West Indies and they donated four brand new computers to the prison. I had bought my first computer back in 1999 and really thought I would never understand how to use it, but gradually over the next couple of years, I had started to master it. I was never allowed near the new computers that were donated: they went into the offices for the warders to enjoy - that made me laugh.

We carried on training for the football game and I was also rehearsing with the Bloom of Light; my days were being filled with positive things when I was unlocked. The 20-hour lockdowns could be torturous at times and I reread Tolstoy's *War & Peace;* it would take me a week to read the whole thing, but it was a masterpiece that I thoroughly enjoyed.

I had another good friend that I used to chat with; his name was Moses, he was serving a life sentence for murder and had been in there for 18 years. He was a small man built like a jockey, and he had a good way about him and used to make me laugh, telling me stories about his life in Jamaica before he came to prison. He would tell me about the political situation in Jamaica, and how it was hard to survive with no money on the outside. I had only been to Jamaica a few times and that had involved smuggling, and now I was incarcerated I was eager to learn more about the country with its 14 parishes and two million inhabitants. Moses spoke patois, a strong mixture of creole with a West African influence. It took me months to begin to understand the Jamaican way of speaking, and although it was English it was difficult to understand at first, but I started to get the hang of it. Moses had 12 children and his family still visited him after all these years. Usually after a couple of years into your life sentence family would start to come less and less, to the point you were lucky to get any more visits, so he was the exception to the rule.

The local radio DJ came to the prison from Roots FM, and spoke with Owen Desmond, who had set up the Reverence for Life Programme they had going on in Jamaica, but with all the killings going on all over the island I think it fell on deaf ears; but good luck to him, he was trying.

I also met Errol Findlay; he was serving time in the GP. He was from Reading St James, a suburb of Montego Bay, and he told me he had broken into the home of Lady Sarah Consuelo Churchill, the aristocrat who was the cousin to Sir Winston Churchill, the great war Prime Minister. She had a house in Montego Bay, and he said he and Lady Sarah began talking, and when she had calmed down, they had started to get along really well, and they ended up having an affair for months afterwards. He said she was extremely kinky, and they enjoyed sex all over her house before she returned to her home in America. I wasn't sure how true it was, but it was a great story. There were nearly 2000 men in the General Penitentiary, and they all had their own stories to tell.

Trying to keep my life and health together as much as possible was utmost on my mind. I was referred to the prison psychologist, a lady called Heather, who had been asked to check on my mental health. I was really cautious about revealing too much about myself at first, as I was not sure how it would affect my sentence, but I started to loosen up after a few weekly sessions. I think she liked the fact that I was a white man and it appealed to her curiosity; we seemed to get on well and I think at the end of the sessions she thought I was pretty well-balanced after the experiences I had been through. But to be honest, I held a lot back, and a lot of the time I would give her the answers she was looking for. It was nice being in the company of a woman who seemed to care though. She was quite old then, in her 60s, so there was no physical attraction, which was a slight disappointment: after all, I was in prison.

Things were grim though. I had trouble even getting a pen to write in my diary; I was constantly trying to get one to keep my diary going. The training for the football match was stepping up a notch, and the prisoners really wanted to beat the warders in the upcoming game. I was covered in grazes from trying to stop the ball from getting past me. One day I took a football directly in my face and it hurt like fuck. I had bruises all over, where the ball would hit me; I would be glad to get this game over and done with. I really started to think it was not such a good idea after I let the ball go past me and into the goalposts for the umpteenth time. My side would hurl abuse at me: 'Wake up pussyhole and watch the ball!' Fuck, what had I let myself in for? Pedro, my Cuban friend, would laugh his head off when he walked by; they all thought I was crazy joining the team and perhaps I was. The Yardies were always trying to get my phone number and my address in London: they wanted to get me involved in many drug capers. My days of dealing drugs were over, but I let them talk and I acted like I was interested. My plans were all about the music. I often wondered how things were going back in Notting Hill with the band I was managing, NRG Fly, David the guitar player, Dandi the bass player, Andy the singer, and Jock the drummer - maybe they had split up, who knows?

Leppo would always come over for a chat when I was in the band's room, and I agreed to do an interview with him. I went over to his cell on the other section and he gave me a pen and some paper, and we started the interview as follows:

Interview with Dennis 'Leppo' Lobban - General Penitentiary

TK: Where were you born?
DL: I was born in Jubilee Hospital Kingston, on the 16th of January 1955.
TK: Where are your mother and father?
DL: Mother abroad, father passed away.
TK: Where did you receive your education?
DL: In Kingston and rural Jamaica.
TK: How long have you been inside prison now?

DL: I have been here 16 years and have spent seven years on Death Row.
TK: Do you feel you have been treated fairly?
DL: No, I was framed.
TK: How do you feel about your sentence?
DL: Extremely upset.
TK: Do you still maintain your innocence?
DL: I do.
TK: Has being a Rasta helped you during your incarceration?
DL: Yes, it has.
TK: How long have you been involved in music?
DL: Many years.
TK: Why have poetry, and how many poems have you written?
DL: Many poems, and it's good for my mind.
TK: You were friends with Peter Tosh, how did this come about?
DL: We were friends from youth.
TK: What do you think the reaction of the people in Jamaica will be if you are set free one day?
DL: I don't believe people will be concerned after all these years.
TK: How do you keep yourself positive?
DL: I read and do the exercises.
TK: When you are free where do you intend to live?
DL: Rural Jamaica.
TK: How do you feel about the situation in Jamaica in 2003?
DL: Things get worse and the youth cannot find jobs.
TK: How do you think violence can be stopped in Jamaica?
DL: You can't stop the violence, people make money.
TK: What message would you like to give to the people outside?
DL: I am an honest man and also amicable.
TK: Do you want society to hear your poems?
DL: Yes.
TK: When you look back on your life, how do you feel?
DL: Very upset.
TK: Do you feel you can add something positive to the outside world?
DL: Yes, by doing my music.
TK: Who are your musical influences?
DL: The Wailers, and Bob.
TK: How do the other prisoners treat you?

DL: Some have manners, and some don't.

TK: You are nearly 50, you were once called a Rude Boy, what have you learned after all these years?

DL: I was a Bad Boy.

TK: You have won many competitions in prison and performed many concerts; how do you feel about that?

DL: I feel uplifted.

TK: Have you seen the documentary Stepping Razor?

DL: I have heard of it.

TK: Are you prepared to tell the full story of what happened on that night, 11th of September 1987?

DL: When I leave here.

TK: Peter Tosh's mother still lives in Jamaica.

DL: I know, but I committed no murder.

TK: You have certain notoriety in Jamaica, do you think that works against you?

DL: No. I am innocent and one day I will be free.

Interview over. Leppo was getting agitated.

I walked back to my cell with the interview in my hand and really started to wonder what had happened on that fateful night when Peter Tosh and two of his friends were killed back in 1987. Leppo was a very guarded man, of quite small build but he carried himself with a superior air around the prison. Everybody knew who he was - he was well known for the murder of Peter Tosh - yet I never saw anybody abuse him or try to attack him. He was a fitness fanatic and he worked out regularly; lots of prisoners doing life sentences would become very lazy, but not Leppo, he had a sharp mind it was hard to work him out. I think he truly believes he will walk out of prison one day and then he will tell his story to the world.

Leppo always claimed he never killed Peter Tosh and two others, Wilton Brown and DJ Jeff Dixon, on that fateful night. Marlene Brown, the woman who was living with Tosh, had a bullet put in her head but by some miracle survived. Peter Tosh was one of the founding members of The Wailers. Tosh was so anti-establishment that his guitar case was shaped like an M16 rifle. Leppo was charged with all three murders of Tosh and his friends at Tosh's home on the Barbican Road in Kingston, where Tosh was throwing a small party back on September 11, 1987. Leppo was a friend of Peter from way back, claiming he had gone to prison on behalf of Peter when a gun was found in Tosh's car. Leppo took the rap, thus preventing Peter from going to jail. Peter was also a black belt and Leppo knew this, and it was claimed Leppo and two friends turned up at Tosh's house with the intention of robbing him after he came back from America with a lot of money. Leppo was alleged to have made them all lie down and executed them one by one with a bullet in the back of the head.

When Leppo gave himself up to the police he came along with a priest. When interviewed he would not reveal the names of his two friends who had been with him the night of the murders, and he was charged with all three murders. He had got a taxi that night, and the taxi driver later turned up in court as a witness, along with Marlene Brown, the survivor. He had gone to the same court where I had been sentenced, Halfway Tree Magistrates, before being sent to appear for trial at the Home Circuit Court.

When Leppo was due to give evidence on his own behalf he claimed he had never even been there on the night, and he reckoned Marlene Brown had fancied him and he rejected her advances, and she was so angry that he believed she was trying to frame him for the triple murders. The jury took less than five minutes to dismiss his alibi and found him guilty, whereupon the judge sentenced Leppo to death. Leppo sat on death row for seven years before his sentence was commuted to life imprisonment.

'Evil is he who holdeth the key to another man's freedom.' Written on a prison wall

Chapter 32
One Love Football Game

It was only a few days away from the football match with the warders and the training became intense: the prisoners were determined to beat the guards. The heat was incredible, and some of the younger players were soaked in sweat from running about so much, but they carried on. I was starting to worry about the game. I felt I was in a no-win position: if we got beaten the Yardies would blame my goalkeeping for sure, and if we beat the guards, I was certain our lives would be made a misery. Fuck me, what had I got myself involved in?

One of the top henchmen in the Shower Posse was beginning to bother me. He was always cussing me, and if I let a goal in, he would scream at me to keep my eye on the ball; he was a nasty piece of work and the whole team seemed scared of him, they always made sure he had the ball. But in fact, he was a good player, so maybe he was just passionate about the game; still, I didn't feel like I was in a good position either way.

Aljoe had kept warning me to be careful when I was out there playing football with them, but I hadn't listened, and I was beginning to regret my foolhardiness in ever getting involved. The football was taking up a lot of my time when I should have been rehearsing with the Bloom of Light; the musicians also started complaining that I was never there. I decided after this match whatever happened I would give football up, it was too demanding, and I was fed up with having the ball kicked at me as hard as they could. I'm sure they enjoyed aiming the ball at me sometimes.

The guards had been training when we were locked down, and they looked like they meant it. My heart sank when I caught sight of Mr Williams, the guard who had taken an intense dislike to me - fuck me, that was all I needed, I hadn't realised he would be playing.

Then disaster struck. A couple of the football players on my team got into an argument the day before the game was to be played; on the pitch they had started to fight and when they got back onto their section of the prison the fight escalated, and one of them pulled a knife and hacked away at the other until he lay dead at his feet. The whole prison was once again put on lockdown, the affair was hushed up and the Governor cancelled the match, which had been due to be played the following day. I couldn't believe it; all the hassle I had been put through was a complete waste of time, and some poor fucker had died because of it. We spent 24 hours on lockdown, and I realised the irony of it all: if we had played, I couldn't have won either way.

'When nothing goes right, go left'

Chapter 33
Skin of my Teeth

After the fiasco with the football, that was me well and truly done with playing: from now on I would stick with my own routine, exercising in my cell and using the weights at the gym in the field. It had reiterated how dangerous this place can be and my mission was to avoid trouble at all costs. I was getting sick and tired of this place; you never knew from one day to the next when trouble would rear its ugly head and trying to get through to some of the inmates was like talking to a brick wall. Not having the luxury of education that we have in a first world country, unable to read or write, many of the inmates could only express themselves through violence.

My own mother had difficulties growing up, and she could barely read and write herself, although later in life she got better. It wasn't that I thought people were unintelligent but if you had not been taught to read and write it made things difficult, and I found some inmates who did not read and write but were very good at reading people and situations; I suppose it heightened other senses that some people had no reason to use. My own schooling had been erratic, but I always took advantage of the classes in any of the prisons I found myself in, even if it was mainly just to occupy my time. The classes they had in General Penitentiary were quite basic, really enabling a lot of prisoners to learn how to read and write. There were also a group of Rastafarians who were highly intelligent and could talk on any and all subjects, and you would often see them around the prison reasoning with each other daily on all kinds of topics. Trying to get them to come to a final conclusion on anything was like trying to nail jelly to a wall; they really debated things to the maximum.

The true Rastas in the prison hated the ones who pretended to be Rastas just by growing the locks and not really knowing anything about Rastafarians; it was just a guise for many to blag the tourists that came to Jamaica, perhaps picking up some silly western woman on the beaches of Negril, Montego Bay or Ocho Rios. But in all fairness, if you were brought up in Jamaica, born into poverty, what would you do? No wonder crime was rampant all over the island: the select few are very rich and the rest live in ghettos. I knew what a ghetto was, I was living in one with some of the worst people Jamaica had. The prison literally was a ghetto beyond a shadow of a doubt. The smells and sights of the General Penitentiary could look horrifying to an outsider, but the human spirit that found itself living under these conditions had to adapt. My own personal worst nightmare would be to find myself back there, on another sentence. Ok, I deserved to be there in the first place; if I hadn't been so desperate, I would never have done it: 'desperate men do desperate things' was spot-on in my case. The way life pans out was a series of events for me which led me to even contemplating doing what I did, but I know it will never happen again. Who am I to judge anybody? Judge not lest you be judged yourself.

Berry was all smiles as he wandered around the prison; he knew all the guards and he made it his job to get along with them - doing a life sentence under these conditions, they wanted to make their own lives as comfortable as possible. In the General Penitentiary, it really was every man for himself. In the summer months, it was so hot and humid, and without the luxury of air-conditioning and ice-cold drinks my throat was so parched I could barely breathe; we were all living in these conditions, but just like on the outside, a select few were not. I remember one day I was walking around the yard and was pulled over by one of the prisoners demanding money off me in a very intimidating way. I just told him to fuck off, and then he smiled, and his whole demeanour changed. I had called his bluff and he knew it, but I was glad it never went any further, as fighting at my time of life was a no-no. When you are placed in a hostile environment on a daily basis, you knew that some would cause you serious harm given the chance, and for others, it was all bravado. There were some serious gangsters in the General Penitentiary who wouldn't give you the time of day, and they never spoke to me, but that was fine by me, I could tell just looking at them.

Jamaica was involved in some high-level crime from the top down for decades. It wasn't any of my business, and I kept well out of another people's business. You would find yourself dreaming of freedom; it was always a good day when somebody got released from prison. I had seen men who had been in the General Penitentiary for 10, 15, 20 years getting released, and it gave me a good feeling to see somebody actually get released - it did happen - because sometimes in your mind you really did wonder if you would get out at all. I carried on rehearsing with the Bloom of Light, and the band's room was my sanctuary away from the rest of the prison. There were actually some fine musicians in the prison who had played together for many years, and it was good to be around them. It was always good to play a gig, it gave you something to look forward to, and the band would rehearse for weeks before to make sure they were tight and sounded great.

I had just finished reading *Marley and Me* by Bob Marley's former manager Don Taylor. Bob Marley was revered like a god in Jamaica, as he should be, for his insightful lyrics and prophetic songs. There are many fine musicians in Jamaica who just never get the break into the mainstream the way Bob did on a global stage. Listening to Irie FM on my radio there were many great songs by artists I had never heard of outside of Jamaica. It was not unusual to have new prisoners descend on the band's room, claiming to be great singers or musicians, but the Bloom of Light members were always reluctant to let anybody in, for fear of losing their place in the band. All the time I was there nobody new joined the band, which was okay by me. I knew them all and there was never any trouble with them.

Many singers would audition for the chance to sing at least one song, and you really felt the passion all of Jamaica has for music; it was their biggest export, along with drugs of course. I enjoyed playing the bongos with the band and I was getting much better after the lessons I received from Pedro the Cuban musician. The band members took the rehearsals very seriously and they loved jamming. I really wish I had been able to record these moments, but sadly at that time, there was no way of doing so. It felt like even for a brief time in the day that you were not in prison, but then when you had to return to your cell after rehearsals the reality would hit you. Aljoe was a joy to stand on stage with and he really was a supreme guitarist; he had picked up the guitar and taught himself from a very early age. With decades of playing within the penal system, it really was his release, and I'm sure he must have dreamed of being a free man one day and playing outside.

The police force and prison warders are paid such a pittance for putting their lives on the line, it breeds rampant corruption. The money my father used to send to help me survive went to one of the guard's bank accounts, and he would then take his percentage before I received the money. Many times, I would be waiting for the money; if they were short of money themselves that month, they would hold onto it for weeks; what could I do? I could get tick off some of the prisoners, but you really had to be careful and make sure they got their money back. There was one prisoner who used to do that, Rasta Beard they called him; he was doing a long sentence for drug offences and he was running a nice sideline in giving credit on goods he sold. He had a very imposing presence and a no-nonsense business head, and he had a small army of younger prisoners who would violently assault anybody who owed him money and never paid up, and they delighted in carrying out his orders. I owed him over 5,000 Jamaican dollars, around 30 English pounds; I used to get food off him and buy craftwork, and he would have it all written down. He was ruthless, but he trusted the UK prisoners because he knew they had money coming in from friends and family back in the UK, and he also knew about the money coming in from Prisoners Abroad.

My money had been due to come in at the end of the month, but this particular month the guard who was due to give me my money was absent from work. When the time came for Rasta Beard to collect his money, he came around to my cell and I didn't have it. I explained that the guard was not around and as soon as he came back, I would get it sorted. Now, Rasta Beard didn't know which guard was bringing my money in, I never told anybody, that was part of the deal; you had to give to the guard your friends or family number back in the UK, and the guard would then send his bank details via phone text, then my dad would transfer the money across to Jamaica to the guard. You were completely at their mercy. I was sure Rasta Beard was wondering if I was trying to pull a fast one, which really was not my style - my father always taught me to pay my debts and not renege on a deal, which I never have, but at this particular time, I was really panicking. I had no means of paying him back and I had no clue as to what was going on with the guard who mysteriously went absent from work.

He never threatened me verbally, but I could tell by his mannerisms that he was contemplating it. He said he would give me another week and left my cell; he was built like a brick shit house, and he was a crafty fucker, he never seemed to miss a trick where money was concerned. He had spies all over the prison who would let him know everything about who had money, and who received parcels. He was on a different section of the General Penitentiary than I was, and I was relieved to see him go back to his own section. I had seen poor fuckers lose their lives over a pittance, and this was big money that I owed. In a Jamaican prison you have to remember they had fuck all, and unless you were well connected you had to fend for yourself. I had been trying to avoid trouble and this was making me slightly uncomfortable, to say the least.

I just hoped the warden returned to work before the week was up.

The stench of the General Penitentiary in the summertime, with the vermin and the rats, was enough to make you want to vomit. When the food came around it was ladled out of a huge drum and would be slopped into your plastic bowl, provided you had one that is. I really could not say any of the meals were enjoyable; the only thing I did like was the Jamaican cornmeal porridge they served occasionally, and I devoured that. We never had jerk chicken, yams, ackee, fried dumplings, unless you had visitors bring it in; some of the lucky prisoners had small stoves inside their cells and could cook their own meals, and if you had money you could buy cooked food from them; constant hunger and thirst were never far away in the General Penitentiary. The week started to fly by and still no sign of the warder; how the fuck was I going to pay back Rasta Beard with no money? I was getting worried, but I had to keep my cool: the worst thing you can show in prison is fear, even if you felt it inside yourself. I was keeping busy with the band and I told nobody about the money I owed and was really sweating about how I could pay the fucker back. I really could not fathom out what had happened to the guard who had gone missing - was he ill? Had he been transferred to another prison? My mind was in overdrive trying to speculate what had happened to him. I really did not want to ask anybody, but things were getting desperate.

Then I ran into the fat fucker Berry who knew everything that went on in the prison; he was all over the prison and also worked on the gatehouse and reception, and he told me one of the guards had been arrested about ten days ago for selling weed to one of the prisoners - fuck me that was me well and truly in the shit once again! I knew it was my guard and there was no way I would get the money back now. What the fuck was I going to do? The next day, on the morning when Rasta Beard was due to come and collect his cash, I spotted him heading towards my section of the prison and I thought, I have got to front this fucker out, if he got into my cell alone with me, I could be in serious danger, if not from him, then from one of his henchmen at some point and I could be a target, no doubt about that.

Rasta Beard was ambling my way with a serious look on his boat race; he was built like Mike Tyson and he had a couple of scars across his face. I decided I would stay outside my cell and reason with him. When he arrived, I kept him out of my cell. 'Where's my money, you white pussyhole?' he shouted. I replied I didn't have it, but I would have it in another couple of days - fuck knows where I was going to get the money, but I had to say something to stall the cunt, and if I'd told him about the arrested guard, he wouldn't have given a fuck. He was in a funny position: he knew he couldn't hit me in full view of the guards who were milling about on my section to witness it - the white man could get him arrested and thrown into the hole. He started barking at me that he would have me dealt with if I never got it sorted in two days' time. I told him no worries, he would be sure to get it.

When he fucked off, I breathed a sigh of relief, but now I was in serious danger: my guard would not be back and I had no way of ever getting any money again from him, and my dad knew nothing about it. I had to find another guard who I could get the money sent to, and that meant finding one who I could trust, which was a proper pain in the arse. I really didn't know who to turn to with my problem, it was such a massive problem I had on my hands. I really didn't trust anybody in this prison. I did trust Aljoe, but that was about it on the Jamaican side. Then bingo! A light went on in my head: the young kid from Bristol, Mikey, he was a decent lad and he must be getting money sent in via a warder. I would approach him and see what he had to say.

Mikey was from the St Pauls area of Bristol. He was a tough looking kid, but he was easy to chat with. I went around to his cell and told him the story. Mikey knew all about Rasta Beard and his way of doing business. I'll give Mikey his due, he pulled out the cash and gave it to me to pay the cunt back. He said he would introduce me to the guard that he dealt with, and I could get the money transferred to him. But first I had to make a phone call to my dad, which was going to cost me money, and Mikey said he would sort it and we gave each other the Jamaican handshake, knuckles to knuckles the way they do to give you strength. Fuck, that was a close call… the kid had proved to me he was a decent fella, and I wouldn't forget it.

The next day the guard who Mikey knew came to my cell. He gave me his mobile and I rang my dad to explain the situation. Fair play to my dad, he sent the money the next day to the warder's bank account. He sent double the money because of the missing money that had gone via the sacked warder. Once again, my father had stood by me and had got me out of this shit. The following day Rasta Beard came around to my cell to collect his money, with a face like thunder, which suddenly changed into all smiles when I pulled his money out. It went from me being a white pussyhole, to him starting calling me by my name,

Tommy. I had to laugh at the change in his attitude. I have seen it many times over the years: no matter who, what, or how long you had owed somebody money it was always forgiven when the cash was paid back. In the drugs world, you have to work on trust - laying things on and waiting for the money to come back is pretty normal in the game. When I got the money from the warder I went around to Mikey and gave him his money back, plus a bonus for helping me out. That really was a close call: I got away with that one by the skin of my teeth.

'Not all forms of abuse leave bruises'

Chapter 34
Howard Marks

I had met Howard Marks in the summer of 2000 at one of the freshers' balls at Oxford University with Manchester DJ Billy Idle, who was working with Howard at the time.

I was with an Irish band called Alchemy, who Virgin Records had shown some interest in, but nothing came of it. I had read Howard Marks' books and was pleased to meet him. We hit it off instantly and Howard was a perfect gentleman, well-educated and sharp as a razor. He had served 7 years of a 25 year sentence in America. He was reputed to be the biggest hash smuggler in the world in the 70s and 80s.

Billy was from Manchester and had been doing door work and DJing at the Hacienda back in the day. It turned out Howard had an office on the All Saints Road in Ladbroke Grove, where I was living at the time. I kept bumping into Howard on Portobello Road, and I used to give him lifts, and we would go out drinking and go to parties. I went to his flat a couple of times and got to know him quite well. He had given up drug smuggling and was now a writer and many other things.

He came to visit me; I was really surprised. He was on business in Jamaica for three weeks. We had a good laugh, and he gave me a couple of hundred US dollars, a bag of clothes and a nine bar of weed. We talked about doing a fundraising gig in the future for the organisation Prisoners Abroad, who did such great work helping men locked up in foreign countries around the world. It ain't easy raising money for unsuccessful drug smugglers, as most of them are, but they do, and I take my hat off to them for the great work they do. It was good to see Howard; he knew how to make me laugh. The prison was awash with the news that Howard Marks had been to see me: they thought I was Mr Big, lol. A lot of the prisoners started to see me in a new light, which suited me if it meant they left me alone.

I was on a high for a few days, but the 20-hour-long lockdowns every day start to get to you. There were no toilets: you had to use a plastic bucket, unlike at the remand centre. I felt as if I was never going to get out. I really was starving and thirsty all the time - the Jamaican summers drained you. I could kill sometimes for a glass of ice-cold water; instead, I had warm tap water in a plastic bottle. This wasn't the Hilton Hotel. I settled into a routine of cleaning my cell in the morning, breakfast, then two hours out, and then locked down until the next day. The cycle repeated itself endlessly. I started to think I would never get out.

Some days in the General Penitentiary you could actually feel the tension in the air. A lot of the prisoners would be more aggressive than usual, the staff were on alert, and it took me months to work out why: a lot of the drugs that came in via being thrown over the wall would be intercepted, and the prison would be on a drought. When the Jamaican sinsemilla that kept the prisoners mellow and less violent was in short supply, the atmosphere in the prison was palpable. It gave me a perfect business opportunity: I had the 9oz of high grade that Howard Marks had brought for me, good old Howard! I had spoken with Aljoe, and he would sell it for me and keep it in his guitar, and we would split the profits, which was fine by me, it had cost me nothing and I trusted Aljoe - better still, so did the guards. He had been so long in the General Penitentiary that he was rarely searched, whereas some prisoners could be walking around the prison and would be pulled and searched often.

Aljoe put the word out, and within a few days business was booming as he sold it for 200 Jamaican dollars per gram. Prison prices were very much higher than on the outside and considering the risk, it was a reasonable price. I usually bought my weed from Rasta Beard, and after about a week he started to become suspicious as to why I wasn't anymore. I told him I was on a health kick and had decided to quit. He was purely thinking about the money he was losing, laughed and said I was crazy, and it wouldn't be long before I would restart again.

Although Rasta Beard was very intimidating, he was a good businessman, and I had a grudging admiration for him; he was many things, but he wasn't stupid. You had to be very careful around him - he never missed a trick - and after all we were taking some of his business away from him. Having a bit more money helped to survive in prison a bit more comfortably. There were many dealers all over the prison; the connected guys sold the crack cocaine and you can imagine what some of those prisoners were like when they were out of their heads on that. You could pass some of them on the section, and the least little thing would turn them aggressive. It really was a tightrope trying to steer clear of trouble, and even when you did try it could still come your way. Most of the guys were not petty criminals, they were hardened drug dealers and killers, hence why they were in the maximum-security unit of the General Penitentiary. The reality of it all was quite unnerving at times and it was like walking on eggshells around some of them.

I tried to keep myself to myself but at times it was virtually impossible, you never knew what people were thinking or could be capable of. I never felt fully at ease when walking around the prison. All the cell blocks were different. One particular cell block was very dark and always made me feel uneasy; gangs would be roaming around when they were unlocked, and it made me want to get out of there very quickly. The prison was very old and at times it was quite spooky. People in Jamaica lived and died by the gun or knife it so wasn't unusual for them, but for me, it was very alien. Five or six guys in very small cells, locked down for 20 hours a day in close proximity, was really asking for trouble. The Yardies themselves were living in ghettos and they had to be aggressive to survive in these conditions. The ones who were feared the most were those that rose to the top, both inside and outside the prison, because of their ruthlessness in dealing with anybody getting in their way.

Prisoners would be kidnapped and tortured in their cells by fellow prisoners, gagging their mouths to stifle the screams, if they owed them money or somebody had a grudge. Suicides were not uncommon either under these conditions. I knew for a fact I could easily be killed, and I am sure it was on the minds of many to actually do it. I was closely watched by the guards for my own safety; it really was like living in a nightmare, and at times I felt extremely vulnerable, especially when away from my section of the prison. Many times, I had to conquer my own demons which came into my head quite frequently. You knew for a fact that you were dealing with hardened killers - this was not a tea party, it was the real deal, and I had to quell the thoughts that were constantly on my mind.

I had no real friends. I was definitely the odd man out, and that alone was scary and disturbed my peace of mind continually when I was roaming around the prison. I knew I had to be on my guard and at times, my nerves were frayed to the point of extreme paranoia; maybe it was in my head at times, but I never felt completely safe. The human rights campaigners would have had a field day with the things that happened in the General Penitentiary on a daily basis. Mr Williams, the guard who disliked me intensely, used to smirk at me when the other prisoners were giving me a hard time; he was such a twat, who enjoyed seeing others suffer. Whenever I saw him it gave me a feeling of loathing, and the feeling was mutual, and he knew it. Some people can just walk in a party and completely ruin it just by their presence. I figured he was just jealous of me, as with a bit of luck, I would be back in the UK the following year, and he would still be working in the General Penitentiary for the next 20 years.

Freedom and surviving were utmost in my mind but there were times when I doubted getting out alive; when you saw a bruised and battered inmate being dragged by his feet to the hospital section, as many times as I did, it's not surprising. Many would be dead or barely alive, and although you did become immune to it, I would give a sigh of relief that it wasn't me. I did emphasise, but there really was not a lot I could do about the atrocities I was seeing. I really had to stop myself from being sick after watching the guards go to work on a prisoner with their batons, going hell for leather - you could hear the bones cracking and popping. I was completely shocked and would have nightmares alone in my cell at night that I would be next; the paranoia was real and not a figment of my imagination. The cell I was spending most of my time in was dark and dank at night, and reading by the dimly lit bulb was affecting my eyesight to the point where reading was becoming difficult. The one thing I loved doing was slowly being taken away from me. I knew I would need glasses on my release. I had to count myself lucky when I thought of some of the sentences that my fellow inmates were serving under these conditions, and it would make me feel slightly better about my own predicament.

The prison was deathly quiet in the early hours of the morning, and you could hear the footsteps of the warders checking the cells to make sure there were no escapes. My mind would be racing just in case they could smell the sinsemilla I had smoked to help try and make me sleep; it was my sedative and quelled my thoughts, lifting me from my surroundings. The warders knew most of the inmates were taking some kind of drugs, and in fact, some of them were on the make, selling it to prisoners, but I was never sure which ones were, and which ones weren't. I wasn't privy to this information like the dons of the prison were. In comparison to most of the prisoners who were serving horrendously long sentences I was the new kid on the block. I met prisoners who had been flogged by the cat of nine tails and still carried the scars. The last flogging had been in 1997, four years before I arrived, but the warders still threatened prisoners with it, and some of the older guys had wounds all across their back that made me grimace when I saw them. Keeping a sense of humour was essential under these trying conditions, and keeping my mind positive could be difficult, but I tried by joining the band, sport and exercise; anything to keep me busy.

Jamaicans are a hardy race, and they really would take liberties with you if you showed any sign of weakness. It was a fine line keeping my emotions under check, and pretending none of this bothered me, when in fact it bothered me tremendously; you just learnt to hide it well. Often the silence of the prison would be broken by the screams of the madmen that I was surrounded by. Knives were all over the prison, toothbrushes were sharpened to a deadly point, some prisoners had machetes hidden that they'd bought from the guards ready to use when needed. Watching prisoners in chains being extradited to America with armed DEA officers who had been flown in specifically for the job, you started to realise how large the drug problem was. I used to wish it was me being extradited, but no such luck, although the unlucky Jamaican who was extradited to the States never went willingly, knowing he was going to be entombed in the American penal system, and virtually buried alive there for the rest of his life. It was hard trying to take all of this in, but at the end of the day, I was a freewheeling, opened-minded spirit who had travelled the world in search of adventure, living in the moment and becoming more aware of my own mortality, and how briefly we really are on this planet. Two days in this place would have been enough for any rationally minded person to make them never want to come back here in a million years.

Travel was my life, and I enjoyed the extreme conditions of testing my mental and physical stamina, seeing and doing things that far removed me from a life of drudgery back in the factories and building sites of the UK. I began to wonder if I had truly chosen the right path, but then I would think my life had been that of a rolling stone for so many years it would have been impossible for me to settle down, and it really was inevitable that things would go wrong and I had to accept my fate, not dwell on the misfortunes that I had brought on myself. It was my spirit that had brought me here; who really in their right mind would have taken the risks I had? It really had been a shit or bust trip for me to Jamaica, and I had been well and truly busted.

Aljoe sold out in about 10 days; we split the profit, and I was happy. I didn't want to push my luck and try to source more weed from someone within the prison: it was too dangerous and to be honest I wasn't greedy, and I knew when to pull out. The extra money came in handy; it allowed me to buy more food and more bedding and cigarettes.

I had to go back to buying my grams of weed from Rasta Beard, which made him happy also. Aljoe stocked up on cigarettes, which he had sold for years; it was far less hassle than dealing drugs.

'Quotation is a serviceable substitute for Wit.' Oscar Wilde

Chapter 35
A Stroke of Luck

I still had a small problem: the $10,000 I had given the police was not my money, and the Jamaican gangster Delroy wanted his money back, or I was a dead man when I got out. This was the last thing I needed, but a few months later he was murdered in a shootout in Trenchtown, and so my problem was solved. I didn't want him to die, but I didn't want to die either. Sometimes I think I have a guardian angel watching over me. I do seem to be lucky in my unluckiness. I had survived three motorbike crashes, two drownings - one in Southampton, the other on the island of Bali, when I forgot to swim between the flags and swallowed lots of water, but luckily one of the Balinese lifeguards spotted I was in trouble and swam out to rescue me - and two drug overdoses, with one more to come in a few years' time, when I finally realised I was finished with heroin.

I'm not quite sure how many people were killed in the penitentiary while I was there, but I had counted at least 20 bodies in those years. When I was originally sentenced to hard labour, one of the warders told me I would be smashing rocks for 12 hours a day on a chain gang, and he laughed. Luckily, he was only joking. I never did a day's work apart from playing the bongos. I now had a bed, a mattress, a pillow, blankets, a small radio and plenty of books. Being locked down for 20 hours a day every day I would have gone crazy without those books. I tried to keep everything positive, but still, when you're surrounded by murderers and rapists you really had to be careful at all times.

Leppo was always coming to speak with me. I was never sure about him and was always wary; after all, he was doing life for three murders. He said he was innocent, but he is still there 31 years later. He suggested we have our photo taken together; he bribed one of the warders and we duly had our photo taken. I look a right state standing next to him. I wonder if he will ever be released. Peter Tosh was an icon in Jamaica, and I can't see them ever letting him out, and if they did, I'm sure somebody would murder him.

Time really drags in prison, but it never stops, it keeps moving forward, although in prison it feels like your life is on hold, which it is really. With the time spent on remand in Rema and the time in the penitentiary, I had been locked up for a year. It may not seem long but imagine being locked up in your bedroom for a few weeks - it can drive you mad.

Jamaica is a very religious country; it has more churches per capita than anywhere in the world. I'm not really religious - I adhere more to the Buddhist philosophy - but I would go to the church just to get out of the cell. Jamaican churches are fun, with lots of laughter and singing, no gloom and doom, and sometimes you would spot a woman who had come from outside. Even just the smell of their perfume was enough to give you an erection. I still love the smell of women and their perfume. It is very hard when you are locked away, you can have wet dreams. I had long ago given up on the solo stuff.

Some of the young Jamaicans were crazy: on the outside they were paid killers and killed many people, sometimes flying to the UK, America and Canada, and shooting somebody before flying back to Jamaica. Life is very cheap in the Caribbean.

I am not joking, this was a seriously dangerous prison to be locked up in: the Yardies are the most dangerous gangsters in the world, rivalling the Italian Mafia and the Mexican drug lords like El Chapo. You did not fuck around with these people if you valued your life, and I was dealing with them on a daily basis. Some of them had been to England, and they used to laugh about the way police were not armed, and say that our prisons were like holiday camps. There are thousands of them living in England, America and Canada, dealing in drugs and murders. Some of the prisoners had guns tattooed on their chests, and lots of them had machete scars all over. A Jamaican will think nothing of picking a machete up and using it on you. They didn't really like fistfights: a knife or a gun is much quicker. They see rich pickings in London, New York and Toronto; they are fearless and will not stop at anything to get what they want. Third world countries breed crime and violence. All Jamaicans love music; Tom Jones, Boy George, country music is surprisingly big in Jamaica, along of course with reggae music, raga, dancehall. They love to dance and party, much like myself.

My grandmother on my mother's side had eight children, four born in Ireland and four in Scotland. On my father's side, the Kennedys came to England in 1874, settling in Warrington. My grandfather was a master bricklayer and died of lung cancer at the age of 42; his name was Tommy. My great-grandfather was called Tommy, and I named my son Tommy. I'm a natural born native of the British Isles and proud of my Celtic roots, but I also appreciate all other cultures and cannot understand racism in any shape or form. I cannot judge anybody, and I think that's why I got on with the Yardies; they liked my sense of humour.

The suburbs in London were full of Jamaicans and Irish, partying together, and lots of mixed-race children came out of those days.

Anything helps the time go by in prison. I started helping in the classroom, helping people to read and write. My schooling was erratic when I was a kid - I had gone to ten schools in Warrington, Scunthorpe, Liverpool, and down south in Fawley, because of my misspent youth. But I had passed my eleven plus and was considered a bright boy until I started to go off the rails when I hit thirteen. If I had my time over again, I would have loved to have studied philosophy and history. I love ancient history and geography. Know your history and be wise: in these days of computers you can learn so much, but you cannot beat reading a book.

I love laughter, and I find the people who make you laugh seem to become lifelong friends. I bare my soul and wear my heart on my sleeve. My father used to say some people will hate you and some people will love you but fuck them if they didn't like you. They can like me or lump me. I do love people; I can get on with a tramp on the street or somebody who is a multi-millionaire. I'm impressed with people who have depth and a good sense of humour, regardless of what they have or don't have.

Life in the General Penitentiary churned on very slowly. Most of the time I was very hungry. I really had trouble eating the food. Sometimes I would get ill for a few days. It was not good, but then I would bounce back and focus on reading and playing with the band, anything positive to get through each day. A few Jamaican English would turn up in the prison some days, from places like Birmingham, Bristol, London, Manchester, Nottingham, Derby. All of them were drug smugglers. There were so many drugs coming through the airports in Jamaica, I think the English police had complained and the Jamaican government had started to crack down on the smugglers; the courts were handing out stiffer sentences. Jamaica was a good landing point for the Columbians in those days. The Yardies would entice people to smuggle drugs across Europe, Canada and the USA. People would be desperate for money, and with the promise of three or four thousand dollars, people were prepared to risk their lives and liberty smuggling drugs out of Jamaica.

A lot of the customs officers were paid off, and 50 or 60 mules would board flights daily, heading out of Jamaica safe in the knowledge they would get through. It was a bit like Russian roulette when you landed in the UK though. Some got through and some didn't, but there were always more people back in Jamaica willing to take the chance or the risk. Old white women and white men usually were never searched, or so the Jamaicans would tell you. The customs in Jamaica were getting wise to this, and they started to make arrests. Anybody who looked suspicious was stopped and searched, and huge amounts of weed and coke were being found on a regular basis. Jamaica was starting to become hot for smugglers to get through in the summer of 2002.

'Time and tide waits for no man.'

Chapter 37
A Surprise Visit

I had just smoked a huge spliff when a warder came to my cell to tell me I had a visit. I was surprised: who could it be? When I got there, I was surprised to see my sister Lynn and her husband Pete. It was a dangerous time to be in Kingston: the elections were going on and many people would get killed; you could hear the gunshots going off all the time outside the prison. It was great to see them, and it was only my second visit in over a year. I caught up on all the family news. Lynn had three kids, Daniel, Donna and Katie. They are all grown up now.

My father had recently survived a heart attack, and I didn't want him to travel with all the stress it would cause. The visit flew by, and the next time I would see them would be a few years later in Portsmouth.

Some of the Yardies would try it on, and if they thought you had something they would try and get it off you, but I was too wise for that. I would politely tell them to fuck off.

A tuck shop opened up. You could buy fruit, cold drinks, food - but it was a nightmare when you bought something, you would have ten or twenty on you. I used to give things to my cellmate next door, Aljoe. He had nothing and never had a visit in over twenty years. Life was really tough if you had no money or friends in the penitentiary. I had given up smoking for the first six months but decided to start smoking the weed; it was too good not to. That got me back on the cigarettes, and it was always a hustle to get them.

I was learning about Rastafari, black history and culture in the Caribbean. I started to understand a lot more about Jamaica. It used to drive me mad sometimes being in prison; there was so much on the other side of the wall that I wanted to see and do. One day I will go back to Jamaica and walk around the outside of that prison wall. Jamaica is a beautiful country and tourists flock there from all over the world. The beaches of Montego Bay, Ocho Rios, and Negril are stunning, as are the weather, the weed, the women, the home of reggae music, ska, dancehall, and its laid-back vibe. It truly is one of the top destinations of the Caribbean.

I was getting fitter, stronger - I was using the gym daily. I had my routine of exercises in my cell and I was reading huge amounts of books on all kinds of subjects. I had made some friends from the prison band, and Aljoe the band's guitarist and my next-door neighbour was my closest friend. We really got on well, he had a good sense of humour and sometimes he would talk for hours.

The warders could be sadistic and thought nothing of beating prisoners with their batons, no matter who was watching. They were always on the make, selling weed to prisoners, bringing mobile phones in. Some of them were ok, but most of them could be right bastards. They wielded power and you knew who was boss. I think the uniforms did it to them. I kept away from them as much as possible: I hate people in authority looking down their noses at you and telling you what to do. We all have our places in life, and I do believe in destiny and some kind of higher power that brings kindred spirits together.

Music was my saviour in the General Penitentiary. I met many people who claimed to know Bob Marley or to have worked with him. The Marleys built a studio, Tuff Gong, in Kingston. I love Jimmy Cliff, Morgan Heritage, Sizzla. 'Thank You, Mama', by Sizzla, was a big tune in 2002. I used to play a lot of gigs in the prison the time I was there - we would be wheeled out to play for visitors that came to the prison or on family day. Friends and family came to visit, and we were allowed to mix with the prisoners whilst we played on a huge stage that was built specifically for the occasion. We would play on Emancipation Day in August, the day slavery was abolished in 1838. We would play on Independence Day on 6th August, the day Jamaica gained independence from England. It was always good to get out of your cell and get up on stage and forget your troubles.

One day they asked me to be a judge in a music competition. Leppo won the dub poetry with 'When Was the Last Time', and John Roberts won the singing with 'Prison Pressure'. We could all relate to that song. The whole event was filmed for posterity.

My friend Moses, who was doing life, told me to get out and write a book about the General Penitentiary. Well, it's 16 years later but I'm finally doing it.

'If you don't take an opponent serious, they surprise you.' Canelo Alvarez

Chapter 38
Christmas

Sadly, my cousin Darren (son of my dad's sister, my aunty Val), got killed in a car crash in 2000 with my friend Ste Hardman. It was a massive funeral: 400 to 500 people attended. Darren was loved by everyone, and I still miss him now; we were like brothers. Our Jack, and his brothers Bernard and Chris, and his sisters Joanne, Alison and Sarah, all rallied around and sent me money in Jamaica to keep me alive. I will be forever grateful.

I have Pakistanis in my family. Joanne married one, and my cousin Gayle married a Japanese guy, and had two kids with him, they lived in Japan for ten years. I have a large family all over the UK and Ireland. My Uncle James and his two sons, James and John, were good boxers. Their sister Donna is now married and living in Ireland. I have family in Devon: my uncle Roy and his wife and their grown-up kids, Roy Junior, Gayle and Tania. We are all close, and I feel blessed.

Friends can drift in and out of your lives, but our family remains tight and constant. I decided that when I got out, I was going to go straight for good this time. My karma had caught up with me and I was paying the price. Life in the penitentiary was dragging along, and I was getting gate fever, badly. You really could lose your life in there; it was like a very close brush with death.

I met some wild characters in the General Penitentiary, men serving seriously long sentences who had no chance of ever being released. I never spoke to anybody about my release date, I kept it to myself - somebody could kill you in a fit of jealousy. A wise man holds a still tongue, especially in there.

When there was a lot of weed in the prison things were calmer; people would mellow out. Sometimes there was a drought on, and you could feel the atmosphere change. There would be a lot of fights and stabbings. Occasionally I was glad when they locked us down at 3:30pm for the night. I really didn't want to die in this rat-infested hell hole, no sir, I had things to do on my release.

When I thought about my time in the General Penitentiary it made me wonder. My friend and next-door neighbour, who had butchered his grandparents with a machete when he was 17, really was one of the gentlest souls I have come across in my lifetime. He always had a smile on his face and was willing to help where he could. He had no hidden agenda; he was just so happy to play the guitar, and it was a pleasure to be on stage with him - his face truly would light up. After 28 years in the General Penitentiary he really didn't know much else, it was his whole world. He had seen how some of the other prisoners would try and intimidate me, but there was nothing he could do, nor did I expect him to. He would still be there long after I had gone, and in the end, in this place, you had to look after number one.

Leppo was a different kettle of fish: he was very confident, brash and forthright. He was not a physically big man, he was quite small and wiry, but he never worried how the other inmates perceived him. He did have a presence and he carried himself like a much larger man: he was a keep fit fanatic and worked out religiously after decades behind bars, and seven years on Death Row. You knew he was mentally strong. I never saw him try to bully anybody or get into any fights, so perhaps he really wanted to be a model prisoner. He knows he has a certain infamous celebrity throughout Jamaica, and he knew if he was ever released the world's media would descend on him; he's just biding his time to see if that will ever happen.

Who really knows what happened the night Peter Tosh was killed? There were supposedly eyewitnesses and Leppo was found guilty in record time, but he always insisted it was a miscarriage of justice and he was totally innocent, and like many prisoners across the world who say they are innocent, he sticks to his story. His poems really are good, and I saw him perform them dozens of times in concerts, and hundreds of times at the rehearsals in the band's room. I got to know him really well, and towards the end of my sentence we would talk for hours. I forgot about his crimes when we became so familiar. The conversations were all about his music and how he performed it. He was a big fan of Mutabaruka, a dub poet in Jamaica who is very radical with his lyrics, and Leppo adopted his style big time. Does Leppo deserve to be free and go and live the rest of his life? I just don't know, but if it was me in that situation, I would want to be free.

The band's room really was the sanctuary for all of the musicians; you heard all the gossip and there were deep bonds and camaraderie between these convicted killers who had played for the Bloom of Light for many decades. In a way I was highly honoured to play with them. I would be at the back on the stage performing with them and occasionally I would sing backing vocals when they played Bob Marley songs. It really was a very surreal experience, the couple of years I played with them, and one that built my confidence for years to come; after all, I'm sure I was the only white man from Warrington who had or ever will play with them, and indeed I would love to play with them again - as a free man of course.

The origin of the Shower Posse was believed to be one of the most violent drug lords in Jamaican history, their leader Jim Brown aka Lester Lloyd Coke, who had died in this very prison while awaiting extradition to the United States in 1990, in very suspicious circumstances. His charred corpse was found one morning in his cell in the General Penitentiary, and it is widely believed he was murdered for he knew far too much about the Jamaican politicians that had helped him during his bloodthirsty rise to the top, supplying colossal amounts of cocaine to the United States. After his death, the Tivoli Gardens Don was followed into the business by his youngest son, 21-year-old Christopher Michael Coke, aka Dudus Coke, who was far more ruthless than his father ever was.

I had never classed myself as a racist, and although I had been taunted for having ginger hair as a kid and suffered terrible racist comments in the General Penitentiary, I really never took them to heart unless I felt my life was in danger. It becomes part of life when you're the odd one out, as I was for sure. I did have fun with people and many humorous incidents occurred that would make me laugh uncontrollably. Being the stage manager for a load of convicts dying to show off their musical skills was always an eyeopener; trying to get them on and off stage was no mean feat and one I took to with relish.

I got to know a lot of people throughout the institution and at times I really did feel the need to pinch myself that I wasn't having a dream, sometimes a nightmare, and other times the whole scenario would blow my mind at the position I found myself in. My life experiences helped me a lot to cope with the General Penitentiary; my spirit was strong and helped me in my darkest moments, especially those first six months trying to get my head around it all, living in a darkened cell on a concrete floor, with no bedding and a plastic water bottle for my pillow. My elbows and knees became accustomed to it and I would fall asleep like I was in a king size bed. Each day was to be conquered, and as torturous as it could be at times, I could see the funny side of it all; otherwise, I really would have gone mad, and without a sense of humour, I would have been well and truly fucked.

Christmas was coming and we had a gig planned for the 12th of December 2002. Artists were going to be playing from the outside, alongside the Bloom of Light, including Egg Nog and Daddy English, and prison performers included Norris Gordon, Serano Walker, Leppo, and John Evans, to name a few; we were all looking forward to it. A lot of the Jamaican prisoners who wanted to be in the band resented a white man taking their place, but for me, it was a way of doing something positive with my time and I ignored their resentments. We rehearsed constantly for weeks prior to the big event. Leppo always wanted his performance to be perfect, and to watch him rehearse you really could tell how seriously he took it all. My hands were hurting from the number of rehearsals we did, hitting those bongos with all the power I could muster to be heard above the rest of the band.

It was a great build-up to the Christmas period. This was my second Christmas in the General Penitentiary, and I just wanted to get it out of the way and into the New Year of 2003, and edge closer to my release date. Mentally this was my main focus and one I wanted with all my being. Berry was running around the prison like the good fairy, ingratiating himself as usual with all the guards and new prisoners to see what he could elicit from them in one way or another; he really did know what was happening on the prison grapevine. I had written a song called 'Kissing My Baby in the Moonshine' for Norris Gordon, who made it sound really good, and I enjoyed listening to him perform the song in the band's room at rehearsals.

Finally, the day of the concert arrived. There was a huge stage that had been built specially for the occasion with great big speakers, and a sound engineer in front of a state-of-the-art mixing desk that had been brought in by the outside performers who were on the bill that day. There were over 300 people from the outside who had come along to see the prisoners perform, and I spotted quite a few good-looking women in the crowd, which in my book was an added bonus to the whole event, and there was a film crew there to add to the atmosphere. It was a brilliant sunny day and all the musicians were in a great mood; after all, this is what they lived for, to play to a live audience. When it was the Bloom of Light's turn to play, we all dutifully took our places on the stage and covered half a dozen songs of Bob Marley and the Wailers, which went down really well, and then the band did three songs of their own, including the song I wrote, 'Kissing My Baby in the Moonshine'. We all got a massive round of applause. We were all buzzing; the event had been a brilliant success. Half an hour later we were all back in our cells, locked down until the next morning, with 'no business like show business' bouncing around in my head.

The following day when we unlocked and met up in the band's room, we were all chatting excitedly. It had been the highlight of our year.

Christmas was coming around in the next couple of weeks and services were held in the church. I used to pop in there just for a break from the usual routine, and occasionally there were women in the congregation, usually well to do members of society, but any sign of gazing at them and you could be disciplined and barred from the church. It used to make me laugh as I gazed around the church nonchalantly, trying not to let my eyes be caught by the warders who were standing around during the services. Some of the prisoners knew their Bible inside out and would attend every and any religious meeting. I found some of them quite creepy, especially those who were doing long sentences for indescribably heinous crimes - deep down you knew they were putting on an act for the parole board, although some prisoners were genuinely brainwashed by the whole religious drama. But who was I to judge? If it brought them comfort and solace, surely it was a good thing. Often the heat outside was unbearable during the height of summer and prisoners would come along just to feel the breeze from the fans that blew gently around the church. Small mercies are something you would be thankful for; things you take for granted outside meant a great deal in the General Penitentiary.

Christmas Day came and it was slightly different from the usual day. I went for a stroll down to the open-air gym and did a workout, then returned to my cell, and Christmas dinner was served: a piece of chicken and rice. I was so hungry I wolfed it down like a starving dog. After we were all locked down a guard came to my cell, unlocked my cell door and told me to go down to collect my Christmas cake, which was a bun and cheese, and to be honest I really enjoyed it. Compared to the usual gruel that was on offer it felt like a 5-star meal. I spent Christmas night reading and smoking a spliff and fell soundly to sleep.

I couldn't stand the smell of the prison, and in the heat when the latrines were overflowing the mosquitos and the rats would be unbearable. Emptying your slops was also a problem - you could get stabbed if you splashed anybody with your bucket, - fights were always caused over this, and I made doubly sure I never splashed anybody with any of my waste. I used to dream of having my own toilet to sit upon. It was very awkward doing it in a plastic bucket with no chain, no disinfectant, lucky if you had toilet paper.

The nights were the worst, locked down from 3.30pm until the next morning. I would get stomach cramps and the rats ran about. I quite often got sick and delirious, and on Boxing Day I collapsed; it all hit me at once. I was throwing up from both ends and really had visions I was dying. I must have fallen on my face and hit a sharp object because when I woke up, I was bleeding badly and was covered in blood. The sick that was coming from my mouth and the waste from my rear end, combined with the blood all over my face, had turned me a deathly white. I had a small broken piece of mirror that Aljoe gave me for shaving, and alone in my cell looking at the reflection I was horrified. I had no clue how long I had been unconscious for. The prison was very quiet, and I reckoned it was the early hours of the morning.

I had been sick a few times in the General Penitentiary, but I had never felt this bad. I knew I had to see a doctor and get this sorted. It was still a few hours before we would be unlocked, and I had to alert somebody to my condition. There was no way of ringing a bell like in a hospital, so I clutched the bars in my cell and shouted out loud that I was in trouble and had to see a doctor. I heard feet approaching and I groaned when I saw who it was - the one guard that detested me turned up at my cell door; it was Mr Williams. Alone in the blackness, I felt my heart sink as I tried to explain my condition to him. He snarled at me that I was just a white pussyhole who thought I was special, and there was nothing wrong with me and that I was trying to waste his time. He said if I didn't keep my mouth shut, he would open the cell door and beat the bumbaclart out of me, and then he turned to leave. I lost my temper and called him a cunt, and as soon as I said it, I immediately regretted it.

He turned around and unlocked my cell door. He was fuming as he entered my cell, drew his baton and struck me on my shoulder, across my back, and around my head; he knocked one of my teeth out, the pain was all consuming, and then I felt nothing, just a blackness came over me.

I came around in the prison hospital. It was daylight. My body was trembling from the pain, and I had trouble focusing my eyes. I wasn't quite sure what had happened, but I soon started to recall the night before, and then I realised where I was. I had been placed in the mad man section of the hospital, with the insane criminals. It was unlike any hospital I had ever entered in my life; I had been in hospitals in India, and once to a leper hospital on the Island of Flores in Indonesia, but this stinking place was the worst I have ever seen. Half the patients were walking around naked mumbling to themselves, there was no clean bedding, there was excrement covering the walls, and no sign of any doctor or nurses. We were just left alone, about 20 of us, in this flea-bitten room that stunk of body odour, shit and piss. I was covered in bruises and blood. Some of my fellow patients were terrifying to look at, never mind being up close to; I was in the depths of despair and actually contemplated suicide, before lapsing back into unconsciousness.

I came around again a few hours later, with one of the guards near my bed. He told me that I was in the wrong section of the hospital, and that his friend Mr. Williams, the guard who had beaten me, was going to arrange for me to seek medical attention in the medical section of the prison, and I would be looked after, but I must keep my mouth shut as to what had occurred, especially where the British Embassy was concerned. I felt so alone and ill; I would have agreed to anything. I told him I would keep my mouth shut if they got me out of there: it was the worst experience I had ever encountered in my time in the General Penitentiary, and I still had another seven months to serve. The thought of it all made me wonder if I would keep my sanity. Later that day two prison orderlies were sent to my bed and they placed me on a stretcher. They carried me out of the psychiatric cell and took me to the main medical section of the prison, which was basically a huge dormitory full of beds, with sick or dying prisoners laid up in them, but at least the patients were compos mentis. I slept fitfully for a few days. I was still covered in blood, my whole body was aching, and I could barely breathe; it was so hot and the noise from the other patients was doing my head in.

The prison doctor eventually came to see me. I explained my symptoms and he told me I had to be cleaned up first; he then told the orderlies to help me to clean up. I was taken to a room barely able to walk while they held me up with their arms under mine. I shuffled along, one foot after the other, and felt humiliated when they roughly undressed me. I was standing there in a dark room naked, and covered in bruises, while they poured cold water over me from the plastic slop buckets used for shitting in. But I was in such a state of filth that the cooling water eased my mind, and it was almost enjoyable.

After they had finished throwing water over me, they threw me a dirty towel and I dried myself off. Fuck, this had nearly broken me in two, but I knew I could not let them know how I was feeling. I had to pull myself together and show no fear whatsoever. The fleeting thoughts of suicide had gone, and now in place was a grim determination to survive and see my family once again; they really were my guiding light.

I was taken back to my bed and the doctor once again came to see me. I felt a bit better. The last couple of days had been hard; I was still feeling sick and had diarrhoea and the doctor told me I had a bad case of gastroenteritis. I was to have lots of fluids, and bananas would be served for me. It all started to make sense. Throwing up out of both ends, my eye had a gash and I was covered in bruises, one of my teeth was missing but fuck it, I was still alive. I stayed in the hospital for another three days and my strength started to return. I was walking about in the ward and eating the bananas which were a luxury I had never been allowed.

I realised I would have to keep my mouth shut about the incident with Mr Williams, and I would have to tread very carefully around him in the future; never again would I answer him back. The British Embassy was not due to visit for another six weeks. I had badly underestimated that I wouldn't be beaten because of the visits from the Embassy, and there was no way I would complain to the Governor or any of the other prisoners, as I am sure my life would have been in danger if I had. So I resolved to forget about it all and soldier on with the rest of my sentence.

Three days before New Year's Eve I was returned to my cell. I was certain Aljoe knew what had happened. I never mentioned anything apart from I'd been in a fall and had a fever, but I was feeling fine, and left it at that. Alone in my cell, I tried to process it all. I had come very close to losing my life: I knew he had beaten me into unconsciousness and for that, I was thankful I had blacked out. He must have panicked, realising I was the white man, and he could have been in serious trouble with the British Embassy. How he had managed to get me to the hospital I never found out. My eye was throbbing, and I was still stiff all over, but the enteritis had gone, thank fuck. I hardly ventured out of my cell for a couple of days, resting up and letting my body heal. Compared to the atrocities that went on in this prison, mine was nothing, but it still made me feel extremely vulnerable and my mind was on overload about the whole event. This was a prison and it almost felt like a large village at times filled with psychopaths and killers who roamed freely when the prison was unlocked. It felt like a time bomb and you just never knew who would set the detonator off. Some of my fellow prisoners were so scary to look at, and you knew a lot of them were capable of extreme violence at the drop of a hat; it really was like the Wild West. Maybe this is why the guards were so sadistic: they had to quell and control any sign of trouble in an instant before the whole prison began rioting. The General Penitentiary had such a fearsome reputation throughout the whole of the Caribbean, law-abiding citizens were terrified just by its name.

I knew it would have to happen, but I really didn't want to run into the guard who had beaten me so badly, Mr Williams, but he came to visit me late at night just before New Year's Eve. I was sleeping when I heard him rattling the bars on my cell door with his baton. I opened my eyes and saw him standing outside my cell door. I felt like a cornered rat: I could go nowhere, it was just him and me alone once again in the pitch black of the prison. My heart was going ten to the dozen and my mouth was dry with fear, and he whispered through my cell door that if I ever stepped out of line again, I would be a dead man, and from now on I must call him sir at all times. I could barely speak as I replied, 'Yes sir.' He gave me a disdainful look and left me there, shaking in fear. I had been terrified that he was going to unlock my cell door and finish me off. The guards' batons were made of the hardest wood in Jamaica, from the Lignum Vitae tree, and they gleamed with polish. The pain they inflicted with them is indescribable, and the mere thought of another beating by him literally left me petrified, half naked with only my flip-flops and shorts for protection. What could I do? I felt my mental health was deteriorating rapidly and he was literally rubbing salt into my wounds. He knew full well he was messing with my mind by putting the fear of god in me. I was so glad when he fucked off.

If it had been outside the prison, just me and him, under different circumstances, I am sure I would have made him realise he had been in a fight, but I was locked down in his prison, alone, a white man, in Jamaica, and I'm ashamed to admit how I felt that night: I was truly in fear for my life. It took ages before my heart stopped racing and I got my thoughts under control. I smoked all my cigarettes in the ensuing hours before we were unlocked in the morning; he had taken all my confidence away from me, and it was something I would have to live with for the rest of my life. The most powerful tool in the hands of a bully is the mind of the bullied, and he had mine that night.

I have never uttered a word about that night to anyone. It was the most frightened I have ever been, since my mother had terrorised me when I was a small child. It had brought back childhood memories of when she had come to my bed late at night with a kitchen knife and jabbed me in the legs after pulling the bedclothes off me; she had threatened to kill me, uttering profanities to me whilst cackling into the early hours of the morning in a drunken stupor. Why she did it I will never know. I had wet the bed in fear, and the childhood memories I had buried in my subconscious for over 35 years came flooding back. I was a total fucking mess in my head; she had abused me for years and fucked my childhood completely, and would laugh about it, as if I deserved it.

Life can be so wonderful and at the same time so brutal. I have lived with my demons for all these years and watched my own life fall into chaos, which led me into drug abuse, alcoholism, and taking huge risks with my reckless behaviour, in and out of prisons, never knowing why, unable to completely sustain relationships with people, running away from problems, unable to hold jobs down, fucking up the good things in my life through my own sheer stupidity, and not-giving-a-fuck attitude. I have always been attracted to the negative things in life, and the weirdos I meet, I feel the most comfortable with. Sometimes I cannot believe I'm still here. I probably have suffered from low self-esteem my whole life, covering it up with crazy escapades, but deep-down searching for something or somebody to heal the pain I carry around with me, locked inside my heart and soul, like a malignant cancerous tumour.

I am a total mass of contradictions; I care for people, sometimes the wrong people, who to my own detriment have shit all over me, or I have shit all over them. I say this not for sympathy but to reveal my own pain to myself, and see it written in words to help me to try to understand myself. But here I was locked up in a Jamaican prison, where nobody gave a fuck about me and the madness running around in my head. Surely there were hundreds of prisoners brought up in the Jamaican ghettos of Kingston with stories a thousand times worse than my own. So, you learn to hide your insecurities with sheer acts of bravado, and you blunder through life trying to deal with your problems in the best way that you can. Maybe I was making myself suffer because this was the way I felt about myself, worthless, and just cannon fodder for the penal institutions. Indeed, I felt I must count myself lucky I had not been sectioned to a lunatic asylum; I must cover things really well and not let people in too close to me to figure out.

Child abuse and neglect runs rampant in many families across the world, and the results are devastating: the prisons are full of abused kids and most of the blame must be placed at the parents' feet for it all. The ones who have given their kids a terrible upbringing must look within themselves and admit they were wrong. Instead of keeping things secret, children should be allowed to express themselves and feel loved and comforted in their own homes. Was my own mother evil? I don't think so. She had a hard life, she drank far too much, she had no idea about parenting skills, she didn't seem to realise the meaning of love, and probably never understood what she was doing to me, and maybe in her mind, it was all a joke. She beat me so badly once in the backyard of our house with her shoe, I was grief-stricken and sobbing my heart out. I ran to a neighbour's house, and my mother dragged me out of their house by my hair, slapping me all the way to our house, shoved me in the bedroom and left me there with no food for the night. She may have forgotten the next day, but I never did, and it was all over nothing.

I am not sure if my sister suffered from my mother, but I think she did. She left home at a very early age and couldn't wait to leave Warrington; there were no happy memories. My younger brother was lucky he missed a lot of it, thankfully. All of this was going through my mind constantly as I drifted off to sleep that night.

The Jamaican sunshine helped to raise my spirits. I was glad when daylight came, and the prison woke up and helped to lift my mood from the previous night. You learn to deal with things. I had spent my life dealing with drama and trauma, and you carry on regardless.

'A friend loveth all the time a brother is born for adversity' King Solomon

Chapter 39
Red Yardie

The start of the new year of 2003 was really slow; my body was beginning to heal, and I just wanted to get on a plane and leave this place behind forever, but it wasn't that simple - first I had to serve the rest of my sentence. I was really hating this shithole with a passion. It felt like purgatory with no end in sight, and the people I had to put up with on a daily basis didn't make it any easier with their constant threats and limited conversations. In the cold light of day seeing Mr Williams strutting around the prison made my blood boil. I had to hide my feelings of hatred whenever I saw him, as he held the keys to my freedom. I had dreams of stamping his head all over and cutting the bastard's throat for what he had put me through, although I knew I couldn't do anything to him: this was not the UK, the rules of this prison were more medieval, and I was alone without any kind of help. I buried my head in my books for weeks and went through the motions.

I was losing interest in the band. Maybe I was suffering from mild depression. Then halfway through January I was coming back from the prison library, and Moses called me over and said, 'What's up, Red?' I replied, 'Nothing.' Moses said, 'Come on man, you been walking around this place for weeks with a long face, and you look like you have something on your mind.' Moses was a good man; we had a lot of chats and he always gave me good advice about the General Penitentiary, and about life in general. He was much older than me, and he hated this place, but he knew how to deal with it after so many years. He was serving life and was well respected in the General Penitentiary. I hesitated; I really wanted somebody to talk to but I'm never the most forthcoming to people in general.

I had a lot of secrets and had difficulty telling people about personal stuff. I was doing a short sentence, and he was doing life, so my problems were minute to his. So I just said that the prison was getting me down. He laughed and said, 'They can build another prison inside of the prison, and then build another prison inside of that. I'm already in prison, it makes no difference. It's the way you cope with it that matters; don't show them it's getting to you.' I thought about what he said and realised he was right; I was walking around with a long face, and if he noticed so would other people.

It made me feel better that another human being had reached out to me and called me by my nickname, Red. I was in the total minority and some people never spoke a word to me; in some ways it wasn't cool to be seen talking to a white man, and I felt that on many occasions. Moses had an easy way about him, and it really raised my spirits. He threw me a packet of cigarettes and said, 'Pay me back when you get some money.' Wow, I was so humbled by the gesture, it made me feel not so alone after all. I said, 'Thanks man, really appreciate it.' I had the money on me though, so I paid him there and then. As I walked back to my cell a new feeling came over me, and I realised I had to snap out of these doldrums and get involved with the band and lift my mood for the better.

Berry was outside my cell when I got back. He really was a smarmy fucker, but he always made good food. He told me his daughter had been, and he had some nice chicken he was cooking up. I knew the score, money would have to change hands, so I placed my order for the evening meal. I carried money with me at all times, wrapped in a plastic bag, but with Berry, I always went to his cell with the money when I knew it was ready: you didn't flash cash around him, the less he knew the better. I never really trusted him. He didn't give a fuck about anybody but himself; he pretended to be your friend if he thought he could get something out of you. He never said what he was in for, but other inmates told me he had killed his wife in a fit of rage, and I could believe it. There was something that was too good to be true about him. He was hugely overweight, weighing in around 20 stone at a guess, and he always had the best of everything. He looked almost white although born in Jamaica, and colour did make a difference the way people looked at you. There was the very dark black skin colour, the mixed race, and there was me.

I lay down and wrote in my diary my conversation with Moses, and I felt a shift in my thinking. It was hard working out who was who in this prison, and I had to use my own savvy to understand how the prison ran, but I was going to make sure I did from now on. I had observed and absorbed as much as I could in the first year, but you could never fully understand the running of this place unless you were connected. There were some hardcore prisoners who you just knew meant business: they had been actively involved in huge import and export of cocaine across the UK, the United States and Canada, and they were ruthless, and you knew never to cross them. In prison they stood out in the way they carried themselves; even the guards seemed to leave them alone. It would be very hard to penetrate into their circle. They were never involved in violence within the prison; it was not their style, they were way above that.

The Yardies were a difficult and fearsome looking race; they had to survive in the best way they could, and it was usually drugs and murder that took them out of their grim upbringings. There was one who stood out: he would work out in the yard gym, he was about 6ft 4in, and he was always surrounded by at least six of his cohorts in the yard. I could tell he was the leader by the way the others fawned around him and laughed at his jokes. He was all muscle and very intimidating looking, but I had my northern sense of humour and when I want to use it, I can chat with anybody. I would find out his name, and when the time was right, I would approach him and introduce myself. He had never spoken to me, but I knew he knew who I was; I stood out just by being me, and he couldn't fail to notice me.

Just before lockdown I went to Berry's cell and collected my evening meal of chicken and rice which he had cooked up in his cell on his little stove. I gave him his money and he smiled and said, 'If you want more, come back tomorrow'. It really was a good meal, never enough but far superior to the shite the prison served up. Your nerves could get run down when you weren't eating properly, and if I had money, I would occasionally buy a meal from him; he had his uses. Rasta Beard was always on the hustle and also sold food, and I preferred to deal with him more than Berry, but Berry was on my section and easier to get hold of.

London Jamaicans from places like Stonebridge in Harlesden, North West London, reputed to be the murder capital of London in the late 90s, Brixton, Tottenham, Notting Hill and Hackney were directly responsible for the crack epidemic that hit London like a ton of bricks. All these areas had a large black population and were well connected to Jamaica. Gun crime went on the increase, and the Metropolitan police were overwhelmed with Yardie gangsters in the capital. They were a new breed, flash, taking huge risks, and anybody who got in their way was dealt with by a bullet. It was hard to keep up with them and Operation Trident was set up by the Met to deal with black on black gun crime that had spread like wildfire right across the UK in largely Jamaican populated areas of Birmingham, Bristol, Nottingham, Manchester, Leeds and Liverpool. The UK was flooded with coke and crack and it made some of them rich beyond their expectations.

The General Penitentiary was full of British-born black Jamaican gangsters who revelled in the Yardie reputation, wearing the best clothes and the finest gold jewellery. Many of them were in the General Penitentiary, and connections were made, and deals struck. There were also the old school Yardies whose parents had come in on the Windrush generation, who only dealt in weed and reggae music, which had also erupted all over the UK. They were cool and much easier to deal with, and I had met a lot of them when I was living in Notting Hill; they loved music and put on great parties. The Notting Hill Carnival had sprung out of the area 36 years previously, something that had been started by the Caribbean community in Notting Hill. A street party of a few hundred had become the largest carnival in Europe by the millennium.

It was the younger new breed of gangster that helped the rise of cocaine in the UK, and I met many of them in the General Penitentiary. We had something in common: they were born and bred in England, and we all were convicted of drugs trafficking, and although I had been duped, I still knew what I was doing. There were crack houses all over London and I had scored from many of them. I knew first-hand the devastation that was caused. They used to laugh and called me Red Yardie because of my long ginger hair, which had grown over the past year. Cocaine and particularly crack cocaine were dealt with in the General Penitentiary; it was expensive and caused a lot of problems between the prisoners, especially for the ones who were totally addicted. A lot of bullying went on, and if you had money you were definitely a target for the bullies who were high on crack. There were a lot of cells cooking up crack around the penitentiary, and they were no-go areas for me. Some of the cell blocks were so dark it was hard to know where you were going, and the sight of someone doing a double life sentence totally smashed on crack really did put me on edge.

Crack, money and power really did change people and it was not for the better. People could be kidnapped and have their mouths gagged to stifle their screams from the guards if money was owed; torture was a good method for debt collecting, families would be contacted, and money would be sent in to pay debts. Machete scars were common in the General Penitentiary. There were all kinds of posses roaming freely around the General Penitentiary, it felt like a minefield some days; my paranoia would be on high alert, this wasn't a figment of my imagination, it was real, deadly real. A lot of the prisoners were squeezed in so tight in the cells it was inevitable there was going to be tension between them, and I had to count myself lucky that eventually I got a single cell. But alone at night was the time when you really had time to think with no interruptions, and my thoughts were my own worst enemy at times. Where was I going to live on my release? How feasible was it that I would stay out of trouble? I was now 42 years old, and what had I achieved really? I had been on the road for so long; financially I had nothing, and no partner, and once again nowhere to live - all these things went through my mind, and on top of it all I was on a mission to succeed in the music business. I knew it wasn't going to be easy, and I sometimes wished I had just settled down, but with my lifestyle and the demons I have carried for years it was virtually impossible for me to hold a relationship down. I would usually fuck things up at some point; but even so, I tried and failed many times. I bore nobody any ill will. Perhaps I blamed my mother too much; I had brought all these things on myself. My mother had been dead over six years, and I'd not seen her for twelve years previously, was I being hard on her? It did drive me nuts at times that I had never spoken to her, reconciled our differences and maybe given her a chance to explain her side of things; it was something I never got to know. The thing about prison is, it gave you loads of time to think things over, and maybe that was a good thing, or maybe not, I was never sure.

Over the next week, I began to use the gym in the yard more frequently. Lots of inmates would use exercise to build their strength and flex their muscles to look more intimidating. I used it to do something with my time and at least try and get fitter. Many times, I would be slightly embarrassed working out alongside dozens of Yardies who were super-fit; I would be huffing and puffing, working out alone, and at times I could hear sniggering, but I carried on anyway. I was waiting for my chance to meet the main man, but he never showed up that week. I guess he had better things to do.

Aljoe had been acting slightly strange again; his eyes were glazed. I'm not sure what medication they gave him, but he did lapse into his own world, and I would leave him alone. In prison, like in life, you have to give your friends space, but in prison, unlike life, you were guaranteed to see them regularly, you had nowhere else to go. If a man made you feel uneasy or had a grudge against you it was a head fuck: you couldn't get away from each other. There were no washing machines and the few clothes I had I had to wash by hand in the blazing sun. There was always a chance of trouble, a man shouting, 'Hurry up white man, I want to use the sinks'; these were around the prison for washing your clothes in, and they were far and few between. Nothing was easy and trying to avoid trouble wasn't easy; the Yardies would argue over anything, and it was a lucky day if it went by without some form of an altercation over some bullshit or other.

I never wanted to feel the guards' batons ever again: that had been one very painful experience I never wanted to repeat. I was constantly aware of the danger. Rasta Beard asked me if I wanted some paintings done, when I was washing my clothes one day, and I told him yes, he could get one of his friends to paint my logo for ZodoA, the company I had started in 1999 after meeting Mentona K, who had to give me the idea for the company name. It was music that had brought me here in the first place; I would never have agreed to have taken the risks I did if it hadn't been for my passion for music. 'Life is stranger than fiction' rang true in my case. Rasta Beard was a funny character but there was something about him I liked, and if he struck a deal, he always came up good. He had to survive, and he took risks transporting drugs around the prison; he was a Mr Fixer for sure. He was a grumpy bastard though, and you had to keep on the right side of him. He had great stories of his life in Jamaica. He had been involved in the weed trade outside, which landed him a ten-year sentence, and he still had five more years left to serve, so he was relentless with his hustles to make money to make his life easier within these prison walls. If you had no money you lived like a peasant in the General Penitentiary.

Machetes are common in Jamaica from the slave days when they were cutting cane, and it was the weapon of choice for many; I would see prisoners who had been in fights with scars all over their body, and missing limbs were commonplace - in the showers you would see up close the damage they inflicted on each other. Rasta Beard had a few on his body, and he would laugh about them and say, 'The other men are dead now.' The death penalty is still in use in Jamaica, although the last hanging had taken place in 1988. It didn't seem to bother Rasta Beard; he talked about killing people with a smile on his face. This was another world for me, and although I had been alive when the last hanging had taken place in the UK, and the Jamaicans were part of the British Commonwealth, they are literally worlds apart in their sense of justice. Rape is commonplace in Jamaica; there were a lot of rapists in the General Penitentiary, and for some reason they never got the same

amount of abuse they would in a British prison - it was really confusing, and I never understood why.

I was doing classes in English. The level of reading and writing was very basic, but anything to keep me on a positive was good for me, and then an opportunity arose: the main man had decided he would join the classes after the Christmas and New Year break, and we were both in the same class. He sat alone at his desk, cutting an imposing figure in the classroom; he seemed intelligent, and after a few weeks, I decided I would take the risk of talking to him. I asked him his name, and he said, 'Why do you want to know, white man?' Shit, this was going to be awkward. I said I was just being friendly, then he broke into a grin and said, 'A man could be dead for asking too many questions in here.' I told him my name was Tommy, from London, and he laughed and said he had been to England many times and had family all over London. It broke the ice and we chatted about the Notting Hill Carnival, reggae music, and parts of London he had been to. He seemed animated and enjoyed talking about his times in the UK. He had a lot of nice pens and I was always short of pens to write in my diary, so I asked him if I could buy some from him, he said, 'No problem, you can have for free,' and he gave me a couple of pens.

He told me they called him The Don. I knew this was not his real name, but I had made the connection and that was the main thing. Once the connection was made, he started to warm to me: people can get bored shitless in the General Penitentiary and if you had different things to say it helped to break up the monotony of it all. I started to help him with the classes: he was a smart guy but had never been to school, like many Jamaicans, who never had the luxury that we take for granted in the UK. Over the weeks I started to get to know him more. People gave him huge respect whenever he was around. He had travelled a lot all over the Caribbean, America, Canada, the UK and South America, he had a sense of humour and he carried himself like the Don he was; nobody dared to speak shite around him.

He was from Tivoli Gardens in West Kingston and had been involved in crime since he was ten years old. I guessed he was in his middle thirties, although I never asked him his age. Outside of classes he would stop and chat with me while his friends would be looking on. He had been in the General Penitentiary for 18 months and was fighting extradition to the United States on cocaine charges. He started to open up about things, how they had transported huge amounts of cocaine by sea and air; he had a network of contacts worldwide and it was all a game to him, he never took coke himself, he said only dogs sniff cocaine and he wasn't just talking about the canine variety that roamed around in airports. He smoked a lot of the finest weed, and he was full of interesting conversations. He never seemed to want for anything, and over the next couple of months, I would say we became friends. The guards were scared of him: they could easily get shot outside of the prison, it wasn't unusual to hear of that happening. I started to visit his cell and was amazed at what he had in there: a colour television, a proper bed, and the best food was brought to him three times a day, cooked by one of his crew. He could make calls anytime he wanted to, and the guards smuggled things in for him and were on his payroll.

One day I was talking with him in his cell when the guard I hated the most, Mr Williams, popped his head in and was just about to say something to the Don when he noticed me; he hesitated to speak, and I froze, fuck me, what was going on here? The Don noticed it, laughed, and said to Mr Williams, 'Relax man, the white man is my friend.' I could tell straight away Williams didn't like it, but he had to swallow it, and he pulled a mobile phone from his pocket and gave it to the Don to make a call. The Don turned to me and said he would see me tomorrow. I took his hint and left the cell, with Mr Williams giving me the evil eye as I left. That cunt was on his payroll; well, now he knew I had friends.

The Don started to give me books to read and in return, I started to help him with his reading and writing. He was a good pupil and a fast learner; his education was very limited, but he had a thirst for knowledge about the world. I asked him to get the *National Geographic* sent in, and he said, 'No problem.' A few days later he had about 50 issues brought in and we pored over them. I was learning alongside him. It was driving Mr Williams mad I could tell; every time I saw him, he was biting his tongue off dying to find out what was going on. I used to laugh thinking about the time he had beaten me, and said from now on I was to call him sir. I did indeed: I started to call him Cur; in my northern accent he thought I was calling him sir, and he never cottoned on. My confidence was coming back, and I knew he wouldn't do anything to me now I was friends with the Don. I asked the Don if he could get Mr Williams to bring his phone to my cell, as I had to speak to my father, and the Don replied, 'Yeah mon', and that night Mr Williams came to my cell and told me I was pushing my luck; but he gave me the phone. I spoke to my dad for thirty minutes. I was buzzing; I assured my dad that everything was fine, asked him how he was, and talked about family matters. After the call was over, I asked Williams how much I owed him, and he said it was fine, the Don had sorted it. I knew it stuck in his craw; I just smiled and said, 'Thanks cur' - oh my, revenge was sweet, and I haven't finished with you yet, I thought!

Things were looking up and I was going to take full advantage of my luck changing. The Don and I were becoming much closer and one day he said he had something for me, and to call to his cell later. After we were unlocked, I went around to his section. I had started to notice I was getting fewer insults. After over a year of abuse from the Yardies who had nothing to do with the band's room, now fewer people were calling me a white pussyhole, which was their favourite insult; it used to wind me up no end, but I had to swallow it. I got to the Don's cell and he pulled out a small black and white television with a little aerial. It was only about 12 inches wide and about 8 inches in depth. He said, 'It's for you, Red.' Wow, I was taken aback but I said, 'Thanks, man.' He had some great connections. Amazingly he was going to send Mr Williams around with the TV later to drop it off. Fuck me, that was the icing on my cake having that cunt bring it over; that was going to do his swede in big time. Sure enough, that night he came over and passed it to me - his face was a picture and I wished I had a camera! Once again, I said, 'Thanks cur', and he fucked off. I was not a big lover of television on the outside, but in here it was like gold dust. Then I realised I had nothing to plug it in to: I had the radio, and I had a small bulb rigged up with wires, but no socket to plug the TV in. Oh well, the gesture was appreciated, and I would speak with Aljoe in the morning; I was sure he would know how to get somebody to set it up. I read a few of the *National Geographics* and fell asleep. In the morning, after we had slopped out our buckets, I spoke with Aljoe about the socket, and he said he knew an electrician who would do it for me for a price, and a few hours later his mate came and sorted it for me. I paid him and switched on the TV. It was quite fuzzy, in black and white, and I found it too annoying to watch, but I decided not to say anything; I didn't want to appear ungrateful.

I had started going to the band's room more and my mood was more upbeat now I knew I had Mr Williams off my case. Aljoe was back to his usual self, his medication must have been working again, and we played some great rehearsals. I was back in the swing and really started to enjoy playing again. I felt so sorry for Aljoe after all these years in prison, he had never had a visit and never had a release date, so the following week I gave him the television and his face lit up with joy, it was worth it just to see his face. He rigged the television up and fuck me, the picture was perfect. Oh well, just my luck, but I was happy for him. I would carry on reading my books safe in the knowledge I had made a good friend, and there weren't that many in there who I could say that about.

A few days later I was talking with Les from Manchester about home, when we noticed another body being loaded in to an ambulance. He laughed and said, 'I bet you're glad that's not you.' I said, 'Fuck off', and he laughed; he was a northerner after all, and he had that piss-taking way about him that you find in the North West. I received a postcard from my Irish mate Peter, who lived in Australia, a good friend whom I had not seen for years, and it was good to know somebody was thinking about me. Various friends had sent me books: Cacker, who had lived in London; and my old school mate Eny sent me *The Evolution of Man* by Darwin, and it made life more bearable. The Cuban guy Pedro was still giving me percussion lessons. I wasn't living on easy street, but I was thankful things were improving in 2003, my year of release. The beggars were doing my box in though - they would be constantly on my case for things. I gave some things away to people I knew were destitute and who didn't try to bully it out of me; after all, what goes around comes around, but it did get on my nerves the persistence of some of them. A lot of them were piss-takers just trying it on.

I got a letter from my brother Anthony telling me he was getting married in February to Paula, and my ex Jo would be going to his wedding with her new boyfriend. I was glad for them all and hoped he would be happy. I was also called out for a visit that day, which surprised me. It was from a Jamaican girl; she was reggae and ska singer Justin Hind's sister. She had met my sister a few months previously and our Lynn had asked her to visit me. Her name was Kadijah and we hit it off on the visit. Fuck, I came away horny as hell, and she said she would write to me soon. It was a nice change to chat with a woman, and a great way to break the day up, totally unexpected. I do love Jamaican women; they are fun and definitely not shy, as I had found out from previous visits to Jamaica.

'Money is the root of all evil.' Biblical Proverb

Chapter 40
Time Waits For No Man

There were so many people in the General Penitentiary, it was vastly overcrowded, and new inmates were arriving daily, with not so many leaving. Those first few months were always the hardest; they gave you nothing and you had to scavenge and fight for everything, and if you had nothing it was going to be extremely hard no matter who you were.

You could tell that lot of the newcomers who had never been in jail were scared to death. If they were weak and never stood up for themselves, they would be bullied and have things taken from them, and it was shocking to watch how the inmates would treat them; even though I had my own problems surviving in this place, if I could help with a kind word or give advice I would. There was one old man who came in and I really did feel sorry for him; he must have been in his sixties, he had fuck all. His name was Horace. He was starving most of the time and I would give him my food; I got him a pillow and started to help him get on his feet until his family could get to see him.

Kingston was a long way from his home in Montego Bay, and he was grateful; he started to run errands for me in the General Penitentiary, and then Berry shocked me one day when he pulled me to one side, and said, 'Red, why are you helping this old man?' I said, 'Why not?' Berry explained, 'Him no good, he is in for child molesting.' Fuck me, I had been helping a child molester, the lowest of the fucking low; that was the problem, everybody mixed freely in the General Penitentiary, and you never knew what people were in for unless they told you.

What could I do? I was in a fucking rage thinking about my own childhood and what that Scottish bastard Bill had done to me, and here was I helping one out. Horace was a little old guy and I didn't have the heart to beat him, but the next time I saw him I told him I knew what he had done, and to fuck off and never come near me again. He looked hurt, but I didn't give a fuck, he skulked off and I never spoke to him again. A few weeks later he was found dead in his cell; it wasn't known if he killed himself or he had been killed, but he wasn't going to be missed by anybody. Just another strange day in the General Penitentiary. There were many cases of rape, child molesters - I just didn't want to know what people were in for, you had to close your eyes to it otherwise you would go mad. This was a strange jail, and you just had to let certain things go.

Rasta Beard shouted me over: 'Here, I got your painting.' He passed it to me; it was my logo ZodoA and it looked great. I gave him the money and tied the logo on my cell door. I thought about where this road had led me since I had started in the music business back in 1999 in Koh Samui, Thailand. My karma had really caught up with me, and I did feel like I deserved the punishment that had been inflicted on me since my arrival in Jamaica. I was well and truly paying the price for my mistakes.

The next day another new guy showed up from Pakistan called Abdul. He was very small and frail, and now lived in Leicester. He had previously served ten years in England for smuggling heroin out of Pakistan. He was very talkative but was scared witless by the Yardies, who had been slapping him around whilst he had been on remand. He was very mild-mannered, and Jamaica was a huge shock for him.

He had to pray five times a day and the guards taunted him over it. His cellmates couldn't stand him, and the Governor had moved him over to my section for his own protection. He too had fuck all, so I gave him my old flip-flops and some soap and toothpaste. He asked me a lot of questions. Any foreigners that came in would look me up at some point and question me about how to survive in there; the British-born Jamaicans too would be horrified by the conditions. The ones who had relatives in Jamaica would be looked after by them and had it much easier.

Abdul was always reading from his Koran. He barely spoke to anybody, but he never stopped when he was around me, which would do my head in. I find it really annoying when people are constantly talking, but I put it down to his nerves and put up with him banging on. He had been talked into bringing coke over to Jamaica, something he said he would regret for the rest of his life. It made me laugh when he was on his knees praying to Allah; he was a drug smuggler, he was probably praying he never got murdered in here. A couple of weeks later Kerry came from the British Embassy. My bruises had healed and the cut over my eye was barely noticeable. It was good to see her, and all the British subjects in the prison would line up to see her. She told me my father was fine and he sent his regards, but better still she brought the money from the Finsbury Park Organisation, Prisoners Abroad, which we were all waiting for which and was a big deal, for many of us had debts to pay in the General Penitentiary, and then we could get more credit. Afterwards, I went to the library and picked out Bertrand Russell's autobiography *The Philosopher*. I figured I must have read well over 300 books in the General Penitentiary by now, which is not that hard when you're locked down for 20 hours every single fucking day.

The weeks seemed to be flying by, it was just the hours and the minutes that seemed to drag along for eternity. Wednesday was always a buzzing day for the visitors would come, and food would arrive for the chosen ones who had a visit. Sometimes I would buy fruit from Berry. He told me one day that somebody was going to write his biography, he really thought he was special. I had to keep in his good books though: he was close to my cell and he did get great food.

I carried on doing the classes, then one day the Don asked me if I could do him a favour. I thought, Oh no, what is he after? He explained that one of his men had been caught with a shit load of weed, and his supply was running low; he asked me to talk with Rasta Beard and ask him to swing by his cell later, he wanted to chat with him. He knew I was dealing with Rasta Beard, but why he asked me to talk with him I had no clue; maybe he was just being friendly. After classes I went and saw Rasta Beard and told him what the Don had said. Rasta looked surprised and said nothing, he just nodded his head. I left and went back to my section and thought no more of it.

I was sweating it was so hot, and when I tried to enter my cell Abdul came over and started yapping away about books. He was becoming a nuisance, but I was far too polite to tell him to fuck off - not my style - but I wished he would piss off and leave me alone. It was becoming a real pain in the arse dealing with him; he was constantly complaining about how bad it was in there, he never left the section, never got involved in classes, the gym, obviously not the Church, and I think he was far too scared to leave, so his world was very small, and I was the only one who took any notice of him. More fool me. When lockdown came, I was glad to get away from him; I didn't dislike him, but I really found him to be irritating at times.

After showering in the morning, I bumped into Rasta Beard. He didn't look happy at all, and I wondered what was up with him. He ignored me when I asked him what was the matter. I was sure it had something to do with the Don, but I thought I had best not push him; after all, it was not my business and curiosity could get you killed in there. Then, from nowhere, I saw the Don appear with a huge grin on his face. Rasta Beard took a quick walk and was gone in seconds. The Don said, 'How's things, Red?' 'Fine man,' I replied and headed back to my cell to eat breakfast. I was getting worried that trouble was brewing between the Don and Rasta Beard and I sure didn't want to get involved. They were both big guys, but the Don carried more power, and the rumours around the prison were that he was extremely dangerous and not a man to fuck about with. They were loosely both my friends, but in reality, I was just the white man who they chatted to. I was lucky they both bothered to talk with me; life was difficult enough as it was without me getting caught up in something I had no idea about.

The days rolled by and the atmosphere in the prison was becoming tenser. There were hordes of crackheads and they were the most dangerous; the ones who smoked weed were the calmer ones, but it was feeling like a drought was on and even they were becoming cranky and volatile. The flashpoint was always around the showers, or where the men were emptying their shit buckets. I stayed in my cell a lot over the next few days. I could feel the tension building up to something; I wasn't sure what it was, but my sixth sense was on overdrive, I was feeling edgy and really uncomfortable. It was quite frightening being around in the General Penitentiary when it was this tense. I was an easy-going man and I hadn't been brought up around guns and violence the way a lot of the Yardies had, and they did kill quite frequently, it was no joke.

Then it happened. Gunshots rang out all over the prison and one of the sections exploded in an orgy of violence. Later I found out that Rasta Beard had taken a knife through his chest: three or four inmates had attacked him, he had pulled out a machete and maimed one of the prisoners before the guard had taken him down. The guards were running all over the place and there was a mass fight going on, on the football pitch, the sirens were going off and the batons were being brought down on prisoners' heads. I was far away from the incident, but I could see it in the distance from my section and it was deeply disturbing. The Alsatian dogs were brought in and they were viciously tearing at the limbs of the fighting prisoners...

It took an hour for it all to calm down, and the prison was once again locked down. It happened so quickly; that was how things went - it was fucking crazy in here without a shadow of a doubt. Locked down, the food was brought to our cells for the next 48 hours. Berry was the prison trustee, so he was allowed out to bring the food to the prisoners. It was a ball ache being locked down for two days and never knowing what was going on. I found out from Berry that Rasta Beard was still alive and had been taken to an outside hospital, and from there he was to be transferred to Spanish Town, the other maximum-security prison in the Parish of St Andrew, along with ten other prisoners. Things like this were a common experience and one I had to deal with whilst residing in the General Penitentiary. Berry had said this was nothing compared to the riot that happened in August 1997 when 16 homosexual men were killed by being either stabbed to death or burned to death, and many were mutilated, and at least 50 were injured terribly. He seemed to find the whole thing funny; he was a creepy fucker at times, and I was glad when he left me alone with my thoughts about the whole scenario.

At that time of the August 1997 riot, the guards had been on strike after a plan to combat Aids, which was a major problem in Jamaican jails. The government planned to introduce condoms because many thought the guards were having sex with the prisoners. The guards were indignant at these suggestions and staged a walkout, and it was believed the guards had left cells doors open on purpose, which had sent the prisoners on a killing spree. Some broke free from their cells by using bricks and bars and went after the gay population, who were segregated. It was terrifying for the prisoners that were being targeted, and because of the strike, there were very few staff on. Many gay prisoners were shoved into their cells with their hands and feet tied up, burned alive with no chance of escape, begging for their lives, but no mercy was shown. Rival gangs took revenge on each other, and with no guards on hand, it was easy to kill your enemies. The riots went on over two days and it took the Jamaican army to bring the prison under control. Friends and family were outside pleading with the guards and soldiers to save their loved ones. It barely made the news; if this happened in the UK it would have been world news. It was no wonder that anyone who was gay in Jamaica wanted to leave.

The two-day lockdown was getting to me big time. Berry would come to my cell three times a day and give me more information on what had transpired, and little by little I started to piece it together. The Don had a weed shortage and he knew Rasta Beard was carrying plenty, and the Don had told Rasta Beard to hand it over. Rasta Beard had refused and so the Don set a plan in action for his posse to have Rasta Beard killed for the disrespect the Don had felt was being given to him.

The Don took no part in the violence and was nowhere to be seen when the attack took place; he just gave the orders. A lot of this was hearsay and I am sure Berry added his twopence worth, but whatever really happened I'm sure Rasta Beard was glad to be alive, and I'm sure the Don was pleased he'd taken decisive action so that the message would reverberate around the prison, adding to his already deadly reputation. A man had nearly lost his life, and several had been injured, all because of the weed; it sounds crazy, but this was the way it was.

It was great when we were finally unlocked, and freedom of movement was allowed again. The aftermath of the whole affair was being talked about around the whole of the penitentiary. I was glad my family knew nothing about this place: my father was a worrier at the best of times, and I never told anybody in the family. I always kept letters upbeat - what was the point of worrying them unnecessarily? The following week I saw the Don in the classroom, and he was all smiles and he never mentioned a word about the whole affair. He was a true leader, his actions spoke for him, and nothing had to be said, especially to the white boy. I had one other problem: Rasta Beard was my connection to buy weed from and he was gone. I would have to deal with somebody else and I wasn't sure if I trusted anyone enough to deal with them. I would keep my ears and eyes open until I felt the time was right to approach somebody.

Abdul was coming out of his shell and speaking to other prisoners besides myself, which was a relief to my ears. Bristol Mikey was his latest victim to talk to, but we all wanted somebody to talk to at times. I can be moody myself and will clam up when I am not in the mood for chatting; we all have foibles that make us different, but the one thing you couldn't show was fear - under these conditions people would take advantage big time. Pedro the Cuban was due to leave soon. I liked him, he was always in a good mood. He came to my cell: 'Hey, Red, I got something for you.' He was holding in his hands the bongos he had played for years. 'These are for you.' I felt honoured and thanked him profusely. Cuba was only 90 miles from Jamaica and it's a country I have always wanted to visit; Pedro invited me to stay in his house in Havana if I ever made the journey after I was released. I would certainly look him up. I wrote his address down in my diary, and he told me, 'We have the most beautiful women in the Caribbean, and you will love it.' He laughed. He spoke good English in a Spanish accent; I would miss him when he went.

'Do not be excessively timid or excessively confident.' Cuban Proverb

Chapter 41
A Glimmer of Hope

A new Jamaican English guy showed up in the General Penitentiary. His street name was Carrot, from Brixton, and we ended up chatting and he asked me where I was from. 'Up north, but I was living in London for many years,' I replied. He said he may be able to help me with accommodation when I was released. Well, I had no place to live and that is the hardest thing, finding a place to live in London, so my interest was aroused when he explained he had a flat in Brixton, and wanted somebody to take care of it so Lambeth Council didn't take it off him. It was still many months until my release date came around, and I said to him, 'No worries, if I can help you I will.' Carrott explained the keys to his flat were in reception, and if I could help him out, he would get them for me. This was music to my ears, but I thought we shall see if he comes good on his word.

People say anything when they are locked up, but I filed it to the back of my mind and would remind him nearer to my release date. Carrot was a jovial guy who had lived in Brixton for many years. He seemed like an old pothead, and I got a good vibe from him. Calm had been restored around the General Penitentiary and the latest influx of weed arrived, either brought in by the warders or over the wall route. It was a much nicer feeling when lots of prisoners were stoned; which reminded me, where was I going to get mine from? Then I realised who I should go to, he would know for sure. I went around to see Moses the Rasta who had given me the packet of smokes. It was always good to see him, and we enjoyed our chats. I mentioned my situation and what I was looking for, somebody to deal with regarding the weed situation. He smiled and got up from his chair outside the cell, went into his cell and returned with a small package which he handed to me. It was wrapped in a piece of newspaper and it felt like three or four grams. 'Here, this one is free for you Red.' 'Good man Moses, I will be back,' and that was the start of my new connection. It was good to do business with someone you could get along with. I sure wasn't going to bother the Don with such things. I hid the package in my underpants and made my way back to my section with a smile on my face.

On my return I spotted Mr Williams. He always stared at me like I was a piece of shite, but I knew I was safe as long as the Don was around; heaven forbid that he got extradited before my release, that cunt would make my life hell, and I had flashbacks of the beating he had given me. When the Don was not around, he walked around slapping his baton on his leg to put the fear into the inmates; he was a first-class cunt who loved the power he carried by his uniform. I ran into Aljoe, who casually said that another gig was being planned in the coming weeks, and I should get back into the band's room for rehearsals. 'Yes, I will be there' - it was a good way of doing something positive and taking my mind off the past events. A few more letters had arrived from home and one that smelt of perfume was from Khadijah; she had sent me photos of her musical friend Ra's talent, Jimmy Galloway. I enjoyed getting letters from her, but I knew it would go nowhere upon my release. I wouldn't be walking out of the gate to meet her, I would be taken by the police in handcuffs, put on a plane and kicked out of Jamaica. But still, it was good of her to write.

Life goes on. I kinda missed Rasta Beard; he was a grumpy bastard, but at least he was alive. He was a Jamaican who had survived for years in Jamaica, and I was sure he would be fine. I was sure that the Don had other things on his mind, fighting the extradition to the States.

I settled back into reading and listening to the radio, catching up on the world news on the BBC World Service, and I went to a lot of rehearsals with the band for the gig that was being planned for visitors from the University of West Indies. They were usually small affairs carried out in the band's room. We would be wheeled out to give a little show, but we enjoyed meeting visitors and it was something or somebody to play to. The weather was good at the moment, a nice sea breeze blowing through the prison, and the sun was not too hot. Some of the prisoners had to work in the brickyards, but we were never allowed outside of the prison, so my hard labour was hitting the bongos, and that was sweet by me. My day was much the same as any other day when things were quiet: clean my cell, do my exercises, classrooms, band's room, lockup at 3.30pm. I'd had enough of the drama and was happy to get through another day without any aggravation. My release date was edging closer, not fast enough by my standards, but nevertheless getting closer.

I thought often of my daughter Sophie, who was now approaching 18, hoping one day we could sort things out. She was growing up fast and would soon be a woman, with kids of her own one day I assumed. I was running into Leppo a lot in the band's room; he always loved performing for the outside visitors, and who could blame him after all these years in prison - it was the only thing he had. A triple life sentence couldn't be easy for anybody. I was sure glad it wasn't me in his shoes. The gig came around and half a dozen people, accompanied by guards, watched us perform our show, sitting down on the chairs in the band's room. Leppo read his latest poems from the stage with great gusto, the visitors applauded and sat around for 30 minutes chatting with us about the music and how they enjoyed it. There was talk about the university helping to build a studio in the General Penitentiary in the future and recording the band onto a CD with a professional producer. I wouldn't be there by then, but the band would, and they were all excited by the thought of being recorded, especially Aljoe. It was all he talked about for weeks afterwards.

The band, the Bloom of Light, which I thought was a great name for a band consisting of men all doing life sentences, was considered to be the best prison band throughout the Caribbean penal system, and it was something to be proud of. It was not an easy life; all the musicians wanted to be free men and perform to larger reggae audiences in Jamaica, but they had to be happy with what they had, and it was more than some of the poor fuckers had in this place.

A few days later Pedro the Cuban was released. We shook hands and he gave me a big hug. I had never seen a smile so happy as his the day he fucked off, and good luck to him. He had survived for over a decade in one of the world's most dangerous prisons, which housed psychopaths, sociopaths, and serial killers from across the Caribbean. I wished him luck on his release and we both said we would see each other again, even though we knew we probably wouldn't. Before he headed to the gates, and his sweet release to board a plane back home to Cuba, Berry came mincing over to say goodbye, but he was too late, he had left the section. I went back into my cell; I wanted to be alone. I picked up one of my books and lost myself in another world before the gruel was to be served for lunch that day.

'I didn't think of all the misery, but of all the beauty that still remains.' Anne Frank

Chapter 42
Hell, on Earth

It was getting close to the Easter weekend of April 2003. I still had another three months to serve and I felt like it was another ten years away: the closer it got, the longer it felt. I was getting gate fever really badly. My whole being was coursing with anticipation to get out of this place in one piece. Things were changing, new faces were arriving, and new faces meant trouble: you never knew who they were, what kind of mood swings they had, how their mental health was and what their charges were, they could be anybody. I tried to avoid talking to new people; it wasn't worth the hassle that they could bring into your life.

The crackheads were dominating the prison violence; men doing life sentences thought nothing of hurting you really badly, taking their frustrations out on you to find a release for their own anger, their own dissatisfaction; to see a man covered in blood was a huge turn on for some. Abdul was an easy target for many; with his Asian ways and small frame he was a figure of fun that many prisoners took advantage of constantly. They called him Batty Boy because of his effeminate manner. I started to take care of his money: he had been robbed so many times he begged me to keep it, which I agreed to. I would dole out bits of money to him when he needed it for something. Luckily, he never smoked; the hassle you got off smokers if they realised you had cigarettes was unbelievable.

In the prison where you were stripped bare of your dignity, and surrounded by crazy inmates; your true colours would be exposed for all to see, and the weak would be picked on without mercy. The Jamaicans shouted at each other constantly; you could never tell if it was anger or not - it's their way of speaking to each other. Even when the older guys were playing dominos it sounded like war, and the way they smashed the dominos down on the board was deafening, the constant shouting and arguing making you jump and putting you on edge.

Abdul must have felt like an insect at times, ready to be squashed by the nearest animal. I was not sure how he was going to survive after I left. He was due out in 2006, three years after me. A guy called Paper Dread was on our section. I think he was mentally ill; he had been suspected of 14 murders throughout the Caribbean. A very strange looking guy, he used to laugh a lot when he saw Abdul coming, who was shit scared of him and would bolt away from him and hide in his cell. I had to disguise my fears and hope that nobody noticed; it wasn't going to be a fist fight, that was for sure, they never had that mentality, it was about picking a stone up, a knife, anything which could inflict real damage and hurt you; they would do it super-quick before the guards got to you. 'Dem mash you up taras clart.' A fistfight just wasn't in their DNA, and that's what really bothered me, and made me super-cautious when arguments erupted. I had seen first-hand the punishment they meted out on each other, with devastating consequences and serious injuries. I had not seen the Don lately; he had stopped coming to classes, and I would see him randomly on the yard, but he had become withdrawn, and never really said too much these days. That had me worried and it worked on my paranoia.

You could never be too careful in this atmosphere: just when you thought things were going well, things could change so rapidly it left you wondering what the fuck had happened. You could run, but there was nowhere to hide. The guards didn't give a toss really, it was a form of entertainment for them which broke their day up; the batons were ever ready to split skulls and break bones with sickening efficiency.

I felt like an albino at times. There was one real albino in the General Penitentiary; he was as white as a ghost with white hair, very weird looking, and I tried not to catch his eye. He had an air of menace about him, and I was no football hooligan constantly looking for a ruck; if I had been I could have found a thousand opponents ready to take me on in seconds.

Berry came over with a smile on his face. His appeal was going through after all these years - he could be going home! He was such a grotesque looking fucker, and I just couldn't take his know-all attitude, but I went along with it to save the hassle of turning him into an enemy; I nodded to him as if I cared. People could get on your nerves very quickly for no other reason than you couldn't get away from them, and you knew everybody was sizing you up or you were sizing them up; there were too many alpha males trying to prove themselves - it almost verged on the homoerotic, which was a joke considering this was a homophobic country. One guy told me I needed to cut my toenails, and I looked at him and said, 'I don't notice guys' feet, I look at women,' and he looked like he wanted to kill me because I made him look a cunt. I would have to be careful around him, he was a nasty-looking fucker doing life. Out of the whole population, I reckon only ten per cent of them you could reason with. This was the maximum-security jail and they were all fucking lunatics; it was like being in an asylum full of them.

Visually, when you looked around the General Penitentiary it looked scary as fuck; you did get used to it, but I never dropped my guard, not once around the inmates, you had to be on your toes always, full stop. The thin veneer of casual friendship could drop in a hairsbreadth if you upset somebody. I never dared to mention my release date, especially to men doing life sentences; in your wildest nightmares you really cannot imagine how volatile these men in the General Penitentiary were. The way they shouted at each other it felt like bombs going off, nobody acted like a pussy and everybody acted like a gangster. Maybe it was a lot of bravado, the way of keeping other men away from you; they were a tough breed of Yardies who stood their ground over every little thing or argument.

Then there were the latent homosexuals; they were the most dangerous, hiding their sexuality from their friends and family, as to be known to be gay would get you murdered in a nano-second, and so they chose to stay in the main population rather than be considered a batty man. They had terrifying tempers that exploded over the least little thing; suppressing their homosexuality must have been one hell of a burden in Jamaica, and I could tell there were many; they were usually the toughest looking motherfuckers around, masquerading as heterosexuals with hair-trigger tempers, ready to wreak carnage over the slightest thing to prove how macho they were. A fight broke out in the showers one day: two enormous Yardies beating the shit out of each other, blood everywhere, smashing each other on the concrete, shouting 'You the fucking batty man, I'm gonna kill you' - you knew one had been found out. The fight would be broken up and one of the prisoners would be shanghaied off the section and placed in the batty man section of the prison for his own protection; if he was lucky enough to have survived the savage assault.

The homosexuals were segregated from the rest of the prison; otherwise it would have been a blood bath. To be even thought of as being gay could get you lynched or burnt alive; in Jamaica you were vermin to be annihilated if you were considered to be gay. In their eyes it was the most unnatural way of living and them ending your life because of it was considered to be doing you a favour. The community at large would all join in with the lynch mob without a second thought. If you were a batty man you deserved to die; it had to be stamped out forever across Jamaica. Living under these conditions, gay men must have been scared out of their minds; no wonder many of them fled to the States and the UK in genuine fear for their lives.

You can only imagine what it was like to be gay in this fortress full of murderers; it literally was hell on earth, with no way out and no reprieve. If one man was caught sodomising another man both would be killed on the spot with machetes or knives - even decapitation was used in some instances - this was the last place you would want to be seen. Homophobia is so prevalent and ingrained in the Jamaican psyche, with no sign of tolerance whatsoever in the near future.

When trouble kicked off, it kicked off, and you had to be prepared to die for it, and there was no fucking way was I prepared to die, to be some form of voyeurism for the onlooking inmates who loved the whole spectacle of bloodshed and violence which broke up the boredom of the day. No thank you, I had better things to waste my life on and it sure wasn't mortal combat with a murderous Yardie over a freaking cigarette or such nonsense. If you walked past someone with your arse in his face when he was sat in a chair on his section, he might scream at you, 'Fucking batty man, get away before I kill you!' - what, was I going to stop and say, 'Excuse me sir, who are you calling a batty man?' Honestly, to try and explain anything fell on deaf ears anyway, so what was the point? I learnt to turn the other cheek many times, just to keep the peace; I wasn't insane or stupid. I never got pushed around, I wouldn't allow it, but with stupid things I just let them slide for the sake of less aggravation. These things happened in some form or other daily for at least 18 months and often times all through my sentence. Even with the Don on my side; not all the inmates knew about that, so sporadic insults would come my way from new prisoners.

Man, I just wanted out of there. I took a lot of shit for the sake of an easy life. Oftentimes it was just a load of prison bluster, but I lived by the motto, 'Better to be safe than sorry.' I never walked freely around the yard holding anything that people would want to take - food, eggs, you kept them out of sight, it was much easier.

Leppo used to make me wonder why nobody attacked him inside the prison. Peter Tosh had been a huge star in Jamaica, friends with Mick Jagger from the Rolling Stones, the world's biggest rock band, and even lived in Keith Richards' house in Jamaica for a time. Peter

Tosh was the biggest name in reggae music worldwide after Bob Marley. Maybe he had gone through shit for the murders, but I never saw it, although Leppo was tough-looking and looked like a man not to trifled with either. It was a strange quandary and I never fully got to understand the Yardie mentality, it was far too way out for me to comprehend.

There are fourteen parishes throughout Jamaica and at least every parish was represented by somebody in the prison, but Kingston was by far the most violent, with the highest murder rate. It was mindboggling, the number of murders committed on such a tiny island, which had the most churches per capita in the world. I just couldn't get my head around it all. There were so many gangs in Kingston dealing in drugs and thuggery it was considered very unsafe for tourists to even contemplate going there.

There was a presentation in the band's room for the superintendent of the prison, Mr Ramsey, for his one year's service at the General Penitentiary. He had previously been at Spanish Town with over 30 years' service; he had some tales to tell I'd bet. The band played whilst the audience applauded, and Mr Ramsey grinned from ear to ear. These little gigs kept the band busy and were something to rehearse for; it was always fun and kept your mind occupied and out of mischief. Time was to be used wisely from now on: having already watched some people leave I knew it was possible, and I sure didn't want any more trouble coming my way. That was a challenge in itself, the way things could change on a daily basis: you had to tread carefully and hope for the best. Thoughts of friends and family started to come to mind more frequently, especially my father, and my daughter Sophie, who prior to my sentence I hadn't seen for quite a few years. We were like strangers, which was something I would have to try and rectify in the future on my return to the UK.

I received another letter from Khadijah telling me she was going to Canada to earn some money for her business, and who could blame her? Money was always tight in Jamaica unless you were part of the Jamaican uptown elite. I heard on the radio Saddam Hussein's regime was toppling, which had to be a great thing for the people of Iraq and the free world. I was formulating in my mind to do a series of gigs with Howard Marks to raise awareness for the charity Prisoners Abroad Organisation; they had really been a lifesaver for me and many others incarcerated around the globe. I wrote a letter thanking them for all their help and sent one off to Howard via his manager Giles. Prisoners Abroad had an office in Finsbury Park and I genuinely wanted to do something to show my appreciation for all they had done. They were a small charity beavering away on behalf of me and thousands of others in the same situation.

You truly found out who your friends were when the shit hit the fan, and I had friends who took the time to write to me. My family had done all they could to alleviate the situation I was in; I had a lot to thank people for. Nigel, one of the Jamaican English guys, was the cousin of Radio One DJ Chris Goldfinger, and could prove to be a useful contact in the future, who knows? All my life had been a gamble.

The band's room was closed over the Easter break and those four days dragged.

The 22nd of April 2003 was my daughter Sophie's 18th birthday. I tried to get a message to my father via Mr Williams' phone, to ask my dad to drop off a birthday card to her, but to no avail, Mr Williams was nowhere to be found, and so it wasn't meant to be. I wondered if I would ever get into her good books.

There was a problem I needed to sort out: somebody back in the UK would have to buy me a return ticket from Jamaica. The Jamaican government would not pay, and if nobody paid for your ticket home you could sit in the prison for years until somebody did. This was a thought that was on my mind and I had to get this rectified asap. I fired off a letter to my dad explaining the situation and hoped he would be able to sort it for me. I was a pain in the arse for him at times, but he always tried his best to help me over the years.

The hunger pains came often, and I could occasionally afford a meal, but mostly I had to rely on the General Penitentiary food. I had lost over two stone in weight, and there wasn't an ounce of fat on me. I was becoming gaunt, and often I would dream of food; I would wake up feeling ravenous. The little things we take for granted outside; I would keep a round of bread in my pocket and often nibble away at it when my hunger became too much, like a Jewish guy in one of Hitler's death camps. It was no joke when you had no money and had to rely on the prison fare; I really couldn't stomach it at the best of times. The times when I had lots of money and ate in good restaurants across the globe were now just a thing of the past, and I would never take anything for granted in the future.

The repetitive daily grind carried on without much incident until the last week of May when a shock came my way. I ran into the Don; his extradition was looking imminent and he remarked that he was worried about being taken from the General Penitentiary to be flown to America and face trial on further charges. His lawyers were fighting on his behalf for him to stay in Jamaica; it was a cat and mouse game with the American DEA which had been going on for months. I was worried about him going, as the guard Mr. Williams would make things hard for me and that was the last thing I needed this close to my release, which was six or seven weeks away. I crossed my fingers for the Don that it would never happen, it was all I could do. I carried on doing rehearsals with the Bloom of Light. Aljoe told me he was approaching his 30th year in the General Penitentiary; fuck me that was such a long time in there. I really admired the way he carried himself throughout my time there; he had never really complained about anything. He was a lost soul permanently reminded of that fateful night when he murdered his grandparents, destined to spend his remaining years in the General Penitentiary until the day he died. If I had been in his shoes, I would have strung myself up, but you never know what you would do unless you were in that situation.

The first week of June I was called into the office, and for the first time ever it was confirmed I would be released on the 8th of July 2003; there had been no mention of it until this time. It was explained that my father had bought me a one-way ticket flying British Airways from Norman Manley International Airport on that date. My heart soared at the thought of this, it was so close. One more month, or 28 days, I had left to survive and put up with these conditions. I kept it close to myself: I really didn't want to tempt fate and any further trouble by revealing when I was going home. In my cell I had been watching flights departing from the Norman Manley International Airport for the last couple of years, and it seemed unbelievable that finally, I would be the one leaving.

Moses was still my connection for the weed, and one day he laughed and told me, 'I like the way you keep your mouth shut in here.' I said, 'Yes, I want to get out alive,' and we both laughed as he passed me another little package of Jamaican sinsemilla, which had kept me going throughout this sentence. Believe me, this was one experience I would never wish on anybody, including my worst enemy. Abdul was coping much better now; he had seemed to be more settled and was even starting to leave the section to walk around the prison. His bottle was returning, and it was good to see; after all, a few years from now and he would have to make some kind of life for himself.

One of the corporals who worked in the classes had passed away a few months previously, Corporal Walters; his name was painted on the school building as a lasting memorial in his honour. That was the only respect I ever saw for somebody's passing in this slaughterhouse they had now renamed the Tower Street Adult Correctional Centre. We all still called it the General Penitentiary; after all, we were all still serving our penance.

I was always short of money and what few clothes I had were by now threadbare, falling to pieces, but I didn't give a toss, my mind was supercharged and fully focused on my release, praying nothing upset that in any way whatsoever. More new guys were arriving from places like Nigeria and Canada, and you could see the fear in their eyes. It was not a pleasant experience being thousands of miles from home, and your only company was testosterone-fuelled Yardies hellbent on giving you a hard time. My heart did go out for them because I knew what lay ahead of them in this third world prison, where life was not valued as much as a packet of cigarettes.

Sunday 15th of June - Father's Day in the UK, and my thoughts were with my father. I hoped he was in good health, and unless something drastic happened I would be seeing him in three weeks' time.

The Don was still worrying about his extradition, but no word had come yet, no date had been given. I think he was just panicking; he knew what would be waiting for him in America and none of it was good. Mr Williams seemed to be avoiding me; he was mainly on other sections of the prison, but occasionally I would see him when I sat around the gravel football pitch. My football days were over, I had learnt my lesson, but it amused me to watch the Yardies kicking the shit out of each other on the pitch. They really took the game to another level; they were as ferocious as fuck and it was a form of entertainment watching them do it. Berry was still waiting to hear about his appeal: justice ran slowly in Jamaica and it could be years before he heard anything. Then thankfully the 1st of July was here; it was International Reggae Day in Jamaica, and in seven days I would be boarding that British Airways flight to the UK. Man, I was counting down the days mentally in my mind. It was hard to keep my mouth closed about my release date, but I was determined not to annoy anybody - with news of your release you really had to be careful, super-careful not to set anybody off. If this had been England your release date would not be a problem to reveal, but here in one of the most dangerous and hostile prisons across the Caribbean Islands I would have been highly stupid to have been bragging about my forthcoming release to all and sundry; one jealous inmate could kill you in a fit of envy, so my nerves were being tested to the extreme. What should have been a joy, I had to hold down until I was safely back in the UK. I promised myself when I landed in the UK I would get down on my hands and knees and kiss the fucking ground in blessed relief.

I was struck by a sudden bout of the flu in the last week. I couldn't believe it. I was unable to eat, and I could barely stand up, I just felt physically drained. I was sure my nerves were ragged; I was just fucked with this place and it was squeezing every little bit of energy out of me, just to twist my mind in one last desperate attempt to make me realise the error of my ways. I was too fucked to go to the gym, I never had the strength to even take a shower, and this July heat was unbearably hot. My cell felt like a sauna, I was so thirsty and all I had was lukewarm water to quench my thirst from the plastic bottles I had in my cell. The sun was so hot you could fry eggs on the floors outside. I felt like I was going to die, and I had to fight with every fibre in my being just to keep from going crazy; even Berry was concerned enough to give me a cooling drink saying, 'You really don't look too good, Red.' Aljoe came to see me on the third day and brought me some hot soup; I was starting to feel slightly better after drinking it out of his plastic beaker. On the fourth day I was feeling much better. By then I was so hot and sweaty I had to go to the hosepipes, take a shower and wash the filth and grime out of me. Within sixty seconds of having the shower, it was red hot again, but I had managed to get rid of this sudden bout of debilitating flu that had completely hit me by surprise.

I had three days to go, and in my cell that night I was wishing and urging for the time to be over. If somebody had given me a pill that would knock me out for those three days, I would have taken it willingly, instead of having to endure the days, hours and minutes I had to put up with in there. I had never wished so hard in my life for this time to come. It was dragging so slowly it was doing my brain in with the excitement I was feeling that I dare not share with others. Sure, people knew I was due out at some point, but they never knew exactly, and it wasn't going to come from my lips. The Don was still there and that was a very good sign for me as I was certain that if he hadn't been then Mr Williams would have beaten me within an inch of my life in a heartbeat if that opportunity had arisen.

I closed my eyes to the violence that was going on around me, I withdrew from prison life, and I very rarely spoke to anybody in the last couple of days. I was like a horse and jockey on the final hurdle; my mind was one hundred per cent focused on release, and getting out of this place of incarceration that had given me the scare of my life. I'd had to put up with being verbally abused by inmates and guards alike over the last couple of years; I had a few friends, and some people had helped me along the way, but ultimately I had been the odd man out, and I did my best to fit in and survive under what I can only describe as terrifying conditions, completely alien to anything I have ever been through in my life. I had been walking on eggshells for two years, never ever sure if I was going to survive; I had no posse behind me, I came into the prison by myself. I had nothing but my determination to get through this, and I have to be honest, it was the hardest time of my life.

On the 7th of July, the night before my release, after lockdown I whispered to Aljoe in his cell next door that I was going home in the morning, and I would give him everything I had. He laughed; he knew I was going home, or at least he had an idea that it was very soon. He asked me to send him some CDs from the UK. I laughed and promised that I would. I lay down in my cell and took my book out, *Howard Marks - Mr Nice*, which I had read many times before, but I knew it would be very hard for me to sleep this night. I was unbelievably excited, and I loved reading about Howard's release in the book.

I could now count Howard as one of my personal friends, as he had taken the time to visit me in Jamaica, and by my book that was a friend indeed. The final hours ticked slowly by. I felt like a man waiting to be awarded a million dollars from the lottery, and for sure I would have been happy to forfeit a million dollars rather than spend any more time in here. I'd had a belly full of it to last me a lifetime. I looked around the cell, and the mosquitoes didn't bother me, and the smell never bothered me, as this was my final night. I would be able to see women, drink beer, walk around a free man and not be locked down by 3.30pm every single day like a caged animal. Was I excited? You fucking bet I was, this was the home straight and the winning post was in sight.

I barely slept - maybe a couple of hours in the early hours - and when finally, the cell door swung open and it was Mr Williams, my heart skipped a beat. 'You go home today, white pussyhole,' he said. I just grinned and said, 'Yes cur.' He looked at me with a disdainful look and carried on to the next cell; fuck him, the horrible cunt, I was going home.

When I got out of the cell, I swept my eyes around the General Penitentiary and realised this was it, my time had come, and a warm relief swept through my whole body like the most intense feeling I had ever felt. I stripped my cell bare and gave all my possessions to Aljoe. By now the other prisoners knew I was going home, and people were shouting 'Good luck!' and some of them were clapping. I couldn't believe it, it almost brought tears to my eyes, I just hadn't expected anyone to be happy for me. I hugged Aljoe and I shook hands with him and Abdul, even Berry and a few others. The Don shouted 'Good luck' and then I headed to the reception by the gate to await the arrival of the immigration police. I walked with my head held high. I had seen things that will remain with me until the day I die, but I had survived, and for that, I will be eternally grateful. I had made a huge mistake and I should have known better.

I was a few stone lighter and my hair had grown down my back, but fuck it, I was going home. I had nothing apart from the clothes I stood in, and to be honest I would have walked out stark bollock naked to get out of there. I had served my time in many prisons in England as a kid, but the feeling I got leaving this place was indescribable. I don't give a fuck what anybody says. I was now ready to carry on with the spiritual journey that Rike had set me on years before, only this time it would be crime free.

To Be Continued…

'Our greatest glory is not in never falling, but in rising every time we fall' Confucius